Gergana Dimova

POLITICAL UNCERTAINTY

A Comparative Exploration

Bibliografische Information der Deutschen Nationalbibliothek
Die Deutsche Nationalbibliothek verzeichnet diese Publikation in der Deutschen Nationalbibliografie; detaillierte bibliografische Daten sind im Internet über http://dnb.d-nb.de abrufbar.

Bibliographic information published by the Deutsche Nationalbibliothek
Die Deutsche Nationalbibliothek lists this publication in the Deutsche Nationalbibliografie; detailed bibliographic data are available in the Internet at http://dnb.d-nb.de.

Cover graphic: ID 79369779 © Hannu Viitanen | Dreamstime.com

ISBN-13: 978-3-8382-1385-9
© *ibidem*-Verlag, Stuttgart 2023
Alle Rechte vorbehalten

Das Werk einschließlich aller seiner Teile ist urheberrechtlich geschützt. Jede Verwertung außerhalb der engen Grenzen des Urheberrechtsgesetzes ist ohne Zustimmung des Verlages unzulässig und strafbar. Dies gilt insbesondere für Vervielfältigungen, Übersetzungen, Mikroverfilmungen und elektronische Speicherformen sowie die Einspeicherung und Verarbeitung in elektronischen Systemen.

All rights reserved. No part of this publication may be reproduced, stored in or introduced into a retrieval system, or transmitted, in any form, or by any means (electronical, mechanical, photocopying, recording or otherwise) without the prior written permission of the publisher. Any person who does any unauthorized act in relation to this publication may be liable to criminal prosecution and civil claims for damages.

Printed in the EU

Soviet and Post-Soviet Politics and Society (SPPS)   Vol. 220
ISSN 1614-3515

General Editor: Andreas Umland, *Stockholm Centre for Eastern European Studies*, andreas.umland@ui.se

Commissioning Editor: Max Jakob Horstmann, London, mjh@ibidem.eu

EDITORIAL COMMITTEE*

DOMESTIC & COMPARATIVE POLITICS
Prof. **Ellen Bos**, *Andrássy University of Budapest*
Dr. **Gergana Dimova**, *Florida State University*
Prof. **Heiko Pleines**, *University of Bremen*
Dr. **Sarah Whitmore**, *Oxford Brookes University*
Dr. **Harald Wydra**, *University of Cambridge*

SOCIETY, CLASS & ETHNICITY
Col. **David Glantz**, *"Journal of Slavic Military Studies"*
Dr. **Marlène Laruelle**, *George Washington University*
Dr. **Stephen Shulman**, *Southern Illinois University*
Prof. **Stefan Troebst**, *University of Leipzig*

POLITICAL ECONOMY & PUBLIC POLICY
Prof. **Andreas Goldthau**, *University of Erfurt*
Dr. **Robert Kravchuk**, *University of North Carolina*
Dr. **David Lane**, *University of Cambridge*
Dr. **Carol Leonard**, *University of Oxford*
Dr. **Maria Popova**, *McGill University, Montreal*

FOREIGN POLICY & INTERNATIONAL AFFAIRS
Dr. **Peter Duncan**, *University College London*
Prof. **Andreas Heinemann-Grüder**, *University of Bonn*
Prof. **Gerhard Mangott**, *University of Innsbruck*
Dr. **Diana Schmidt-Pfister**, *University of Konstanz*
Dr. **Lisbeth Tarlow**, *Harvard University, Cambridge*
Dr. **Christian Wipperfürth**, *N-Ost Network, Berlin*
Dr. **William Zimmerman**, *University of Michigan*

HISTORY, CULTURE & THOUGHT
Dr. **Catherine Andreyev**, *University of Oxford*
Prof. **Mark Bassin**, *Södertörn University*
Prof. **Karsten Brüggemann**, *Tallinn University*
Prof. **Alexander Etkind**, *Central European University*
Prof. **Gasan Gusejnov**, *Free University of Berlin*
Prof. **Leonid Luks**, *Catholic University of Eichstaett*
Dr. **Olga Malinova**, *Russian Academy of Sciences*
Dr. **Richard Mole**, *University College London*
Prof. **Andrei Rogatchevski**, *University of Tromsø*
Dr. **Mark Tauger**, *West Virginia University*

ADVISORY BOARD*

Prof. **Dominique Arel**, *University of Ottawa*
Prof. **Jörg Baberowski**, *Humboldt University of Berlin*
Prof. **Margarita Balmaceda**, *Seton Hall University*
Dr. **John Barber**, *University of Cambridge*
Prof. **Timm Beichelt**, *European University Viadrina*
Dr. **Katrin Boeckh**, *University of Munich*
Prof. em. **Archie Brown**, *University of Oxford*
Dr. **Vyacheslav Bryukhovetsky**, *Kyiv-Mohyla Academy*
Prof. **Timothy Colton**, *Harvard University, Cambridge*
Prof. **Paul D'Anieri**, *University of California*
Dr. **Heike Dörrenbächer**, *Friedrich Naumann Foundation*
Dr. **John Dunlop**, *Hoover Institution, Stanford, California*
Dr. **Sabine Fischer**, *SWP, Berlin*
Dr. **Geir Flikke**, *NUPI, Oslo*
Prof. **David Galbreath**, *University of Aberdeen*
Prof. **Frank Golczewski**, *University of Hamburg*
Dr. **Nikolas Gvosdev**, *Naval War College, Newport, RI*
Prof. **Mark von Hagen**, *Arizona State University*
Prof. **Guido Hausmann**, *University of Regensburg*
Prof. **Dale Herspring**, *Kansas State University*
Dr. **Stefani Hoffman**, *Hebrew University of Jerusalem*
Prof. em. **Andrzej Korbonski**, *University of California*
Dr. **Iris Kempe**, *"Caucasus Analytical Digest"*
Prof. **Herbert Küpper**, *Institut für Ostrecht Regensburg*
Prof. **Rainer Lindner**, *University of Konstanz*

Dr. **Luke March**, *University of Edinburgh*
Prof. **Michael McFaul**, *Stanford University, Palo Alto*
Prof. **Birgit Menzel**, *University of Mainz-Germersheim*
Dr. **Alex Pravda**, *University of Oxford*
Dr. **Erik van Ree**, *University of Amsterdam*
Dr. **Joachim Rogall**, *Robert Bosch Foundation Stuttgart*
Prof. **Peter Rutland**, *Wesleyan University, Middletown*
Prof. **Gwendolyn Sasse**, *University of Oxford*
Prof. **Jutta Scherrer**, *EHESS, Paris*
Prof. **Robert Service**, *University of Oxford*
Mr. **James Sherr**, *RIIA Chatham House London*
Dr. **Oxana Shevel**, *Tufts University, Medford*
Prof. **Eberhard Schneider**, *University of Siegen*
Prof. **Olexander Shnyrkov**, *Shevchenko University, Kyiv*
Prof. **Hans-Henning Schröder**, *SWP, Berlin*
Prof. **Yuri Shapoval**, *Ukrainian Academy of Sciences*
Dr. **Lisa Sundstrom**, *University of British Columbia*
Dr. **Philip Walters**, *"Religion, State and Society", Oxford*
Prof. **Zenon Wasyliw**, *Ithaca College, New York State*
Dr. **Lucan Way**, *University of Toronto*
Dr. **Markus Wehner**, *"Frankfurter Allgemeine Zeitung"*
Dr. **Andrew Wilson**, *University College London*
Prof. **Jan Zielonka**, *University of Oxford*
Prof. **Andrei Zorin**, *University of Oxford*

* While the Editorial Committee and Advisory Board support the General Editor in the choice and improvement of manuscripts for publication, responsibility for remaining errors and misinterpretations in the series' volumes lies with the books' authors.

Soviet and Post-Soviet Politics and Society (SPPS)
ISSN 1614-3515

Founded in 2004 and refereed since 2007, SPPS makes available affordable English-, German-, and Russian-language studies on the history of the countries of the former Soviet bloc from the late Tsarist period to today. It publishes between 5 and 20 volumes per year and focuses on issues in transitions to and from democracy such as economic crisis, identity formation, civil society development, and constitutional reform in CEE and the NIS. SPPS also aims to highlight so far understudied themes in East European studies such as right-wing radicalism, religious life, higher education, or human rights protection. The authors and titles of all previously published volumes are listed at the end of this book. For a full description of the series and reviews of its books, see www.ibidem-verlag.de/red/spps.

Editorial correspondence & manuscripts should be sent to: Dr. Andreas Umland, Institute for Euro-Atlantic Cooperation, vul. Volodymyrska 42, off. 21, UA-01030 Kyiv, Ukraine

Business correspondence & review copy requests should be sent to: *ibidem* Press, Leuschnerstr. 40, 30457 Hannover, Germany; tel.: +49 511 2622200; fax: +49 511 2622201; spps@ibidem.eu.

Authors, reviewers, referees, and editors for (as well as all other persons sympathetic to) SPPS are invited to join its networks at www.facebook.com/group.php?gid=52638198614
www.linkedin.com/groups?about=&gid=103012
www.xing.com/net/spps-ibidem-verlag/

Recent Volumes

211 Li Bennich-Björkman; Sergiy Kurbatov (Eds.)
When the Future Came
The Collapse of the USSR and the Emergence of National Memory in Post-Soviet History Textbooks
ISBN 978-3-8382-1335-4

212 Olga R. Gulina
Migration as a (Geo-)Political Challenge in the Post-Soviet Space
Border Regimes, Policy Choices, Visa Agendas
With a foreword by Nils Muižnieks
ISBN 978-3-8382-1338-5

213 Sanna Turoma, Kaarina Aitamurto, Slobodanka Vladiv-Glover (Eds.)
Religion, Expression, and Patriotism in Russia
Essays on Post-Soviet Society and the State
ISBN 978-3-8382-1346-0

214 Vasif Huseynov
Geopolitical Rivalries in the "Common Neighborhood"
Russia's Conflict with the West, Soft Power, and Neoclassical Realism
With a foreword by Nicholas Ross Smith
ISBN 978-3-8382-1277-7

215 Mikhail Suslov
Russia's Ideology of Authenticity
Varieties of Conservatism in Russian History from the Late 19th Century to the Present
With a foreword by Mark Bassin
ISBN 978-3-8382-1361-3

216 Alexander Etkind, Mikhail Minakov (Eds.)
Ideology after Union
Political Doctrines, Discourses, and Debates in Post-Soviet Societies
ISBN 978-3-8382-1388-0

217 Jakob Mischke, Oleksandr Zabirko (Hrsg.)
Protestbewegungen im langen Schatten des Kreml
Aufbruch und Resignation in Russland und der Ukraine
ISBN 978-3-8382-0926-5

218 Oksana Huss
How Corruption and Anti-Corruption Policies Sustain Hybrid Regimes
Strategies of Political Domination under Ukraine's Presidents in 1994-2014
With a foreword by Tobias Debiel and Andrea Gawrich
ISBN 978-3-8382-1430-6

219 Dmitry Travin, Vladimir Gel'man, Otar Marganiya
The Russian Path
Ideas, Interests, Institutions, Illusions
With a foreword by Vladimir Ryzhkov
ISBN 978-3-8382-1421-4

To M & M

Table of Contents

Figures 9

Tables 10

Appendices 10

1 Uncertainty as a Multi-Dimensional Concept: A Brief Summary of the Argument 11

2 Uncertainty: A Critical Overview 41

3 Uncertainty in Non-Democracies 71

4 Uncertainty in Democracies 101

5 Inter-Institutional Uncertainty 117

6 Democratic Uncertainty 141

7 Historically Induced Uncertainty 155

8 Verbally Induced Uncertainty 181

9 Future Research on Political Uncertainty: A Plea for a More Integrated Approach 219

Figures

Figure 1.1: Uncertainty as a Chain Process: The Cash in the PM's Night Stand Story 19
Figure 1.2: Uncertainty as a Chain Process and Uncertainty as a Nested Phenomenon 23
Figure 1.3: Continuum of Institutional Strength and Uncertainty 26
Figure 1.4: Hypothesized Types and Levels of Uncertainty in Democracies and Non-Democracies 28
Figure 3.1: Impact of Investigations on the Severity of Sanctions Imposed on the Government 84
Figure 3.2: Procedural and Substantive Uncertainty in Democracies and Non-Democracies 89
Figure 3.3: The Accountability Pyramid in Russia: Relative Sanctioning Effectiveness of Forums 91
Figure 3.4: Incidence of Investigations of Media Accusations Levelled at the Government 93
Figure 4.1: Uncertainty in Elections 104
Figure 4.2: Uncertainty in Inter-Electoral Accountability 104
Figure 4.3: High Inter-Institutional Uncertainty: Sanctioning Effectiveness of Forums in Germany 105
Figure 4.4: Specialization of Forums According to Issues 108
Figure 4.5: Translating Inter-Institutional Uncertainty into Substantive Uncertainty 115
Figure 5.1: Two Examples of Patterns of Inter-Institutional Interactions 118
Figure 5.2: Patterns of Institutional, Societal and Governmental Conflict 124
Figure 8.1: Relations between Constraints on Blame Avoidance Strategies, Verbal Uncertainty and Perceptual Uncertainty 181
Figure 8.2: Government Responses to Public Allegations in Germany and Russia 182
Figure 8.3: Distribution of Incompetence and Misconduct Charges in Russia and Germany 194
Figure 8.4: Distribution of the Types of Accusers in Russia and Germany 195

Tables

Table 3.1: Impact of the Type of Investigation on the Incidence of Government Sanctions for Both Incompetence and Misconduct Charges 90
Table 3.2: Types of Uncertainty in Non-Democracies 97
Table 4.1: Factors Inducing or Reducing Inter-Institutional Uncertainty 106
Table 5.1: Sources of Inter-Institutional Uncertainty: One Dominant and Several Alternative Views 123
Table 6.1: Duality of Representative Democracy 143
Table 6.2: Uncertainty in Electoral Democracy and in Extra-Electoral Democracy 151
Table 7.1: The Impact of the Historical Uprisings and Corresponding Developments during the 1989 Transition in Hungary 164
Table 7.2: Juxtaposition of the Communist Party Reformers' and the Hard-liners' Perceptions of Various "Reference Points" 172
Table 8.1: Logistic Regression: Predictive Model of Government Responses in Germany 197
Table 8.2: Logistic Regression: Predictive Model of Government Responses in Russia 199

Appendices

Appendix 8.1: Description of the Number of Articles and Accusations 208
Appendix 8.2: Measurement of Key Variables 208
Appendix 8.3: Overview of Key Variables 216

1 Uncertainty as a Multi-Dimensional Concept
A Brief Summary of the Argument[1]

As I write this manuscript in the early stages of a coronavirus pandemic, I stare at the face of uncertainty. I am very uncertain as to whether I should make an international trip. According to one classical definition of uncertainty, I experience the "inability to assign probabilities to the likelihood of future events" (Stevens 2014, p. 432). I am uncertain about the probability of negative consequences, if I decide to take the trip. At that point, the probability of catching the virus constitutes the ultimate "state of uncertainty as existing for an event when no numerical probability of the event occurring can be assigned" (Knight 1920 cited in Cyert and DeGroot 1987, p. 3). The very existence of two very stark, mutually opposed scenarios, to travel or not to travel in the midst of a ranging pandemic, and the inability to assign precise probabilities to either of them, creates a high degree of uncertainty. Having a choice is very unsettling, but having an ill-defined choice is even more unnerving. This relatively simple scenario multiplied itself endlessly during the pandemic as people asked themselves whether they should cancel their vacation plans, whether they should go to the shops and whether they should send their children to school. Suddenly, the whole planet was overwhelmed by uncertainty — and that is by no means an uncertain statement.

The pandemic brought with itself the concept of uncertainty defined as "heightened unpredictability" not only in terms of personal choices. Uncertainty was also unleashed as the belief in the power of science to predict the rise and spread of the pandemic was shattered. Before the eyes of the public, epidemiologists argued, disagreed, sometimes even contradicted their own past statements about the deadliness of the virus, its infectiousness, whether

---

[1] I thank Laurence Whitehead and John Keane for their invaluable feedback on the first chapter. I thank Christopher Harding for his excellent research assistance with the bibliography for the entire book.

wearing face masks was beneficial and how long the virus survives on metal surfaces. The idea that science is not an unambiguously reliable source of guidance augmented the sense of uncertainty. As doubt was cast on the precision of scientific knowledge, it became clear that the utilisation of scientific knowledge in politics and public policy was, to a degree, subjective and political, and therefore it was rife with uncertainties as well. A rift between science as a monolithic body and scientists as a heterogeneous community was laid bare. It became clear that politicians handpicked the scientists, whose advice they wanted to follow, thus undermining the belief that "science-based" policy is unequivocal. This realisation did not decrease uncertainty either.

While 2020 was the year when the notion of uncertainty reasserted its powerful grip, it was by far not the only instance when uncertainty reigned supreme. The pandemic heightened the importance of studying uncertainty, but it did not create uncertainty per se. It created the urgent necessity to talk about uncertainty. But the questions have been long overdue, long before the pandemic made its point. Here are some of them: is uncertainty borne out of people's inability to imagine such a powerful exogenous shock to the world? Does uncertainty stem from newness, in the sense that scientists by default do not have enough data to gauge the nature and the extent of a new phenomenon and a new threat? Or is uncertainty related to the lack of sophisticated methodology to assess the already available data? Alternatively, is uncertainty so endemic, systemic and pivotal that no matter how much data is available, there will still be a large, unfathomable margin of error in any prediction? Finally, could uncertainty be fueled by the diverse and often conflicting reporting of an event in the media? These are only a small number of the questions that the present book raises.

The book provides a comprehensive and methodological understanding of uncertainty in politics, but it relates it to uncertainty in many disciplinary fields. This introductory chapter builds upon the accumulated inter-disciplinary knowledge to create a framework for studying political uncertainty in particular. To do so, it performs a comprehensive overview, which critically analyses the sources, types, definitions and the measurements of uncertainty.

Looking at the available scholarship, it is fair to conclude that there is a great degree of variation on understanding "uncertainty" as a concept.

Uncertainty: Two Main Claims of the Book

Before positing what the book claims, it is important to state what it does not claim. The main argument is not that uncertainty is invariably dangerous, insidious, destructive or that it is entirely knowable. On the contrary, it is fully possible that uncertainty breeds many positive aspects of life. John Keane (2022) makes a convincing argument to this effect. The book argues, however, that to the extent that political uncertainty should and could be conquered, it should be subject to a comprehensive and systematic analysis. Thus, it makes two main claims: (1) that we need to view uncertainty as a multidimensional, integrated concept and (2) that we need to consider new types of uncertainty.

The first claim — conceptualizing uncertainty as a multidimensional concept — is borne out of the understanding that the multiplicity of existing types of uncertainty should not be viewed individually but collectively. It is also based on the contention that most political processes should not be conceived as a one-stage event but as a chain of events. Even when these events are very minor, they still need to be differentiated because they embody different types of logic and a different type of uncertainty. Viewing the pandemic through the lens of only one type of uncertainty would be misguided. Many of the existing types of uncertainty could be applied to it: (1) endogenous vs. exogenous uncertainty, because the virus came from outside of the countries and was an external shock, but it was resolved endogenously within each country; (2) procedural vs. substantive (or output) uncertainty, because sticking to the procedures of dealing with the virus implied a different kind of uncertainty from the uncertainty underlining the outcomes of implementing this procedure; (3) known vs. unknown uncertainty, because the uncertainty related to how people reacted physically to the virus was less known than the uncertainty related to how much people were afraid of the virus and were willing to follow government advice; (4) state vs. effect vs. response uncertainty is also a useful concept because it captures the difference between the inability to assign probabilities to the spread of the pandemic, to the effects of the pandemic, and to the various response options respectively.

Of all these types of uncertainty, the book focuses on two already established types of uncertainty-institutional and substantive; and it adds three more types: inter-institutional, verbally-induced and historically-induced types of uncertainty. The reason why the book singles out institutional and substantive types of uncertainty is that they have been instrumental in gauging uncertainty in new democracies, but also because the study of the uncertainty-reducing effects of institutions has been fundamental in the fields of international relations, public policy and public administration: "To cope with uncertainty, institutions align incentives for information revelation; to handle difficult problems, institutions create incentives for diverse problem-solving approaches; and to harness complexity, institutions adjust selection criteria, rates of variation, and the level of connectedness" (Page 2008, p. 115). Whether institutions are perceived as a procedure — and this is mainly the procedure of elections — or whether institutions are taken at face value — as government departments, NATO, European Unions, etc. — they all have one 'magic' quality, which is usually put at the centre of studying uncertainty — they equalise expectations about how things should be done.

Institutions reduce the unpredictability of coordinating multiple people, who undoubtedly have diverse and often incompatible ways of doing things. While institutional uncertainty is about how things are done, substantive uncertainty is what has actually been done. It would be one-sided to study only institutional uncertainty without studying substantive uncertainty because that would presume that outcomes always follow institutional rules, which will be a severely reductionist argument as it will automatically exclude a myriad of other causes. Thus, not only viewing institutional and substantive uncertainty together, but viewing the relation between the two of them is paramount. The book takes a step in that direction, although more research correlating the different types of uncertainty in a systematic way is needed.

Apart from building on scholarly wisdom about institutional and procedural uncertainty, the present analysis underscores the astuteness of existing actor-based accounts of uncertainty. In the context of the book, actor-based uncertainty is presented in a new light. A decision does not have to be made collectively — such as an electoral vote, for example — to influence a collection of people. Imagine, for example, the disastrous effect that a pilot's error of judgment can have on the fate of a flight. This view will chime in with the conclusions of the scholarship on the impact of individual leaders. Even if the counterargument holds that leaders are a product of structural circumstances and express a collective identity, the argument about the uncertainty inducing power of individuals still holds because the individuals triggering havoc need not be high-placed or elected. This person could be a nameless driver who causes a small incident on the highway, thus changing the plans of possibly hundreds of people in the cars behind him. It could be an anonymous terrorist who blows up a marketplace, thus changing not only the lives of its victims but those of their families as well. Actor-related uncertainty is important to recognise and to study.

The media age is the main reason why actor-related uncertainty is more important nowadays than ever. Media platforms can augment individual claims, so it does not matter whether a claim is made by one person or a majority of the population. Through the media, this claim can reach a sizeable share of the population. In this case, the number of makers or triggers of the event is irrelevant because the event becomes known to many people. Before the advent of the media age, people had to congregate physically or sign petitions to have the ear of the government or society. Alternatively, they had to have access to the relatively closed circle of newspaper, TV and radio networks. With the advancement of telecommunication technologies, these impediments are almost obsolete. People can make claims in easily accessible platforms, and sometimes these claims "travel." They can be "picked" by more popular outlets. Alternatively, the makers of the claims can email or send electronically compromising material. Such information "dumps" are not uncommon. They can range from Wikileaks to an arguably authentic video taken in the residence of the former Bulgarian prime-minister Boyko Borisov, which showed a drawer in his nightstand packed with 500 Euro notes, gold bars and a pistol. It takes only one person to blow the whistle, and technology has diminished the importance of how powerful that person is. That is why individually induced uncertainty matters, especially in the Media Age.

If we already have such a long list of types of uncertainty—fifteen and counting—why should we include three more types? The ones introduced in the book are: verbally-induced uncertainty, inter-institutional uncertainty and historically-induced uncertainty. The first type of uncertainty is verbal uncertainty, or verbally-induced uncertainty. It denotes the uncertainty not only whether someone is telling the truth or not, and fake news has made the possibility of this uncertainty more probable. Verbal uncertainty is also the uncertainty induced by various blame avoidance strategies, which seek to interpret and re-interpret events. If we exclude verbal uncertainty, we exclude the possibility that words uttered in the media can change the public perception of the world.

This neglect of blame avoidance strategies as a source of uncertainty is puzzling but easy to explain. Blame avoidance strategies exists as a separate and self-sufficient sub-field in communication and the public policy fields and integrating it in the study of uncertainty would constitute not only a disciplinary bridge but a disciplinary breach. To understand the link between uncertainty and blame avoidance, we need to imagine certainty before and after blame avoidance utterances. Image, for example, that the pictures of the Bulgarian Prime Minister's cash-packed drawer were published and the prime minister had not said anything or he had confessed to possessing a huge amount of cash, some gold bars and a pistol. The level of uncertainty would have been smaller as most people would have most likely accepted this as a fact.

Now imagine that the prime minister said, as he actually did, that this is a set-up, and that it makes no sense for him to keep cash in his nightstand, when he had a safe in the corridor. Furthermore, he said that the prolific quantities of cash did not tie in with the "ascetic" way of life portrayed in the video overall. And finally, he added, the person who took the video knew exactly which was the drawer with the cash, and opened it, when there were several identical drawers. All these facts, the prime minister concluded, proved that the maker of the video put the cash and the gold in his drawer to compromise him and to destabilise the government (DarikNews, 2020).

From this point on, the number of people who "bought" Borisov's version of events shot up. It does not particularly matter who these people were. What counts, from the point of view of uncertainty, is that an alternative version of events came into existence, and it sparked an avalanche of supportive comments under the online articles reporting the prime-minister's version of events. What this means in terms of uncertainty is that the prime minister's utterance has sown the seeds of doubt. It has moved the discussion from the sphere of facts as observed through pictures into the sphere of opinion as manifested through verbal statements. Where there is doubt, there is uncertainty.

The second—and most consequential—type of uncertainty that the book introduces is inter-institutional uncertainty. Inter-institutional uncertainty is the uncertainty arising from the interaction between institutions. While institutional uncertainty tends to focus on institutions in general or on very specific institutions, such as elections, it neglects to understand how the dynamics between the institutions unfold. This is a consequential omission because institutions neither exist in isolation, nor do they all embody the same rules. In fact, most of the accountable institutions tend to check and balance each other, which means that they are expected to compete rather than cooperate. This element of competition between institutions raises the level of uncertainty. But even if institutions cooperate, it is unclear what will come out of that cooperation. The very choice whether institutions will cooperate or compete further complicates uncertainty, which I call inter-institutional uncertainty.

The third type of uncertainty introduced in this book is historically-induced uncertainty. The purpose of creating this category of uncertainty is to ensure that decision makers and decision takers portrayed in political science do not suffer from amnesia. It is unrealistic to expect that future predictions should be based on all sorts of factors anchored in the present, while omitting past behaviour. This does not mean that power-holders are particularly wise in "learning from history," as it has been proven that they rarely learn from history (Wilsford 1994; Greenhalgh et al 2011). Neither does historically-induced uncertainty imply a path dependent or a deterministic argument. Rather it is a rationalization purporting that people may look back to pick clues for present and future behaviour. This is especially applicable to transitional and formerly authoritarian countries because they lack a clear system of signalling popular discontent, and thus occasional uprisings in the past offer important information about public support in the present.

Having briefly described the three types of uncertainty the book introduces, it is important to go back to my original claim that uncertainty needs to be perceived as a multi-stage and a multi-dimensional concept. No single type of uncertainty can "capture" all uncertainty. This is so because life unfolds as a process rather than as a single event. Even a single event—such as a pandemic—could be dissected into a process consisting of a series of sub-events. This is not splitting hairs. It is a methodological exercise which acknowledges that the beginning and the end of an "event" is ultimately the result of a subjective decision of a researcher. It is essential to differentiate between these smaller sub-events because each of them is likely to express a different type of logic and uncertainty. This view acknowledges the distinctiveness of each stage of the process and the inter-connectedness between all stages in the process. To demonstrate the explanatory utility of the approach of perceiving uncertainty in processes as multi-stage chain events, I briefly apply it to the above-mentioned case of the nightstand of the former Bulgarian Prime Minister Borisov.

Figure 1.1: Uncertainty as a Chain Process: The Cash in the PM's Nightstand Story

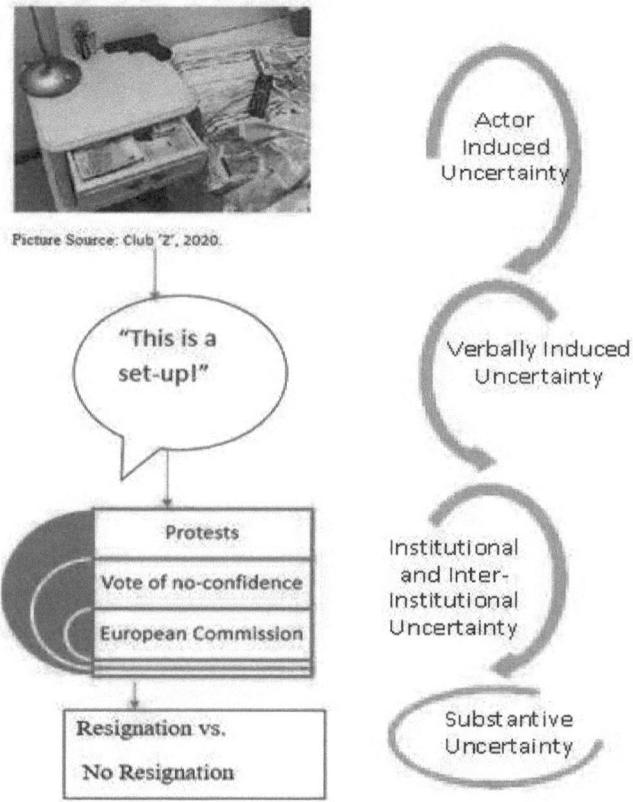

As figure 1.1. suggests, political life in Bulgaria went up in flames with the explosive photos and videos showing pictures from the former prime minister's bedroom. The material was compromising in that it insinuated that the then prime minister was much richer than he had admitted. The secrecy and the abundance of the cash hinted at its unsavoury origin. This accusation testifies to the power of a single person or a small number of people with the access to compromising material to cast a big shadow over the government. This is the uncertainty injected into political life by political and other actors in the first stage of this process.

The second stage in this illustrative case is the strategy for spinning the story. Mr. Borisov came up with a few arguments why the possessions could not have been his but were inserted there by ill-wishers. In this stage, it is the verbal framing of the pictures that introduces another level of uncertainty. In the next stage, institutional uncertainty arose because it was unclear how the accusations would play out within the Bulgarian parliament, the European Commission, and the anti-corruption protests that erupted. But the point I want to make is that inter-institutional uncertainty was equally as important, as it reflected the dynamics not within but among the Bulgarian parliament, the European Commission, and the anti-corruption protests. It could be argued that the institutional responses were linked: because the photos were not condemned by the EU and the EU gave Bulgaria huge loans just a few days after the pictures emerged, the Bulgarian parliament turned down a vote of no confidence in Mr. Borisov, and the protests lost steam. This move by the European Union reduced the political uncertainty unfurled by the photos. In the end stage — which comes fourth in figure 1.1.- there were only two substantive outcomes, a resignation of the government or a lack thereof. The government did not resign. This case illustrates that a fundamental difficulty of conceptualizing uncertainty is to find the balance or the sum between the different types of uncertainty involved in multi-stage and multi-dimensional processes.

Why Should We Study Uncertainty as a Process?

The book examines uncertainty as a political process. This approach presents several considerable advantages in comparison to existing approaches. One current approach to uncertainty is to pick one or a few types of uncertainty (for example, institutional, perceptual or endogenous) and see how they apply to economic or political processes, or how they are generated by them. The reverse approach is to focus on a very narrow interaction, which is usually a single shot game and to analyse the uncertainty inherent in it. Both of these methodological approaches — studying uncertainty as type or as a single shot game — carry two dangers: that some types of uncertainty are omitted and that the relationship between the different types of uncertainty is underexplored. For example, if one sets out to study institutional uncertainty, they may miss out the uncertainty inherent in verbal interactions. If they study uncertainty as a single-shot game, they may miss how uncertainty unfolds over a number of games that do not presuppose fixed structures underlying all games. Analysing uncertainty in a process helps avoid both dangers. It enables the researcher to include a variety of types of uncertainty, which emerge in the consecutive stages of the process. At the same time, it enables the scholar to observe and analyse the parameters, determinants and causality between the different types of uncertainty arising in different situations.

Studying uncertainty as a political process (rather than as a single type or a single shot game) is achieved in this book by approaching uncertainty through the lens of government accountability. The book studies the types, sources and constellations of the types of uncertainty, when the government is publicly alleged in the media. The huge importance and diversity of uncertainty was revealed to me while I was writing my book Democracy beyond Elections: Government Accountability in the Media Age (2019). In a way, the present study is a logical continuation of this book. I was surprised how uncertain it was whether the government would be held accountable for media allegations or not. Above all, I was struck by how decentralized a process accountability was. While studying which groups make the accusations, which groups pursue the accusations, which forums investigate the accusations, the enormous repercussions of this decentralization dawned on me. The idea of studying uncertainty gathered speed while I was describing the various groups that are interested in pursuing various types of allegations, on the one hand, and the various forums, which enable them to do so, on the other hand. The degree of uncertainty was finally revealed to me when I realized how uncertain it was how these accountability seekers will pair up with the accountability forums. It is this particular "pairing up" that was the best argument to pay greater attention to uncertainty through the lens of accountability. In retrospect, it becomes evident that it is particularly suitable to study uncertainty through the process of accountability for the three reasons described below.

First, approaching uncertainty through the lens of accountability is both productive and illuminating because accountability is a chain process consisting of well delineated stages, or sub-events: an accusation, verbal response, investigations and sanctions. The benefit is that it is easier to "capture" different "pure" types of accountability in the separate sub-stages. Thus, one can isolate the importance of actors in the stage of accusation-making, the importance of verbal uncertainty in the stage of blame shifting, to identify inter-institutional types of uncertainty, to tease out the uncertainty of matching accusers to forums in the investigative stage, and to think of sanctions in terms of substantive uncertainty in the sanctioning stage. This approach also has the advantage of being a linear process in the sense that the accusation cannot come before the investigations, for example.

The second reason is that viewing uncertainty as a sequence embedded in the accountability process makes methodological sense. Deconstructing a process into sub-stages and then deducing the types of uncertainty embedded in each sub-stage is diametrically opposed to settling on one type of uncertainty first and then trying to figure out how this particular type of uncertainty is manifested in various processes. The methodology used in this book is easier to track down as it unfolds in a relatively easily observable sequence of stages, rather than as a compilation or an aggregation of events or spheres, which are difficult to disentangle.

From a methodological point of view, it is wiser to study uncertainty as a chain process rather than uncertainty as a nested phenomenon. From a pragmatic point of view, however, it may be hard to tell the difference. For example, in The New Despotism, Keane (2020) suggests that institutional uncertainty — as manifested in the pretence to follow democratic rules while undermining them — is heavily connected to ambiguities in many other spheres of life, such as the economy and the media. This beckons the question whether a high degree of institutional uncertainty can only co-exist with high degrees of other types of uncertainties. Relatedly, another interesting and pressing inquiry is whether institutional uncertainty can exist independently in a single sub-stage of a process and whether it is only functional insofar other uncertainties play a supporting role. The graphical representation of the two approaches to uncertainty is depicted in figure 1.2.

Figure 1.2: Uncertainty in a Chain Process and Uncertainty as a Nested Phenomenon

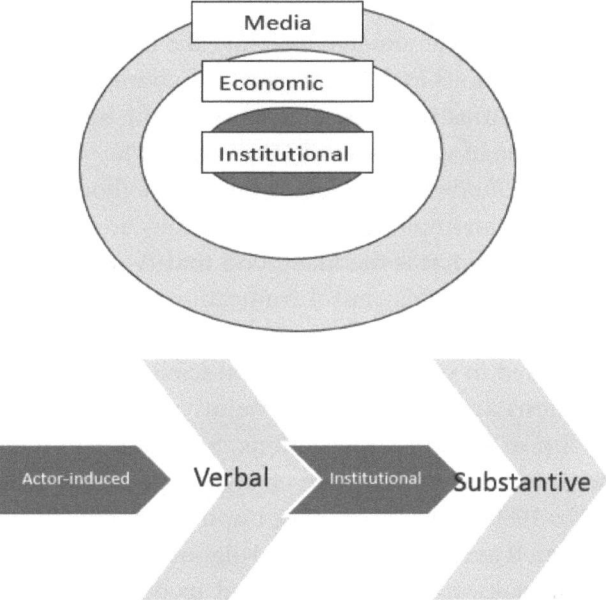

Future research should study the precise degree of causal connection between the various types of uncertainties. Can we view uncertainty as a nested phenomenon or as a chain process? Are uncertainties in different spheres of life, uncertainties caused by different factors and uncertainties measuring different dimensions linked? When does one type of uncertainty imply another type of uncertainty? For example, one could argue that the fact that the Russian president exerts a lot of power over the prosecutorial office could be interpreted both in terms of institutional and inter-institutional uncertainty. Institutional uncertainty is prevalent because there is so much informal influence that it is very uncertain whether the prosecutor will follow the formal rules of the office. However, this finding, which is gauged in terms of institutional uncertainty, can also be conceived as inter-institutional uncertainty, which measures the unpredictability arising from the interaction of the presidential institution and the office of the prosecutor general.

The third advantage of studying uncertainty in connection to analysing government accountability is that it is possible to embed uncertainty within substantive debates in political science. Too often uncertainty is either studied in the abstract or is applied exclusively to economic phenomena. Isolating the notion of uncertainty from thorny questions in political science is counter-productive. By contrast, all theories in political science could be interpreted to gauge the degree of uncertainty in the world. The studies employing quantitative methodology report on the likelihood that a particular variable has an impact on an outcome they are interested in. In a sense, they ask: what is the likelihood that A causes B, and how certain are we about this causal connection? But uncertainty features only implicitly in such analyses. Explicitly, uncertainty is rarely embedded in substantive political science debates. Some notable exceptions are studies of uncertainty as it relates to political parties, political violence, legislations, Supreme Court decisions, deterrence, elections and regime change (e.g., Mueller and Rauh 2017; Combs 1980; Stephenson 2005; Lupu and Riedl 2013; Schedler 2013; O'Donnell and Schmitter 2013; Kilgour and Zagare 1991).

In this book, uncertainty is linked to three political science questions: the EU accountability deficit, the process of presidentialisation of the accountability process and the phenomenon of the multiple accountability disorder. Chapter three highlights the lack of uncertainty guiding the relations between the president and other institutions, when investigating the government in Russia. By showing how the president has monopolized the investigative and sanctioning process, it presents a novel perspective on the debate over presidentialisation. Chapter four throws light on the EU democratic deficit from the point of view of the EU investigating the German government. Learning whether the EU has a disproportionate power over holding the incumbents to account provides a novel point of view on democratic accountability. Chapter five links uncertainty with the thorny issue of the interaction between institutions and how they impact democracy.

Why Should We Study Uncertainty in Democracies and Non-Democracies?

The book takes a comparative approach to the study of uncertainty. It is the first study that presents an explicit and integrated analysis of uncertainty in democracies and non-democracies. It is generally assumed that uncertainty "behaves" differently in democracies and non-democracies, both in terms of its intensity and its type. Interestingly, Schedler (2013) suggests that both in consolidated autocracies and in non-consolidated democracies, institutional certainty is high. Figure 1.3., which is reproduced from Schedler's seminal work on political uncertainty, posits that high uncertainty is prevalent both in authoritarian regime crises and in democratic regime crises. In general, it is argued that "strong institutions create deep certainties, weak institutions much less so" (Schedler 2013, p. 23). So measured in terms of intensity, uncertainty is the same in diametrically opposed regimes. The logical question that arises then is whether this high degree of uncertainty is of the same type in democracies and autocracies. Is a high degree of institutional uncertainty manifested similarly in dictatorships and non-dictatorships? For example, Schedler's analysis explains convincingly that institutional uncertainty is high in electoral authoritarianism because of the threat of rivals, the threat of rebels, the threat of retaliation and ignorance (Schedler 2013, p. 23). Given the lack of a similarly thorough comparative analysis of the high degree of institutional uncertainty in competitive regimes, should we assume that the above factors that lead to institutional uncertainty in authoritarian regimes are simply nullified in competitive regimes, or do they still apply to a degree?

Figure 1.3: Continuum of Institutional Strength and Uncertainty[2]

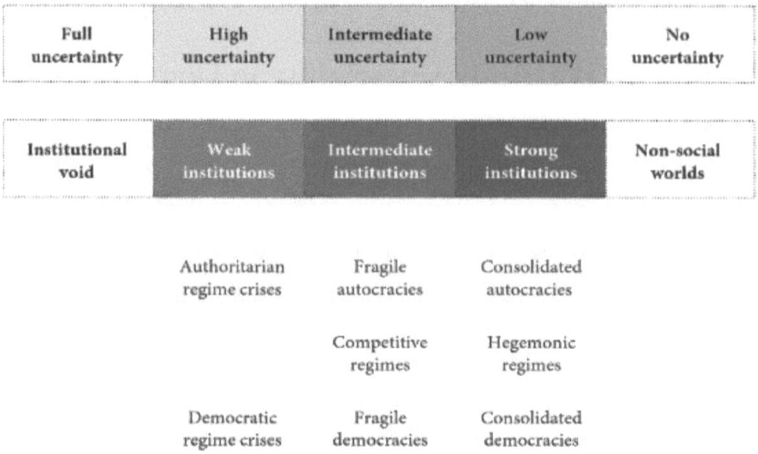

Full uncertainty	High uncertainty	Intermediate uncertainty	Low uncertainty	No uncertainty
Institutional void	Weak institutions	Intermediate institutions	Strong institutions	Non-social worlds
	Authoritarian regime crises	Fragile autocracies	Consolidated autocracies	
		Competitive regimes	Hegemonic regimes	
	Democratic regime crises	Fragile democracies	Consolidated democracies	

It is not necessarily so problematic that uncertainty in non-democracies is studied more extensively than uncertainty in democracies. The problem is that uncertainty is often studied using different explanatory paradigms, and it is consequently not clear how they translate from one regime type to another. The study of uncertainty is somewhat one-sided but this one-sidedness could be avoided by juxtaposing and analysing the regime types in conjunction. For example, it is argued that regime uncertainty is high in authoritarian countries and that it results in "political actors, who must make strategic decisions while assigning positive probability to the breakdown of democratic institutions without being able to foresee the subsequent institutional arrangements" (Lupu and Riedl 2013, p. 1,346). In the absence of a comparative analysis of regime uncertainty, we are led to believe that by implication it is non-existent in consolidated democracies. However, the recent literature on democratic backsliding (Cianetti, Dawson and Hanley 2018) and the demise of democracy (Runciman 2018) seem to suggest that regime uncertainty should not be automatically written off in democracies. For example, Mechkova, Lührmann and Lindberg (2017, p. 163) suggest that "in 2013 alone, five countries went from autocracy to

---

2   Figure 1.3. is reproduced from Schedler 2013, p. 24.

democracy, and nine went the other way. This volatility suggests a fair amount of uncertainty as to how robust the democratic gains of the last four decades or so actually are." Furthermore, there is the argument that developing democracies are set to suffer from economic uncertainty, because their small economies are particularly viable to exogenous shocks and to the market volatility of the global economy (Lupu and Riedl 2013, p. 1,346). But developed and well globalized economies are also very exposed to exogenous shocks. Does it mean that they suffer from uncertainty as well? By focusing on uncertainty separately and individually in different regime types, we fail to trace whether factors that contribute to uncertainty in one type of regime feature in another type of regime, without causing the same uncertainty. We also fail to see how the variations both in the types and the degrees of uncertainty co-vary across established and non-established democracies.

Figure 1.4. makes some tentative suggestions about the variation in the intensity and the nature of uncertainty. It conjectures that institutional uncertainty — that is the likelihood that actors will comply with institutional rules — is high in non-democracies, but actor-based, inter-institutional and verbal uncertainty is low. Conversely, institutional uncertainty in democracies is low, but actor-based, inter-institutional and verbal uncertainty is high. This logic is empirically tested in chapters three and four. But this is just the beginning of thinking about uncertainty as a multi-dimensional process. We need a systematic analysis of the causal links between them.

Figure 1.4: Hypothesized Types and Levels of Uncertainty in Democracies and Non-Democracies

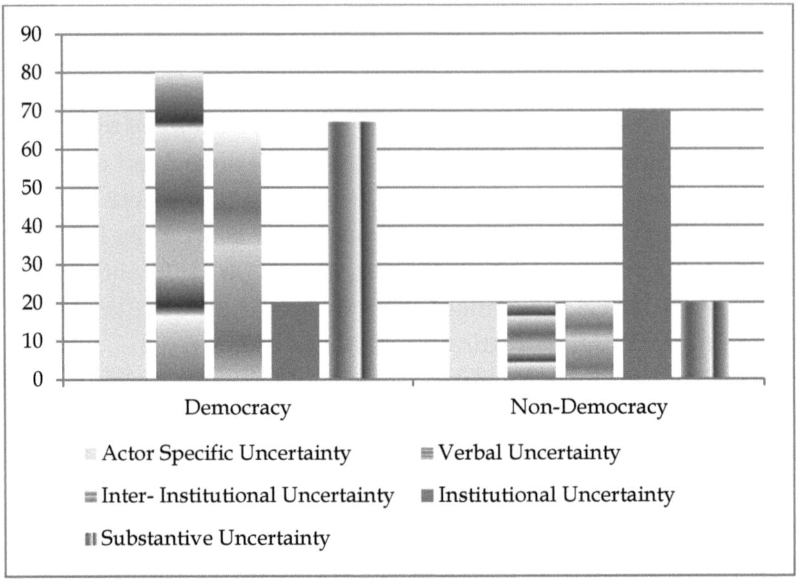

[Bar chart showing uncertainty levels by type for Democracy and Non-Democracy:
- Democracy: Actor Specific Uncertainty ~70, Verbal Uncertainty ~80, Inter-Institutional Uncertainty ~65, Institutional Uncertainty ~20, Substantive Uncertainty ~68
- Non-Democracy: Actor Specific Uncertainty ~20, Verbal Uncertainty ~20, Inter-Institutional Uncertainty ~20, Institutional Uncertainty ~70, Substantive Uncertainty ~20]

Uncertainty and Political Science as a Discipline

Uncertainty is intrinsically linked to the larger question about whether political scientists can predict phenomena or simply explain them retrospectively. Political science does not have an outstanding track record of predicting things. It failed to predict the end of communism, the outcome of the Brexit referendum (Hay 2017) and most scientists failed to predict the rise of President Trump (Blakely 2016), for example. Trump's victory was so surprising that some pundits asked whether it did not "destroy political prognostication forever" (Cillizza 2020). Without a doubt, prediction is more attractive than explanation. "Harry Truman once joked that he wanted to hear from a one-armed economist because he was sick of hearing "on the one hand ... on the other ..." (Tetlock, Mellers and Rohrbaugh 2014, p. 138). Even if explanations can furnish a sense of order in an inherently chaotic world, predictions provide a sense of control in an unsettlingly variable future.

But there is more to the soothing sense of control that predictions can contribute: predictions can alter our behaviours so we can avoid negative outcomes: "we explain in order to give ourselves a more informed perspective on how we might intervene to produce better outcomes in the future (our interest is prospective)"(Hay 2017, p. 184). Predictions can have many practical implications. Certainly, predicting the onset of political violence is important (Mueller and Rauh 2018). So is predicting Supreme Court decisions (Ruger et al 2004). The practical significance of political science has been highlighted by the rise of the political risk industry. Firms, such as Eurasia Group, The Economist Intelligence Unit and Control Risks, are employed by businesses and governments to predict the risk associated with certain investments and policies.

Given the attractiveness of predictions, and political science's unconvincing record of making predictions, the question arises "is political science obsolete"? If the discipline can offer explanations only after the phenomena in question have transpired, is this "retrospective explainability" (Taleb 2007) or "retrospective intelligibility" (Fernando, Smith and Perez 2021) good enough? Certainly, if meteorologists could not predict a thunderous storm that could affect the path of a plane, we would be less likely to respect meteorology as a discipline. Similarly, if medicine is powerless to predict the progression of a disease, but it can only say how the disease developed after it has spread, that would cast a big cloud over its value added. Shall we judge political science by means different from those employed in the natural sciences? And if we do so, and political science fails the test, does it mean that it is an obsolete discipline in this respect and an obsolete subject to study at universities?

There is no easy answer to this question, but I will nevertheless provide four arguments that could be used to salvage political science as a discipline. One way out of this conundrum is to conjecture that the natural world, just like the social world, is indeterminate and unpredictable. Heisenberg's uncertainty principle, which applies to quantum physics, roughly states that "one cannot assign exact simultaneous values to the position and momentum of a physical system. Rather, these quantities can only be determined with some characteristic "uncertainties" that cannot become arbitrarily small simultaneously" (Stanford Encyclopedia of Philosophy, 2001). If probabilities and predictions are impossible or approximate in physics, it would be similarly acceptable to acknowledge the same uncertainty in regard to political science. However, if the challenge is not to be entirely predictive but to be at least similarly predictive to the degree that natural sciences are, however approximate their predictions, we will need other lines of defence.

Thus, we turn to the second argument: political science has become a lot more forthcoming in terms of its relationship with uncertainty. This openness and acceptance of uncertainty has been manifested in its purported effort to make political science more "sciency" by incorporating statistical methods, analysis of large scale data and game theoretical methodology, among others. By doing so, political science has avoided being an all or nothing science, in the sense that events either happen or not or that causes either impact outcomes or not. The discipline has made real progress in reporting uncertainty both in terms of error terms, coefficients, confidence intervals, causal weights and R2. "R-squared (R2) is a useful measure of uncertainty because it represents the proportion of the variance for a dependent variable that's explained by an independent variable or variables in a regression model... So, if the R2 of a model is 0.50, then approximately half of the observed variation can be explained by the model's inputs" (Fernando, Smith and Perez 2021). Knowledge of what portion of the outcome is explained by a model constitutes a huge reduction of uncertainty. The regression coefficient measures the strength of the correlation between two variables. It reduces uncertainty because it shows to what extent the outcome is dependent on a particular cause. It helps the research avoid the perfidy of all or nothing causal relations.

As mentioned, political science has also become more disciplined and open about uncertainty through resorting to statistical analysis, which has enabled it to take advantage of past trends through collecting and analysing data, thus determining the probability of future occurrences. The error term in regression equations reduces uncertainty because it shows what portion of the theoretical model of the phenomenon we try to explain differs from the actual empirical phenomenon. Additionally, by being able to assign probabilities to various outcomes, political science has tamed uncertainty, or at least has shown that it has made an effort to control it. By doing so, it should have won the public confidence as a value neutral discipline, whose value added is to present the world in probabilistic terms, and leave the ultimate judgments to politicians who will make decisions in explicitly and openly value-laden terms. This effort has somewhat backfired, as I conjecture later, but it nevertheless has proved that political science has become more systematic about reporting and assessing uncertainty.

The third line of defence of political science is to discount the value and feasibility of prediction. Prediction could be even conceived as an illegitimate goal: "The notion of prediction (which might be neutral in the natural sciences) here generates the wrong — indeed, an illegitimate — expectation" (Hay 2017, p. 184). A "perfect prediction" is something we know to be impossible in a probabilistic world (or even in a deterministic world where we know we shall never have knowledge and measures of every possible influence) (King 1991, p. 1,048). What would be the grounds for not expecting political science to predict phenomena in the same way as natural sciences do? Why would an equivalence between the natural and human world be false? Chapter two discusses several reasons to treat predictions related to humans as infeasible: imagination, the lack of imagination (Black Swans), social coordination and doubt in other people's sympathy.

The power of imagination makes the human world less predictable than the natural world. Clouds arguably do not change their minds, they are going where the wind blows them, but people have a will, and desires and a brain and, in this sense, they can resist the flow of life's winds, metaphorically speaking. Paradoxically, the opposite reason, the limited capacity to imagine various scenarios, such as the 9/11 attacks and World War I, or the reluctance to do so, also makes the human world less predictable. The element of social coordination, and the infinite number of permutations and variations in which human beings can come together and react to a trigger event also makes the human world less predictable. People aggregate in a less predictable way than objects. It is much less certain what would happen if you put five people in a room as opposed to putting five chairs in a room. Finally, the human world is less predictable because there is never a guarantee that the people making value judgments, such as politicians and business elites, will be benevolent. Their fickle sympathy and empathy create uncertainty, which the natural world arguably does not harbour. As a result, prediction is less realistic and, consequently, political science is less to blame for failing to make predictions.

The fourth line of defence of political science is to revamp the meaning of prediction. Dowding and Miller (2019, p. 1.001) outline two types of predictions-pragmatic and scientific—and argue that political science should only make scientific, but not necessarily pragmatic predictions:

> We outline the difference between the two types—'pragmatic' and 'scientific' prediction—and explain why it is important to separate them for political science. Pragmatic prediction is the probabilistic forecasting of types of future events (such as elections, coups d'état or civil wars). Assessing how good those predictions are is based on how closely the assigned probabilities match what actually happens. Scientific prediction we define as the logical implication of a theoretical model, such as 'the greater the number of veto players in a system, the greater the stability of public policy'... Pragmatic predictions forecast future events and need not be explanatory. We argue that while good pragmatic predictions are important and useful, good scientific prediction should remain the principal desideratum for positive political science.

Whatever we think of the four arguments in defence of the arguably poor prediction record of political science, there are two issues that need to be considered. The first consideration is how to convey uncertainty to the public. The question is whether the average TV viewer is capable of grasping a degree of confidence intervals, and even whether media consumers are willing to be bothered with the technicalities of prediction. At the same time, the media should think carefully whether they have the ethical obligation to report statistical polls and other predictions in probabilistic terms, so they are more accurate. The second consideration is how to hold the forecasters to account. Without a system, which publicly, credibly and systematically reports on the extent to which predictions pan out empirically, forecasters are at liberty to make any predictions. The unlimited opportunity to report even false predictions could be harmful to the political process because it allows biased pollsters to sway the political opinion before elections. It also gives the predicting industry a bad name and makes it less reliable in the future. Some scholars have suggested conducting forecasting tournaments to impose methodological rigor and public accountability to this field (Tetlock et al 2014).

Outline of the Book

In the following chapters, the book lays out some theoretical considerations about uncertainty and proposes several new ones. Chapter two reviews critically the sources and types of uncertainty. It proposes that the chief differentiations between the sources of uncertainty are perceptual, which relate to the way individuals perceive reality, and environmental, which relate to the factors that make reality hard to predict. Of the environmental sources of uncertainty, the major distinction is made between man-made sources of uncertainty and those that are not caused by humans. The chapter proposes that technological innovation is by far the most analysed source of man-made uncertainty, or manufactured risk. It reviews and juxtaposes three different treatments of the link between scientific progress and uncertainty. According to it, science affects uncertainty because: (1) the side effects of scientific progress cast doubt on the objectivity of science; (2) the uncertainty introduced by science is managed by imagination; and because (3) technological innovations could be countered by a very uncertain collaborative communal effort. In this vein of thinking, the chapter inquires whether manufactured risk is a known unknown or an unknown unknown, which is also often identified as a Knightian uncertainty. At this point, the chapter proceeds to suggest one new source of uncertainty — the social fragmentation that has ensued due to various factors. The chapter suggests that institutional and procedural types of uncertainty constitute two of the major types of uncertainty. It introduces verbal, inter-institutional and historically-induced uncertainty as worth considering as well.

Chapter three applies the suggested types of uncertainty to non-democracies. It argues that inter-institutional uncertainty in Russia is very low because the balance between the institutions, which hold the government to account, is heavily skewed in favour of the president. Institutional uncertainty, by contrast, is high because the office of the prosecutor general is informally managed by the president. Sanctions are personalized and favour the president's allies because the president dismisses them but later appoints them to equally attractive positions. This means that substantive uncertainty, which measures the range of possible outcomes, is very small. Although some types of uncertainty vary in intensity, all in all, this multi—dimensional analysis points to a relatively small degree of uncertainty in the accountability process.

Chapter four reviews uncertainty in the accountability process in a democracy. In contrast to the previous chapter, which categorized the types of uncertainty according to the milieu in which they take place, such as verbal, inter-institutional and substantive, this chapter is more focused on gauging uncertainty in terms of the effect it has in estimating an outcome. In this case, the outcome in question is whether the European Union has a disproportionate influence on holding the German government to account. The results suggest that inter-institutional uncertainty in Germany is high because many accountability institutions are effective and motivated to investigate and sanction the government. How do we then estimate the likelihood whether the government will be held to account and by whom? The chapter suggests that there are two types of factors: uncertainty reducing and uncertainty inducing factors. The uncertainty reducing factors make it easier to estimate the EU's influence in the accountability process. In this case study, the nature of the allegations, the identity of the person making the accusations and the ranking of the accused officials reduce perceptual uncertainty because they are not subjective and are easy to observe. By contrast, the uncertainty-inducing factors make it harder to estimate whether the EU's influence will influence the outcome. These uncertainty reducing factors are the following: the perception of the legitimacy and independence of the prosecutor, the public perception of the allegation and the calculus performed by the government to avoid investigations. All these factors are a matter of judgment and are hard to observe because they involve the aggregated opinions of a lot of people.

Chapter five discusses exclusively inter-institutional uncertainty, which is the main type of uncertainty proposed in this book. It challenges the dominant wisdom that when multiple mechanisms investigate the government, these institutions will invariably compete in a vicious manner. The chapter disputes the assumptions implicit in the existing scholarly argument, which posits that institutions will care about their public image and that the public will customarily expect that the government is sanctioned. If both conditions do not obtain, institutions will not always compete. Uncertainty arises as it is unclear whether accountability forums will compete or cooperate, as it is uncertain which societal groups will pair with which societal forums to pursue which governmental policy. This is due to the fragmentation of the forums and the fragmentation of the public discussed in chapter two.

Chapter six poses a more general question, namely whether uncertainty in democracy is a fundamental and permanent feature of the democratic system or whether it is related to certain processes, such as the accountability process. It argues that it is both. It suggests that democracy is underpinned by antagonisms. Examples of such antagonisms include the promise versus reality of democracy, episteme versus doxa (Urbinati 2014), phylogenesis (public maturation) versus ontogenesis (individual maturation) (Hegel 2012), calculable and manageable actuality versus (Derrida 1984). Because it is unknown when, under what conditions and which of these antagonisms will prevail, uncertainty is permanent. In addition to this permanent uncertainty inherent in democracy, there are different types of uncertainty that can be applied to the process of accountability, as the book has argued. Uncertainty, whether verbal, inter-institutional, institutional or substantive, arises because political conflict is decentralized, the public is fragmented, the relationship between the representatives and the voters is varied, and the legitimacy of the various solutions to political conflict is called into question. Under such conditions, uncertainty is naturally rife.

The result is a democratic process in that is non-linear and unpredictable.

Chapter seven argues that there is a link between perceptual uncertainty experienced by political actors and historical events. More specifically, it suggests that popular uprisings taking place during a communist regime reduced the uncertainty that power holders experienced during the transition from communism to democracy. For example, the 1956 popular revolt in Hungary highlighted the public lack of tolerance for the communist regime. Consequently, the power holders were less uncertain about their public support and were more inclined to give up power peacefully. In the Soviet Union, where such uprising did not take place, the communist rulers tended to overestimate their power, and perceptual uncertainty was higher.

Chapter eight suggests that verbal responses are a powerful tool for shaping perceptual uncertainty. This is quite natural because no single person has complete information about the whole world so the majority of a person's decision making is made on the basis of what one hears, not on the basis of what one sees. The power of words to shape perceptual uncertainty has been underexplored. While the chapter highlights the link between verbal responses and perceptual uncertainty, its main core is to inquire what constraints shape the verbal responses themselves. In other words, can power holders say anything at all, or is the scope for spinning somehow constrained? The chapter finds out that the incumbents' blame avoidance techniques in a democratic and a non-democratic country are shaped by different factors. In Germany, government strategies are mostly likely to admit blame, if the accusation is one of incompetence and if there is a formal investigation of the government. By contrast, the process of account-giving in Russia is affected by the identity of the accuser rather than the type of accusation. Chapter nine offers some suggestions for future research. The most important suggestion is to seek the integration of various types of uncertainty.

Bibliography:

Blakely, J. (2016) Is Political Science This Year's Election Casualty? Lessons Learned from the Failures of Predictive Modelling. *The Atlantic.* Available at: https://www.theatlantic.com/education/archive/2016/11/is-political-science-another-election-casualty/507515/ [Accessed: January 24, 2023].

Cianetti, L., Dawson, J., Hanley, S. (2018) Rethinking "Democratic Backsliding" in Central and Eastern Europe — Looking beyond Hungary and Poland. *East European Politics* 34 (3), pp. 243-256. Available at: https://doi.org/10.1080/21599165.2018.1491401.

Cillizza, C. (2020) *Did Donald Trump Destroy Political Prognostication Forever?* Available at: https://edition.cnn.com/2020/08/11/politics/christopher-beha-nate-silver-2016-donald-trump/index.html [Accessed: August 15 2020].

Club 'Z' (2020) *The NSO will Conduct an Internal Investigation due to Alleged Photos from Borisov's Bedroom.* Available at: https://clubz.bg/100131-nso_shte_pravi_vytreshna_proverka_zaradi_predpolagaemi_snimki_ot_spalnqta_na_borisov [Accessed: July 30, 2020].

Combs, M.W. (1980) Supreme Court and Capital Punishment — Uncertainty, Ambiguity, and Judicial Control. *Southern University Law Review* 7 (1), pp. 1-41. Available at: https://www.ojp.gov/ncjrs/virtual-library/abstracts/supreme-court-and-capital-punishment-uncertainty-ambiguity-and.

Cyert, R.M., DeGroot, M.H. (1987) *Bayesian Analysis and Uncertainty in Economic Theory.* Totowa: Rowman & Littlefield.

DarikNews (2020) *Borisov about the New Video from His Bedroom: Someone Stood next to Me and Arranged It (VIDEO).* Available at: https://dariknews.bg/novini/bylgariia/borisov-za-noviia-klip-ot-spalniata-muniakoj-e-stoial-do-men-i-e-aranzhiral-video-2233535 [Accessed: August 16, 2020].

Derrida, J. (1984) *Margins of Philosophy.* Chicago: University of Chicago Press.

Dowding, K., Miller, C. (2019) On Prediction in Political Science. *European Journal of Political Research* 58 (2), pp. 1,001-1,018. Available at: https://ejpr.onlinelibrary.wiley.com/doi/abs/10.1111/1475-6765.12319.

Fernando, J., Smith, A., Perez, Y. (2021) *R-Squared Formula, Regression, and Interpretations.* Available at: https://www.investopedia.com/terms/r/r-squared.asp [Accessed: January 24, 2023].

Greenhalgh, T., Russell, J., Ashcroft, R.E., Parsons, W. (2011) Why National eHealth Programs Need Dead Philosophers: Wittgensteinian Reflections on Policymakers' Reluctance to Learn from History. *The Milbank Quarterly* 89 (4), pp. 533-563. Available at: https://www.milbank.org/wp-content/files/documents/featured-articles/pdf/Milbank_Quarterly_Vol-89_No-4_2011.pdf.

Hay, C. (2017) Explanation, Prediction, Causation—An Unholy Trinity? Appreciative Comments on the Philosophy and Methods of Political Science. *Political Studies Review* 15 (2), pp. 180-186. Available at: https://doi.org/10.1177/1478929917693640.

Hegel, G.W.F. (2012) *The Phenomenology of Mind*. 2nd edn. Mineola: Dover Publications.

Keane, J. (2022) Thoughts on Uncertainty. *Journal of Social and Political Philosophy* 1 (1), pp.1-13. Available at: https://www.euppublishing.com/doi/abs/10.3366/jspp.2022.0003

Kilgour, D.M., Zagare, F.C. (1991) Credibility, Uncertainty, and Deterrence. *American Journal of Political Science* 35 (2), pp. 305-334. Available at: https://www.jstor.org/stable/2111365.

King, G. (1991). "Truth" Is Stranger than Prediction, More Questionable than Causal Inference. *American Journal of Political Science* 35 (4), 1047–1053. Available at: https://doi.org/10.2307/2111506

Lupu, N., Riedl, R.B. (2013) Political Parties and Uncertainty in Developing Democracies. *Comparative Political Studies* 46 (11), pp. 1339-1365. Available at: https://journals.sagepub.com/doi/abs/10.1177/0010414012453445.

Mechkova, V., Lührmann, A., Lindberg, S.I. (2017) How Much Democratic Backsliding? *Journal of Democracy* 28 (4), pp. 162-169. Available at: https://www.journalofdemocracy.org/articles/how-much-democratic-backsliding/.

Mueller, H., Rauh, C. (2017) Reading between the Lines: Prediction of Political Violence Using Newspaper Text. *American Political Science Review* 112 (2), pp. 358-375. Available at: https://www.researchgate.net/publication/321806772_Reading_Between_the_Lines_Prediction_of_Political_Violence_Using_Newspaper_Text.

O'Donnell, G., Schmitter, P.C. (2013) *Transitions from Authoritarian Rule: Tentative Conclusions about Uncertain Democracies*. Baltimore: John Hopkins University Press.

Page, S.E. (2008) Uncertainty, Difficulty, and Complexity. *Journal of Theoretical Politics* 20 (2), pp. 115-149. Available at: https://journals.sagepub.com/doi/abs/10.1177/0951629807085815.

Ruger, T.W., Kim, P.T., Martin, A.D., Quinn, K.M. (2004) The Supreme Court Forecasting Project: Legal and Political Science Approaches to Predicting Supreme Court Decision-Making. *Columbia Law Review*, 104, pp. 1150-1209. Available at: https://deepblue.lib.umich.edu/handle/2027.42/116230.

Runciman, D. (2018) *How Democracy Ends*. London: Profile Books.

Schedler, A. (2013) *The Politics of Uncertainty: Sustaining and Subverting Electoral Authoritarianism*. Oxford: Oxford University Press.

Stanford Encyclopaedia of Philosophy (2001) *The Uncertainty Principle*. Available at: https://plato.stanford.edu/entries/qt-uncertainty/ [Accessed: July 30, 2020].

Stephenson, M.C. (2006) Legislative Allocation of Delegated Power: Uncertainty, Risk, and the Choice between Agencies and Courts. *Harvard Law Review* 119 (4), pp. 1,035-1,070. Available at: https://www.researchgate.net/publication/298917444_Legislative_allocation_of_delegated_power_Uncertainty_risk_and_the_choice_between_agencies_and_courts.

Stevens, E. (2014) Fuzzy Front-End Learning Strategies: Exploration of a High-Tech Company. *Technovation* 34 (8), pp. 431-440. Available at: https://www.sciencedirect.com/science/article/pii/S0166497213001624.

Taleb, N.N. (2007) *The Black Swan: The Impact of the Highly Improbable*. 2nd ed. London: Penguin Books.

Tetlock, P.E., Mellers, B.A., Rohrbaugh, N. and Chen, E. (2014) Forecasting Tournaments: Tools for Increasing Transparency and Improving the Quality of Debate. *Current Directions in Psychological Science* 23 (4), pp. 290-295. Available at: https://journals.sagepub.com/doi/abs/10.1177/0963721414534257.

Urbinati, N. (2014) *Democracy Disfigured: Opinion, Truth and the People*. Cambridge: Harvard University Press.

Wilsford, D. (1994) Path Dependency, or Why History Makes It Difficult but Not Impossible to Reform Health Care Systems in a Big Way. *Journal of Public Policy* 14 (3), pp. 251-283. Available at: https://www.cambridge.org/core/journals/journal-of-public-policy/article/abs/path-dependency-or-why-history-makes-it-difficult-but-not-impossible-to-reform-health-care-systems-in-a-big-way/D4A5351CF18DE00D9317D163B530BA78.

2 Uncertainty
A Critical Overview

Although uncertainty is not a well-defined and a well-developed field of study, there are still a myriad of typologies of uncertainty and a number of suggestions about the sources of uncertainty. For example, uncertainty is categorized as endogenous, exogenous, environmental, perceptual, substantive, procedural, formal, informal and actor-based, among others. The sources of uncertainty are assumed to be technological innovation and the scientific revolution, a transmutable reality, weak institutions, imaginative scenarios, a curtailment of the welfare state, a lack of complete knowledge about the world as well as the limited cognitive capacity of human beings. All of these are reviewed and systematized below.

As a general observation, three trends should be noted from the outset:

(1) There is no clear differentiation between the sources of uncertainty and the types of uncertainty. In some cases, the types of uncertainty denote the sources of uncertainty. For example, institutional uncertainty is a type of uncertainty but the institutions are also the source of uncertainty;

(2) One source of uncertainty may trigger more than one type of uncertainty. For example, technological innovation triggers different mechanisms for creating existential uncertainty as well as economic uncertainty;

(3) Various criteria for defining uncertainty are used. Thus, uncertainty may be defined in regard to the milieu in which it takes place, such as institutional uncertainty. It could be defined as to the origin of the source, such as exogenous uncertainty. It could be gauged as to the unit of analysis and the level of aggregation, such as actor-based versus fundamental uncertainty. It could be defined as to the effects that uncertainty induces, such as effect uncertainty. There is neither a clear overlap across these categorizations, nor a distinct demarcation between them.

After analysing the existing sources and types of uncertainty, the chapter advances the proposition that we need to consider three new types of uncertainty: historically induced uncertainty, i.e. how historical experiences limit the level of uncertainty experienced by actors in the present; inter-institutional uncertainty, which pertains to the uncertainty arising from the lack of clarity which of the many institutions will prevail on a particular occasion, and verbal uncertainty, which denotes how the politicians' verbal utterances confuse the public. The chapter echoes the book's central claim that scholars should be interested in a comprehensive and multi-dimensional vision of uncertainty.

Definitions of Uncertainty and Risk

The most accessible definition of uncertainty, which is available in the online Merriam Webster dictionary, provides a fairly good idea of the spread of the meanings of the word. According to it, uncertainty is the state of being uncertain, and being uncertain means: "1. a: not known beyond doubt; b: not having certain knowledge; c: not clearly identified or defined; 2: not constant; 3: Indefinite, indeterminate 4: not certain to occur; 5: not reliable." This range of meanings is reflected, to a certain extent, by the usages of uncertainty in academia and in science. Broadly speaking, the existing definitions of uncertainty could be divided into two categories: those that believe that uncertainty describes the nature of things and those that argue that uncertainty denotes the limited ability to find out about the nature of things.

Most of the definitions, however, fall into the latter category pertaining to the uncertainty in recognising and evaluating the nature of things. For example, Milliken (1987, p. 136) defines uncertainty as "an individual's perceived inability to predict something accurately. An individual experiences uncertainty because he/she perceives himself/herself to be lacking sufficient information to predict accurately or because he/she feels unable to discriminate between relevant data and irrelevant data." In another definition, still viewing uncertainty through the eyes of the actors, uncertainty is defined "as the imprecision with which political actors are able to predict future interactions" (Lupu and Riedl 2013, p. 1,344). According to Keynes, uncertainty is an inverse function of the weight of the evidence and the logic used to assess it (Keynes 1979 cited in Brady 2016). In economics, "uncertainty" refers to situations in which probabilities are neither known, nor can they be deduced, calculated, or estimated in an objective way" (Gilboa, Postlewaite and Schmeidler 2008, p. 173). In the field of literature, "the word "uncertainty" derives from the [Latin] verb cernere, which means 'to distinguish, to mark out, to separate one thing from the rest, to discern"; "Uncertainty is an ability to draw the lines that define one thing in distinction from something else" (Aggarwal-Schifellite and Siliezar 2020). In short, it is evident that when it comes to explicitly defining uncertainty, most definitions focus on the perceptions and knowledge of the nature of things.

The difference between risk and uncertainty is that "risk refers to decision-making situations under which all potential outcomes and their likelihood of occurrences are known to the decision-maker, and uncertainty refers to situations under which either the outcomes and/or their probabilities of occurrences are unknown to the decision-maker" (Park and Shapira 2017, p. 1). North's seminal distinction is worth noting:

> By uncertainty, I mean here a condition wherein one cannot ascertain the probability of an event and therefore cannot arrive at a way of insuring against such an occurrence. Risk, on the other hand, implies the ability to make an actuarial determination of the likelihood of an event and hence insure against such an outcome. In the modern world, insurance and portfolio diversification are methods for converting uncertainty into risks and thereby reducing, through the provision of a hedge against variability, the costs of transacting (North 1991, p. 106).

Sources of Uncertainty: Existing Explanations

Having briefly considered the definitional side of uncertainty and the difference between uncertainty and risk, it is interesting to note that if the definitions of uncertainty are juxtaposed against the sources of uncertainty, it becomes evident that there is a discrepancy. The definitions are mostly about cognitive and perceptual dimensions. On the other hand, the literature on the sources of uncertainty pays a significantly greater attention to the uncertainty arising from the nature of things. This emphasis on the uncertainty of the nature of things could be a matter of disciplinary inclinations. Perhaps political science and economics prefer to focus on the structural sources of uncertainty for fear that focusing on perceptual uncertainty will turn them into some sort of 'psychoanalysis': "studying perceptions alone would reduce the study of organizations to a "problem of psychoanalysis of actors" (Milliken 1987, p.134). Apart from psychology, it is perhaps neuroscience and biology that will be more inclined to analyse the limitations of the way people process environmental factors. For example, Clark (2015, p.169), a neuroscientist, argues that our brains do not perceive reality and then make models of it, but that the reverse process is in order: our brains create multiple simulations of reality and then select the most realistic option based on the data they perceive.

The sources of uncertainty vary significantly. These categorisations, however, are never compared or contrasted. Currently, each scholar of uncertainty is at freedom to pick and choose their sources of uncertainty without feeling the need to explain or justify his or her choice. As a result, there has never been a rigorous discussion that ranks and compares the different perspectives, such as perceptual vs. environmental, and the corresponding views on the various sources of uncertainty, such as newness, limited cognitive abilities, technological advancement, curtailment of social welfare, inability to know the opponent's preferences, etc. The link between the types of uncertainty and the sources of uncertainty is currently broken or non-existent.

The central cleavage in these categorisations seems to be the perceptual vs. environmental dichotomy, because it inquires whether uncertainty should be measured objectively or whether it should be measured subjectively through the eyes of the people perceiving it. This is a valid question. If people are subjected to uncertainty but they do not perceive their situations as uncertain, then environmental uncertainty plays a role. On the other hand, if the situation is perceived as uncertain but it is not, then people would act upon their perception of uncertainty, so perceptual uncertainty is important. It is my impression that the solution to this quandary is made not on the merits of perceptual versus environmental uncertainty as such but based on the goals of various studies. The analyses which take a more actor-centred approach or elite-centred approach are more likely to stay on the perceptual side of uncertainty, whereas studies which study aggregate social and political phenomena err on the side of the environmental sources of uncertainty. The perceptual vs. environmental dichotomy is sometimes referred to as the antagonism between ontological and epistemological uncertainty: "our future is always uncertain — and uncertain ontologically (it could, and at the moment of its making, can be made differently) not (just) epistemologically (we do not know enough to know how it will turn out)" (Hay 2020, p.191).

Economic approaches to uncertainty are also very cautious about the distinction between uncertainty as a perceptual problem and uncertainty as a quality of the world: "The discussion of uncertainty is closely related to probability, and different conceptions of probability underpin the different ways in which uncertainty has been expressed. One important distinction is made between the theories of probability in which "probability is a property of the way one thinks about the world, a degree of belief, and those theories where probability is a property of the real world" (Dequech 2004, p. 265). Perceptual versus environmental uncertainty has also been named aleatory versus factual respectively: "Aleatory uncertainty refers to a factual uncertainty... Epistemic uncertainty refers to an uncertainty existing because the mind has its opinions... and because it cannot apprehend more than a limited sphere" (Perlman and McCann 1996 cited in Dequech 2004, p. 366). Hayek (1945, p. 519) offers an epistemic source of perceptual uncertainty: "the knowledge of the circumstances of which we must make use never exists in concentrated or integrated form, but solely as the dispersed bits of incomplete and frequently contradictory knowledge which all the separate individuals possess." What is astounding about perceptual uncertainty is that it can arise even if the facts are indisputable and the people analysing them are intelligent (The Enlightened Economist, 2019). This is so because the world contains a "hidden half" even to the most astute observers (Blastland 2019).

Game theoretical models are most likely to emphasize perceptual sources of uncertainty, but they also consider the impossibility to compile exhaustive information. According to them, uncertainty arises from the "1) the lack of all the information which would be necessary to make decisions with certain outcomes, and 2) limitations on the computational and cognitive capabilities of the agents to pursue unambiguously their objectives, given the available information" (Dosi and Egidi 1991, p.145). In this sense, perceptual uncertainty relates not only to the lack of complete information about environmental events, but also to the ability to perceive and analyse it. It can imply a competence gap in problem-solving (Dosi and Egidi 1991, p. 146). This competence gap exacerbates perceptual uncertainty, especially when the task is to compute the fallout and the repercussions from various actions. Agents may feel uncertain how to compute the political costs of government actions, rather than not knowing the specific government actions: "We consider two types of uncertainty. The first type, which we call political uncertainty, relates to uncertainty about whether the current government policy will change. The second type, which we call impact uncertainty, corresponds to uncertainty about the impact a new government policy will have on the profitability of the private sector. In other words, there is uncertainty about what the government is going to do, as well as uncertainty about what the effect of its action is going to be" (Pastor and Veronesi 2012, p.1220). In most game theoretical models, however, uncertainty pertains to the impossibility to calculate the patterns of coalition formation (Pillai and Rao 2014), the optimal strategies of actors, even when the rules of the game are fixed (Székely and Rizzo 2007) or to not knowing the preferences of one's opponents (Kilgour and Zagare 1991).

Interestingly, the pandemic injected another element into the analysis of perceptual uncertainty. It taught us that uncertainty could be a question of beliefs and goals as well. People who wanted to go back to work argued that the data is uncertain. Thus, the logic was reversed because it was not the limitations of the perceptions that impeded the fulfilment of the agents' goals, but the opposite scenario was at work: the agents' goals defined their perceptions.

Another lesson from the pandemic related to perceptual uncertainty is that uncertainty can arise from aspects related to the bias of the data, the reporting of the data and the processing of the data, not only to its completeness, as argued before. At the beginning of the Covid-19 crisis, the biggest problem was the lack of reliable data coming from China. Epidemiologists seemed to process the scarce data points in different ways and came up with differing conclusions about the rate of infection of the virus. Subsequently, there were wide disparities in government reporting, especially as far as the death rates were concerned. Various governments reported and calculated death rates differently to the point of making a comparison of death rates even across European countries impossible (World Health Organization, 2020). In addition, the government was accused of disclosing data selectively and some people distrusted official sources. The media also was accused of sensationalising the data. As a result of all these factors—a lack of data, manipulated data, diverse scientific analysis of data, skewed government reporting of data, and one-sided or incomplete media reporting of data—a lot of uncertainty has arisen. People were confused about the seriousness of the virus, and some even contended that it did not exist. Before Covid, existing analyses of the sources of uncertainty have underscored the inherent incompleteness of data, meaning that data are never fully attainable, even if everyone makes sincere efforts to compile and report it. The pandemic threw light on a different source of uncertainty, namely that the data may be present and complete, but the way the data are analysed and reported is amiss.

Having briefly discussed the causes of perceptual uncertainty, the present review chapter turns to the discussion of environmental uncertainty. Davidson's categorization of environmental uncertainty into 'immutable' and 'transmutable' is instructive in this respect. Basing his characterization on Keynes, Davidson (1999, p. 482) suggests that "transmutable or creative" environment can be changed by people: "Keynes' uncertain future involves a creative economic reality in the sense that the future can be permanently changed in nature and substance by actions of individuals, groups (e.g., unions, cartels), and/or governments, often in ways not completely foreseeable by the creators of change." This type of transmutable reality renders perceptual uncertainty irrelevant, because even if agents had all the complete data and the full mental capacities to extrapolate predictions from it, they will still be unable to do so. The reason is that creativity and entrepreneurship can model reality, and because by definition they are hard to predict, uncertainty is rife.

In contrast to a transmutable reality, a predetermined or immutable type of environment is "not susceptible to change induced by human action. The path of the economy, like the path of the planets under Newton's classical mechanics, was determined by timeless, immutable natural laws... This does not preclude an economy that is moving or changing over time. It does mean that all future movements and changes are already predetermined by the fundamental real parameters of the system and cannot be changed by human action" (Davidson 1999, p. 479). In this sense, a predetermined reality lends itself to prediction more naturally, because if agents have complete information about these natural laws, and the mental capacity to figure out how they will play out, they can assign possibilities to future outcomes with more confidence. Consequently, uncertainty is easier to tame. It seems that a lot of these predictions rest on the fact that natural laws have only one possible consequence and agents cannot pick and choose which path events will follow. In general, the dichotomy between transmutable and immutable reality hinges precariously on the assumption that only human action can transform reality, and if humans were held back, nature will follow a scripted scenario that is easy to decipher. This assumption should be open to interpretation.

Currently, the literature is in general agreement that one of the best markers between a transmutable and immutable reality, and the corresponding sources of uncertainty, is the notion of manufactured risk as flashed out by Giddens (1999). It should be noted that the study of uncertainty, especially as far as scientific knowledge is concerned, is mostly framed in the notion of risk, not uncertainty:

> Manufactured risk refers to risk situations which we have very little historical experience for confronting. Most environmental risks, such as these

connected with global warming, fall into this category. They are directly influenced by the intensifying globalization... The best way I can clarify the distinction between the two kinds of risk is as follows. In all traditional cultures, one could say, and in industrial society right up to the threshold of the present day, human beings worried about the risks coming from external nature—from bad harvests, floods, plagues or famines. At a certain point, however—very recently in historical terms—we started worrying less about what nature can do to us, and more about what we have done to nature. This marks the transition from the predominance of external risk to that of manufactured risk (Giddens 1999).

Of all the sources of a transmutable reality and manufactured risk, technological and scientific progress have received by far the most attention in the literature. Technological advancement has been credited by students of uncertainty, especially economists, as the most consequential development causing uncertainty. The consequences of scientific progress have been interpreted slightly differently by various students of uncertainty. Here we will review and compare the analysis of the impact of technological change on uncertainty as conducted by Beck (1992), Hiskes (1998), and Beckert and Bronk (2018).

Beck's analysis of risk and uncertainty is particularly useful in explaining the connection between technological progress and risk. He proposes that scientific progress has made dangers less predictable because "the afflictions they produce are no longer tied to their place of origin—the industrial plant. By their nature, they endanger all forms of life on this planet" (Beck 1992, p. 22). While scientific progress has made it possible to have large atomic plants and big factories, it has also unleashed the dangers of "nuclear fission or the storage of radioactive waste" (Beck 1992, p. 22). The fallout of such dangers is notoriously hard to calculate because of the large externalities involved (Gonzalez and Saarman 2014). This means that such dangers have concentrated benefits but highly dispersed costs, and the beneficiaries and the victims of these policies do not coincide. Consequently, the dangers are inherently incalculable.

This incalculability of dangers afflicting society, which is a form of environmental or structural uncertainty, has created lots of perceptual uncertainty or at least a lot of doubt as it has become clear that there are a lot of interests and subjective judgments in estimating the fallout of these dangers and "distributing the risk" from them across society. Once trust in rationality is broken, the uncertainty in managing the unwanted aftershocks of modernization and technology sets in. Doubt creeps in that the businesses, politics and ethics will favour the victims of the dangers, not the producers of the dangerous atomic plants. This distrust is borne out of the large uncertainty surrounding the "always competing and conflicting claims, interests and viewpoints of the various agents of modernity and affected groups, which are forced together in defining risks in the sense of cause and effect, instigator and injured party. There is no expert on risk" (Beck 1992, p. 29).

From the point of mixing and matching various types of uncertainty, Beck's analysis of reflexive modernization stands out. His treatment of uncertainty, and of risk more specifically, puts environmental and perceptual uncertainty — the two major types of uncertainty- in close and even causal proximity. Environmental uncertainty in this case could be related to the side effects of modernization and perceptual uncertainty results from the muddled criteria and processes for deciding who stands to lose from these side effects. By emphasizing the reflexivity of this process, Beck essentially underscores the inter-play between environmental and perceptual uncertainty.

In contrast to Beck, who traces how technology creates perceptual uncertainty, Beckert and Bronk (2018) focus on how technology creates uncertainty that is overcome through imagination. They also place technological progress in the larger context of a competitive capitalist system. The authors acknowledge that the element of innovation in the capitalist system significantly increases its indeterminacy and by doing so, they paint a picture of a transmutable reality discussed above. The authors' view is useful because innovation is placed within context. According to them, it arises because the capitalist system puts people in competition against each other, encourages maximizing behaviour, which values "the new commodity, the new technology, the new source of supply, the new type of organization." As a result, a creative destruction (Schumpeter 2013, p. 83) ensues that changes the system from within. It is this constant endogenous change that accounts for its indeterminacy: "The radical indeterminacy implied by innovation and novelty constitutes a major problem for economic actors: How are they to make decisions, and coordinate their actions with others, if they cannot know what future will follow? How can they form expectations of the future that may legitimately guide them?" (Beckert and Bronk 2018, p. 3).

The authors suggest that there is another reason, however, that drives indeterminacy, and it is the novelty and the process of imagining of new options. This factor is entirely man-made, but it is slightly different from the entrepreneurship discussed above, in that it places a stronger emphasis on imagination. These "imaginaries" or "fictional expectations" break away from the rationalization as a mode of disciplining uncertainty. In this sense, the creation of uncertainty comes from the "abilities not usually associated with rational thinking, such as the "ability to visualize counterfactuals, to place oneself in the shoes of another (the basis of sympathy), and to colour perception analysis by playing with new metaphors" (Beckert and Bronk 2018, p. 3).

This verbal and emotional aspect of uncertainty in an economic context is both surprising and highly valuable. It breaks away from the mode of rational thinking of economic agents and attributes to them qualities that are akin to humans as viewed in psychology and other contexts.

> When the future is demonstrably indeterminate thanks to widespread innovation and complex interdependencies, those attempting to model decision making need to analyse the role of shared narratives and fictional expectations in guiding beliefs and behaviour. They should be attentive to the importance of fashionable theory, political or market power, emotional contagion, and rhetoric in determining which narratives and models will succeed in performing the future and coordinating behaviour (Beckert and Bronk 2018, p. 9).

Beckert and Bronk's idea about "fashionable theory, political and market power" is very similar to Beck's suggestion that conflicting interests, businesses, politics and ethics determine the risks of technological progress. In this sense, it contains an element of reflexivity. The study is also useful in pinpointing the double role of the rising power of imagination—it is both a result of indeterminacy and a cause of indeterminacy. This situation where the solutions to reducing uncertainty constitute also the reasons for increasing uncertainty is hard to manage but it needs to be acknowledged.

Hiskes chooses to emphasize the social aspects of the creation and the management of technological risk. He suggests that "the growth of scientific knowledge is the result of a communal process. This means that no one scientist "discovers" knowledge alone but builds his or her hypotheses on the work of others and awaits the confirmation of the results through the further research of fellow scientists" (Hiskes 1998, p. 12). This is a very "social", community-oriented view of scientific progress, and it underscores the endogenous nature of manufactured risks. This assessment of scientific progress—painfully familiar to most scientists—is very different to the view of the origin of progress introduced by Beckert and Bronk, who emphasize the competitive nature of capitalism and entrepreneurship. These views are not incompatible, of course, but it is important to be aware of them as they present two sources of scientific progress, which in turn creates uncertainty.

The importance of Hiskes' treatment of scientific progress is that he presents a fundamentally different perspective how to manage it as well. He argues that dealing with risk is an essentially social process. He illustrates this point by giving the example of the "gapers' block". The gapers block is a situation where an accident in the highway—which is a technological issue, if it is caused by a malfunctioning vehicle—is exacerbated by a social element where drivers in passing cars slow down to observe the site of the accident. This slowing down creates a congestion. Hiskes' point is that the resulting congestion is ultimately a problem of social coordination. It is a problem of social coordination because most passers-by do not care about the long queues of cars they are creating by slowing down. Hiskes (1998, p. 10) defines this as the NIMBY—not in my backyard-phenomenon. It requires people to be told to push the speed peddle. Perhaps they could be shamed into being portrayed as inconsiderate. They should be made aware that there are many cars behind them, and some drivers may be in a hurry. No single person could do that on his/her own. That is why it requires an intervention that is larger than an individual, and possibly includes a government agency or another type of organization. The main point here is that the negative side effects of scientific progress should be managed socially, thus leaving "behind the excessively rationalistic and methodologically individualistic presumptions that stand behind liberal politics... the resulting communalistic approach to risk is also more amenable to the true nature of democratic politics" (Hiskes 1998, p. 13).

Bauman is one of the thinkers who revolutionises the thinking about the man-made sources of environmental uncertainty by shifting the discourse from technological change to social forms. In a way, Bauman created uncertainty with a human face. The bottom line is that uncertainty arises because the individual feels unable and ill-equipped to find "individual solutions to socially produced problems" (Bauman 2000, p. 14). The reasons for uncertainty are four-fold:

1. Forms have short term life expectations and do not serve as frames of reference for human behaviour
2. Separation of politics and power
3. Curtailment of state endorsed insurance against individual failure
4. Disappearance of structures that ensure long-term thinking

Bauman's liquid modernity is different from Beck's reflexive modernization because in the former case the individual cannot find solutions to problems produced by society while in the latter case society cannot find solutions to problems produced by big businesses riding on the achievements of science. Yet, the individual dimension that Beck outlines in his notion of uncertainty is different from the individual dimension that rational choice thinkers and economic theorists see in uncertainty. Beck's individual is uncertain because he or she does not know whom to rely in cases of illness or loneliness. The structures that used to support ill or lonely people, such as a well-functioning welfare state, are in decline and no new support structures have replaced them. The economic agents are uncertain not because there is no one to turn to for help, but because they lack complete information or cognitive abilities to process that information. Perhaps this difference in the fundamentals of the individual perception of uncertainty is due to the fact that individuals taking different roles in society experience uncertainty differently: businessmen, on the one hand, and consumers of the economic goods, on the other hand, are involved in different kinds of uncertainty. In this sense, as pointed out, Bauman's achievement is that he has shown the human side of uncertainty.

It would have been a taxonomic heaven if the neat categorizations of environmental versus perceptual uncertainty, and between man-made and nature-inflicted sources of uncertainty map neatly onto other categorizations. But it is arguable whether they do. Let's take the differentiation between the exogenous versus endogenous origins of uncertainty, in which exogenous factors come from outside of state borders or from outside of a social group and endogenous factors originate from within a state or a group. So, should risk manufactured by technological and scientific progress be classified as endogenous or exogenous? There could be two views on that. On the one hand, technological progress is endogenous to modernization and industrialization, and in this sense, it is clearly not caused by exogenous factors, such as floods and earthquakes. On the other hand, manufactured risk is exogenous to any particular state or discipline because the scientific community and collaboration have long transcended nation-state borders and disciplinary divides. This shows that taxonomies do not always go hand in hand.

Take another example of the lack of taxonomic overlaps of uncertainty and its sources. Is manufactured risk a formal or informal source of uncertainty? The differentiation between formal and informal sources of uncertainty denotes formal institutions, such as government and international agencies, and informal sources, such as personal conflicts, "political, social, and economic structures of conflict; diverse aspects of political and civil society; and policy legacies, bureaucratic structures, and state efficacy" (Alexander 2002, p. 146). Given this definition, can we say for sure that scientific progress is an entirely formal process, taking place on the pages of journals and in conference rooms but not through personal friendships (and animosities) and that scholarly reputation is not also made through word of mouth? Future research should analyse whether the sources of uncertainty are mutually exclusive, collectively exhaustive, and whether they are partially overlapping. It should also delineate the patterns of these overlaps, if any.

Underlying the scholarship on manufactured risk and uncertainty, the question looms whether events that are thought to be exogenous are not in fact man-made or manufactured. The idea of the Black Swan is extremely pertinent to this inquiry. The Black Swan is defined as a "highly improbable consequential event that has three attributes: unpredictability, consequences, and retrospective explainability" (Taleb 2007). The Black Swan metaphor is meant to convey the idea that there are phenomena that exist but are thought by people not to exist. These extremely rare events are highly impactful on a global scale. Uncertainties created by Black Swan types of events are known as "Knightian uncertainty" after the University of Chicago economist Frank Knight, who came up with this idea based on his observations of the stock market (Knight 2006). "Knightian uncertainty" is unknown uncertainty, as opposed to known uncertainty. Known uncertainty stems from not knowing the parameters of particular variables. It is a quantifiable type of uncertainty. Unknown uncertainty is the inability to image the variables themselves. The attacks on the World Trade Centre are considered the prototypical Black Sawn events. Because they were truly unimaginable, the issue of parameters does not even come up for consideration.

If the definition of a Black Swan event posits that these events are hard to imagine, it is easy to conclude from this definition that such events are not caused by people because people cannot imagine them, let alone execute their plans. It turns out that the "unimagineability" of the Black Swan event is very tentative. Obviously, the 9/11 masterminds imagined the attacks to the last detail, even if to the rest of the world they were not conceivable. Therefore, to count as a Black Swan event, a source of uncertainty needs to be imagined only and only by a very few people in the world. But if we follow and extend this logic, great scientific discoveries, such as the phones and the law of gravitation, were also triggered by a leap of the imagination of a very small number of people. And if we extend this logic even further, Bronk's emphasis on the role of imagination should come to mind. Is the invention of the steam engine and the 9/11 attacks equivalent in terms of being improbable Black Swans, but different only in terms of the desirability of the havoc they had wreaked? If this is the case, then we should rethink the criterion of improbability as a defining characteristic of Black Swans.

It should be noted that the basis of my challenge to the Black Swan theory diverges from Tetlock and Gardner's criticism, which posits that "9/11 was not unimaginable" because there was plenty of information in security circles to this effect: "In 1994 a plot to hijack a jet and crash it into the Eiffel Tower was broken up. In 1998, the US Federal Aviation Administration examined a scenario in which terrorists hijacked FedEx cargo planes and crashed them into the World Trade Center. The danger was so well known in security circles that in August 2001, a government official asked Louise Richardson, a Harvard terrorism expert, why no terrorist group had ever used an airplane as a flying bomb" (Tetlock and Gardner 2016, p. 7). To reiterate, in contrast to Tetlock, my criticism is that a Black Swan event is not unimaginable, but that it was imaginable to a small number of people.

Other Sources of Uncertainty: Fragmentation

In my view, one source of uncertainty, which has not been touched upon in the literature is the phenomenon of fragmentation. Fragmentation means that there are more parts to a whole, and as a consequence, it is harder to put all parts together and to be certain what combinations will arise. Imagine, for example, that you are presented with a puzzle, whose pieces have been collated and stuck together. There is no doubt that a clear picture emerges. Now imagine that the puzzle is broken up into its myriad constituting pieces. It is very unclear what picture will emerge. In real life, there is most likely more than one picture that can emerge from all these pieces. Uncertainty abounds.

The specific type of fragmentation that I have in mind pertains to the law of gravitation (Dimova 2019, pp. 87-89). The fragmentation of the public means that the public is no longer a homogenous and an ideologically monolithic whole, much like the puzzle described above. The public is a motley amalgamation of a series of separate islands of issue-minorities, whose interests, activity and collaboration are hard to predict. The logic behind linking public fragmentation and uncertainty is that if the public is not homogenous, then the variations in which the various 'fragments' of the public get together multiply. There are many possibilities, which in turn means that less definite probabilities could be attached to each scenario. Predictability is smaller and uncertainty is greater.

Before I delve into the particular sources of uncertainty, however, it is important to compare how this mechanism of fragmentation presents an entirely different approach to the existing mechanism of uncertainty. Of all the mechanisms of uncertainty analysed above, fragmentation is most similar to the collaborative process described by Hiskes. It is similar because both Hiskes (1998) and I see the social dimension of uncertainty. Like Hiskes, I view uncertainty as a problem arising out of collaboration. The difference is that I believe that the source of uncertainty is modernisation, marketisation, globalisation, which lead to public fragmentation, while Hiskes zooms in on technological advancement. Viewed from the perspective of the early sources of uncertainty, my approach is similar to the one introduced by Bauman (2000), Giddens (1999) and Beck (1992). All these approaches believe that modernity and interrelated phenomena are the sources of uncertainty. To me, however, uncertainty is not so much existential, such as the lack of reliable support structures (Bauman2000), or the creeping doubt accompanying the subjectivisation of science (Giddens 1999; Beck 1992). I argue that the mechanism is triggered by the creation of segments of the public, and it is difficult to predict which segments will be mobilized and whether they will collaborate. In the end, the link between fragmentation and uncertainty presented here is similar as a process to Hiskes's, and similar as a source of uncertainty to Bauman, Giddens and Beck's suggestions. It is, ultimately, a view of its own.

Uncertainty: Existing Typologies

The primary current differentiation between the types of uncertainty is between substantive uncertainty, which denotes the outcomes of a political game, and procedural uncertainty, which denotes the rules of the game (Croissant and Haynes 2015). Procedural uncertainty, which applies to procedures, or rules, as the name suggests, could be construed as an umbrella term that encompasses various types of procedures, including institutions. Institutional uncertainty could be a subtype of procedural uncertainty, but institutional and procedural types of uncertainty are sometimes used inter-changeably. There is a palpable scholarly agreement about the importance and workings of institutional uncertainty. Institutions are thought to reduce uncertainty by stabilising expectations: "They do not turn humans into machines, but they do render their interactions predictable within reasonable bounds" (Schedler2013, p. 23). The stabilising force of institutions has been widely acknowledged in the field of international relations (Rosendorff and Milner 2007; Rathbun 2020; Montgomery 2006). Institutions have been instrumental in reducing uncertainty in formal modelling as well: "To cope with uncertainty, institutions align incentives for information revelation; to handle difficult problems, institutions create incentives for diverse problem-solving approaches; and to harness complexity, institutions adjust selection criteria, rates of variation, and the level of connectedness" (Page 2008, p. 115). One original formulation of political uncertainty posits that uncertainty is tied to the rotation of authority in a democracy: "While the right to exercise public authority happens to be theirs today, other political actors with different and perhaps opposing interests may gain that right tomorrow, along with legitimate control over the policies and structures that their predecessors put in place. Whatever today's authorities create, therefore, stands to be subverted or perhaps completely destroyed-quite legally and without any compensation whatever-by tomorrow's authority" (Moe 1990, p. 227). This is not the case for business structures, however, because no permanent change of power holders is necessarily anticipated.

Institutions provide certainty by ensuring the repetition of games and reducing the costs of transaction. To reduce uncertainty, institutions need to be evolutionary devices as opposed to sticking to a permanent set of rules. They should constantly negate bad practices and reinforce good practices. They should be adaptive:

> Throughout history, institutions have been devised by human beings to create order and reduce uncertainty in exchange. Together with the standard constraints of economics they define the choice set and therefore determine transaction and production costs and hence the profitability and feasibility of engaging in economic activity. They evolve incrementally, connecting the past with the present and the future; history in consequence is largely a story of institutional evolution in which the historical performance of economies can only be understood as a part of a sequential story. Institutions provide the incentive structure of an economy; as that structure evolves, it shapes the direction of economic change towards growth, stagnation, or decline (North 1991, p. 97).

One of the most popular definitions of uncertainty belongs to Przeworski (1991) who defined democracy as "institutionalized uncertainty." For him, a central distinction between democratic and non-democratic politics is the uncertainty introduced by elections; actors "know what is possible and likely but not what will happen" (Przeworksi 1991, p. 12). Procedural uncertainty in transitional democracy is considered the reduced likelihood that the country will revert to non-democratic rule and it is measured behaviourally when democracy is considered "to be the only game in town." One limitation of this approach is that it has been applied mostly to elections: "electoral competition is open and its outcomes are indeterminate. Democratic elections admit substantive uncertainty" (Przeworski 1986 paraphrased by Schedler 2013, p. 26). Such exclusive focus on the procedural and substantive sources of electoral uncertainty does not align with the realisation that elections are a central but not exclusive form of representation (Dimova 2019, p. 59). Furthermore, this focus is also misplaced when the goal is to explain inter-electoral accountability, not electoral accountability. The focus on procedural uncertainty needs to be expanded and diversified. It should include non-electoral forms of government as well.

There is a danger that substantive uncertainty could be misinterpreted because the term has been used in several ways. Apart from differentiating between the rules of the game and the outcomes of these rules, substantive vs. procedural uncertainty is also used to denote the lack of information about outcomes and the cognitive limitation to process this information respectively (Dosi and Egidi 1991, p.145). Substantive uncertainty should not be confused with structural uncertainty. Structural uncertainty means "a lack of complete knowledge on the part of the economic agent about the very structure of the economic problem that the agent faces," in contrast to "parametric uncertainty... that is a lack of complete knowledge ex ante about the values that specific variables within a given problem structure will take on ex post" (Langlois 1994, p. 120).

How does the notion of structural uncertainty relate to the notions of "state uncertainty, effect uncertainty and response uncertainty" introduced by Milliken (1987)? It seems that structural uncertainty is most similar to state uncertainty, which is a type of "environmental uncertainty" defined as "the inability to assign probabilities to the likelihood of future events." Effect uncertainty denotes "an inability to understand or predict the future consequences of decisions." Effect uncertainty is sometimes named causal uncertainty as different authors choose to emphasise either the cause or the effect of the causal chain, but to keep the same logic (Iaydjiev 2006). Response uncertainty "is associated with attempts to understand what response options are available to the organization and what the value or utility of each might be" (Milliken 1987, p. 135).

Finally, some authors argue in favour of the distinction between market uncertainty and event uncertainty. Under market uncertainty, a person is certain about his or her preferences, endowment, etc., but would be uncertain about the demand and supply of others. Under event uncertainty, the person would be uncertain about his or her endowment because of exogenous factors, such as tax cuts, wheat crop, etc. (Hirshleifer, Jack and Riley 1992, pp. 242-243). Others see the most meaningful distinction between the types of uncertainty to be between regime uncertainty, economic uncertainty, and institutional uncertainty. Regime uncertainty is about political competition and competitors, economic uncertainty is about outcomes and the elites' ability to respond to them, and institutional uncertainty is about the rules of political interaction and their durability (Lupu and Riedl 2013, p. 1,343).

Some scholars believe that the defining characteristic of uncertainty is its intensity. They argue that "strong uncertainty, in contrast to the weak variety, is characterized by the absence of unique, additive and fully reliable probability distributions, used either explicitly or implicitly by individuals" (Dequech 2008, p. 1). The categorization of uncertainty is consequential as it affects how we measure it. Some measures use counts of the word "uncertainty" and its variants such as volatility, volatile, uncertain, uncertainty, risk, risky in experts' reports or in news reports (Economic Policy Uncertainty 2020; Baker et al 2020). They construct quarterly indices of economic uncertainty for 143 countries from 1996 onwards using frequency counts of "uncertainty" (and its variants) in the quarterly Economist Intelligence Unit (EIU) country reports. The EIU reports discuss major political and economic developments in each country, along with analyses and forecasts of political, policy and economic conditions. They are created by country-specific teams of analysts and a central EIU editorial team.

Uncertainty: New Typologies

As the current review chapter demonstrated, there are already plenty of types of uncertainty, such as epistemic, ontological, exogenous, endogenous, formal, informal, institutional, structural, response, effect, regime, environmental, procedural, substantive, to name just a few. Despite this great variety of options, however, the book introduces and analyses the following three additional types of uncertainty: inter-institutional, verbal, and historical. It introduces them because they are important but neglected.

The biggest and most consequential analytical switch that the book makes is to shift the focus from institutional to inter-institutional uncertainty. Institutional uncertainty is no doubt the sine qua non of uncertainty, and it should remain so. But focusing exclusively on institutional uncertainty, without considering inter-institutional uncertainty, relies on one sweeping and factually incorrect assumption: that there exists only one set of institutional rules. Perhaps, if we are interested in viewing the strength of the institutional rules — weak versus strong (Schedler 2010), this is a correct assumption. If we view institutional uncertainty in terms of the rules of elections only, this is a correct assumption (Schedler 2013). However, if we view uncertainty as it pertains to several institutions in between elections, this is an incorrect assumption.

Uncertainty arises from the diversification of the means for holding the government to account. The diversification of forums leads to uncertainty for the simple reason that there is a long menu of options, and it is unclear which option will be chosen. To exemplify it, if the public wants to hold the government to account, it is not limited to participating in elections, but it can choose to use the courts, to engage in protests, to partake in deliberative forums; in addition, there are parliamentary committees, parliamentary questions, audit committees, internal governmental investigations and international investigations. Uncertainty stems from not knowing which of these forums will be chosen, whether just one or a few forums will be chosen, and whether these forums will compete or collaborate.

Of course, all these forms for holding the government to account have existed before. The diversification of forums emerged not because the forums have recently come into existence but because the public's realization of their existence, usefulness and specificity has increased. This growing awareness was invoked by two main occurrences — the realization that elections have imperfections, and that therefore alternative forms of accountability should be sought, and because the accountability revolution:

> diversified and expanded the supply of representation in three main ways. First, and most importantly, the accountability revolution diversified the forums that potential accountability-holders can use to hold the government to account. Second, the accountability revolution drove the accountability turn by highlighting the importance of holding specific ministers or parts of the government to account. Third, it acknowledged the importance of multiple logics and multiple criteria for holding the government to account. This diversification meant that new opportunities were created to pursue government accountability because the forums, the account-givers and the accountability criteria were more specific. It also meant that there could be a

better synergy between the account-holders, the nature of the claim and the specific logic of the accountability forum. The accountability revolution is mainly linked to a paradigm in public administration called New Public Management, but it also connects with such developments as Europeanization and decentralization. The impact of the accountability revolution has been extensively researched in public administration studies but it has not been fully understood in the context of democratic theory" (Dimova 2019, pp. 60-64).

Chapters three, four and five operationalize inter-institutional uncertainty in various ways.

As far as verbal uncertainty is concerned, it should be noted that the nomination "verbal uncertainty" refers to the source of uncertainty, rather than the milieu in which it takes place (such as institutional uncertainty) or who experiences it (such as perceptual uncertainty). It is puzzling why the verbal utterances of politicians as a source of uncertainty have been ignored. By disregarding verbal representations of reality, it is implied that the problem of perceptual uncertainty arises because people are confused as to the manifestations of reality, not by the representation of reality. But most people do not have access to the tiniest pieces of the manifestations of reality. Most of the information that they have access to is reality as described by newspapers, journalists, neighbours, family members and politicians. Consequently, it will not help at all to clarify the situation, and reduce perceptual uncertainty, if various politicians have various accounts of reality. If incumbents and opposition leaders, for example, have conflicting versions of a problem, uncertainty must arise. Uncertainty arises especially for those people who watch more than one channel, or frequent news sites of varying ideological leanings.

Verbal utterances and uncertainty are indirectly analysed in the field of international relations, which focuses on the perception of and the credibility of threats. "Scholars in international relations have long given threat perception a central role in theories of war, deterrence and competence, alliances, and conflict resolution" (Stein 2013). The interpretation of "signals" that various countries give out is the key to this field because the signals implicitly create a lot of uncertainty. The uncertainty mostly revolves around the issue whether states issue threats in earnest or not, but the logic could easily be extended to inquire whether conflicting signals create uncertainty. The link between verbal accounts and the confusion they create is somewhat discussed as relational uncertainty (Knobloch and Solomon 1999) in the field of psychology. In this book, we presume a degree of a positive correlation between politicians' statements and the uncertainty they induce for the public, although this link should be studied more in the future. The chief question is: what are the constraints to politicians' utterances? Can everybody say anything at all, and thus create an unlimited degree of uncertainty? To what extent are verbal statements the decisional result of self-interested politicians, and to what extent do they reflect reality? This is the subject of chapter eight.

Historically induced uncertainty is also largely disregarded in the literature. But why should it be assumed that all the factors that political actors consider are situated in the present? More precisely, why should it be assumed that people's past actions should not be considered when making judgements about their present motivations and attitudes? This is not an argument postulating that past actions pre-determine present choices, rather it is an argument suggesting that knowledge of people's past actions provides more data points to estimate their present positions. Thinking about past uprising to estimating present governmental support is an especially pertinent issue for non-democratic countries because they have no other sources of gauging public support, yet this is a fundamental importance to them. Non-democratic power-holders lack a clear estimate of public support because they do not allow a free expression of opinion or independent polling agencies. Chapter seven argues that past uprisings reduce the uncertainty as to the public support of the regime during the transition from communism to democracy. It uses as case studies Hungary, which experiences the 1956 uprising, and the Soviet Union, which did not have any popular rebellions. It conjectures that, as a result, Hungarian communist leaders suffered from less uncertainty than their Soviet counterparts.

Bibliography

Aggarwal-Schifellite, M., Siliezar, J. (2020) Three Ways of Dealing with Uncertainty. *The Harvard Gazette*. Available at: https://news.harvard.edu/gazette/story/2020/07/3-takes-on-dealing-with-uncertainty [Accessed: January 26, 2023].

Alexander, G. (2016) Institutionalized Uncertainty, The Rule of Law, and The Sources of Democratic Stability. *Comparative Political Studies* 35 (10), pp. 1,145–1,170. Available at: https://journals.sagepub.com/doi/abs/10.1177/001041402237946?journalCode=cpsa.

Baker, S.R., Bloom, N., Davis, S.J., Terry, S.J. (2020) *Covid-Induced Economic Uncertainty*. National Bureau of Economic Research, No. w26983, pp. 1-17. Available at: https://www.nber.org/system/files/working_papers/w26983/w26983.pdf.

Bauman, Z. (2000) *Liquid Modernity*. Cambridge: Polity Press.

Beckert, J., Bronk, R. (2018) *Uncertain Futures: Imaginaries, Narratives, and Calculation in the Economy*. New York: Oxford University Press.

Beck, U. (1992) *Risk Society: Towards a New Modernity*. Frankfurt: Sage Publications.

Blastland, M. (2019) *The Hidden Half: How the World Conceals Its Secrets*. London: Atlantic Books.

Brady, M.E. (2016) *How Should the Post Keynesian School Define 'Uncertainty'? The Only Correct Answer Is to Use Keynes's Own Definition Given in Footnote 1 on Page 148 of Chapter 12 of the General Theory: Uncertainty Is an Inverse Function of the Weight of the Argument*. Available at: https://ssrn.com/abstract=3438090 [Accessed: January 26, 2023].

Clark, A. (2015) *Surfing Uncertainty: Prediction, Action, and the Embodied Mind*. New York: Oxford University Press.

Croissant, A., Haynes, J. (2014) *Twenty Years of Studying Democratization: Vol 1: Democratic Transition and Consolidation*. Abingdon: Routledge.

Cyert, R.M., DeGroot, M.H. (1987) *Bayesian Analysis and Uncertainty in Economic Theory*. Totowa: Rowman & Littlefield.

Davidson, P. (1999) *Uncertainty, International Money, Employment and Theory: Volume 3: The Collected Writings of Paul Davidson*. London: Palgrave Macmillan.

Dequech, D. (2004) Uncertainty: Individuals, Institutions and Technology. *Cambridge Journal of Economics* 28 (3), pp. 365-378. Available at: https://doi.org/10.1093/cje/28.3.365.

Dequech, D. (2008) *Varieties of Uncertainty: A Survey of the Economic Literature*. Anais do XXXVI Encontro Nacional de Economia. Available at: https://www.anpec.org.br/encontro2008/artigos/200807211223070 [Accessed: January 26, 2023].

Dimova, G. (2019) *Democracy beyond Elections: Government Accountability in the Media Age*. Cham: Springer Nature.

Dosi, G., Egidi, M. (1991) Substantive and Procedural Uncertainty. *Journal of Evolutionary Economics* 1 (2), pp. 145-168. Available at: https://www.researchgate.net/publication/226294602_Substantive_and_Procedural_Uncertainty.

Economic Policy Uncertainty (2020) *World Uncertainty Index (WUI)*. Available at: https://www.policyuncertainty.com/wui_quarterly.html [Accessed: July 31, 2020].

The Enlightened Economist (2019) *Everything We Don't Know*. Available at: http://www.enlightenmenteconomics.com/blog/index.php/2019/03/everything-we-dont-know/ [Accessed: August 14, 2020].

Giddens, A. (1999) *BBC Reith Lectures 1999 – Risk*. Available at: http://news.bbc.co.uk/hi/english/static/events/reith_99/week2/week2.htm [Accessed: January 26, 2023].

Gilboa, I., Postlewaite, A.W., Schmeidler, D. (2008) Probability and Uncertainty in Economic Modeling. *Journal of Economic Perspectives* 22 (3), pp. 173-188. Available at: https://pubs.aeaweb.org/doi/pdfplus/10.1257/jep.22.3.173.

Gonzalez, T., Saarman, G. (2014) Regulating Pollutants, Negative Externalities, and Good Neighbour Agreements: Who Bears the Burden of Protecting Communities. *Ecology Law Quarterly* 41 (1), pp. 37-79. Available at: http://www.jstor.org/stable/24113661.

Hay, C. (2020) Brexistential Angst and the Paradoxes of Populism: On the Contingency, Predictability and Intelligibility of Seismic Shifts. *Political Studies* 68 (1), pp. 187-206. Available at: https://journals.sagepub.com/doi/full/10.1177/0032321719836356.

Hayek, F.A. (1945) The Use of Knowledge in Society. *The American Economic Review* 35 (4), pp. 519-530. Available at: http://www.jstor.org/stable/1809376.

Hirshleifer, J., Jack, H., Riley, J.G. (1992) *The Analytics of Uncertainty and Information*. Cambridge: Cambridge University Press.

Hiskes, R.P. (1998) *Democracy, Risk, and Community: Technological Hazards and the Evolution of Liberalism*. New York: Oxford University Press.

Iaydjiev, I. (2016) Negotiating Uncertainty: Crisis, Change, and International Institutions in the Global Financial Crisis of 2008-2009. *St Antony's International Review* 11 (2), pp. 38-68. Available at: https://www.jstor.org/stable/26229146.

Inglehart, R. (1997) *Modernization and Postmodernization: Cultural, Economic, and Political Change in 43 Societies.* Princeton: Princeton University Press.

Kilgour, D.M., Zagare, F.C. (1991) Credibility, Uncertainty, and Deterrence. *American Journal of Political Science* 35 (2), pp. 305-334. Available at: https://www.jstor.org/stable/2111365.

Knight, F.H. (2006). *Risk, Uncertainty and Profit (Vol. 31).* Mineola: Dover Publications.

Knobloch, L.K., Solomon, D.H. (1999) Measuring the Sources and Content of Relational Uncertainty. *Communication Studies* 50 (4), pp. 261-278. Available at: https://www.tandfonline.com/doi/abs/10.1080/10510979909388499.

Langlois, R. (1994) Chapter 17: Risk and Uncertainty. In *The Elgar Companion to Austrian Economics.* Cheltenham: Edward Elgar Publishing. Available at: https://doi.org/10.4337/9780857934680.00026 [Accessed: January 26 2023].

Lupu, N., Riedl, R.B. (2013) Political Parties and Uncertainty in Developing Democracies. *Comparative Political Studies* 46 (11), pp. 1,339-1,365. Available at: https://journals.sagepub.com/doi/abs/10.1177/0010414012453445.

Merriam-Webster Dictionary (2020) *Uncertain.* Available at: https://www.merriam-webster.com/dictionary/uncertain[Accessed: January 26, 2023].

Milliken, F.J. (1987) Three Types of Perceived Uncertainty about the Environment: State, Effect, and Response Uncertainty. *Academy of Management Review* 12 (1), pp. 133-143. Available at: https://doi.org/10.2307/257999.

Moe, T.M. (1990). Political Institutions: The Neglected Side of the Story. *Journal of Law, Economics, & Organization*, 6, pp. 213-253. Available at: http://www.jstor.org/stable/764990.

Montgomery, E.B. (2006) Breaking out of the Security Dilemma: Realism, Reassurance, and the Problem of Uncertainty. *International Security* 31 (2), pp.151-185. Available at: https://doi.org/10.1162/isec.2006.31.2.151.

North, D.C. (1991) Institutions. *Journal of Economic Perspectives* 5 (1), pp. 97-112. Available at: https://pubs.aeaweb.org/doi/pdfplus/10.1257/jep.5.1.97.

Page, S.E. (2008) Uncertainty, Difficulty, and Complexity. *Journal of Theoretical Politics* 20 (2), pp. 115-149. Available at: https://journals.sagepub.com/doi/abs/10.1177/0951629807085815.

Park K.F., Shapira Z. (2017) Risk and Uncertainty. In: Augier M., Teece D. (eds) *The Palgrave Encyclopaedia of Strategic Management*. London: Palgrave Macmillan. Available at: https://doi.org/10.1057/978-1-349-94848-2_250-1 [Accessed: January 26, 2023].

Pastor, L' and Veronesi, P. (2012) Uncertainty about Government Policy and Stock Prices. *The Journal of Finance* 67(4), 1219–1264. Available at: http://www.jstor.org/stable/23261358

Pillai, P.S., Rao, S. (2014) Resource Allocation in Cloud Computing Using the Uncertainty Principle of Game Theory. *IEEE Systems Journal* 10 (2), pp. 637-648. Available at: https://ieeexplore.ieee.org/document/6813595 [Accessed: January 26, 2023].

Przeworski, A. (1991) *Democracy and the Market: Political and Economic Reforms in Eastern Europe and Latin America*. Cambridge: Cambridge University Press.

Rathbun, B.C. (2020) *War and Chance: Assessing Uncertainty in International Politics*. New York: Oxford University Press.

Rosendorff, B.P., Milner, H.V. (2007) The Optimal Design of International Institutions: Uncertainty and Escape. In: *ML Busch & ED Mansfield (eds), The WTO, Economic Interdependence and Conflict*. London: Edward Elgar Publishers. Available at: https://nyuscholars.nyu.edu/en/publications/the-optimal-design-of-international-institutions-uncertainty-and--3 [Accessed: January 26, 2023].

Schedler, A. (2010) Taking Uncertainty Seriously: The Blurred Boundaries of Democratic Transition and Consolidation. *Democratization* 8 (4), pp. 1-22. Available at: https://www.tandfonline.com/doi/abs/10.1080/714000225.

Schedler, A. (2013) *The Politics of Uncertainty: Sustaining and Subverting Electoral Authoritarianism*. Oxford: Oxford University Press.

Schumpeter, J.A. (2013) *Capitalism, Socialism and Democracy*. Abingdon: Routledge.

Stein, J. G. (2013) *Threat Perception in International Relations*. Oxford: Oxford University Press.

Székely, G., Rizzo, M. (2007) The Uncertainty Principle of Game Theory. *The American Mathematical Monthly* 114 (8), pp. 688-702. Available at: https://www.researchgate.net/publication/233489226_The_Uncertainty_Principle_of_Game_Theory.

Taleb, N.N. (2007) *The Black Swan: The Impact of the Highly Improbable*. 2nd edn. London: Penguin Books.

Tetlock, P.E., Gardner, D. (2016) *Superforecasting: The Art and Science of Prediction*. London: Random House.

World Health Organization (2020) *Cross-Country Analysis – How Comparable Is COVID-19 Mortality Across Countries?* Available at: https://analysis.covid19healthsystem.org/index.php/2020/06/04/how-comparable-is-covid-19-mortality-across-countries/ [Accessed: January 26, 2023].

3   Uncertainty in Non-Democracies[3]

This chapter complements the existing treatments of uncertainty in non-democracies by offering new evidence and a new conceptualization. Most of the debate about uncertainty in transitional democracies, hybrid regimes and consolidated authoritarian regimes hovers around the issues of substantive and procedural uncertainty. This emphasis is well placed but somewhat limited as it mainly pertains to the electoral procedure. This chapter builds upon this typology by applying the substantive and procedural types of uncertainty to non-electoral forms of holding the government to account. In particular, it refreshes the view of substantive uncertainty by gauging it not in terms of the number of possible outcomes, but in terms of the types of possible outcomes. It conjectures that some outcomes may resemble punishment of alleged officials, but in fact they just simulate accountability (as elections simulate delegation). Furthermore, the chapter showcases the idea of procedural uncertainty in new light by examining how the prosecutorial office is dominated informally by the president, thus undermining formal institutional rules.

Most substantively, the chapter applies empirically the idea of inter-institutional uncertainty, which it introduces and advances throughout the book. Inter-institutional uncertainty is conceptualized as the uncertainty which institution of accountability will prevail in sanctioning and investigating the government. Based on the empirical results, it concludes that inter-institutional uncertainty in Russia is rather low because the president has virtually monopolized all processes of investigating and sanctioning the government. Overall, the chapter follows the analytical framework introduced in chapter one to assess the two main claims of the book: (1) that we

---

3   Some parts of the material in this chapter have been adapted from chapter seven, titled "The Presidentialisation of Government Accountability in Russia: Crisis or Transformation of Democracy?" from my book *Democracy beyond Elections: Government Accountability in the Media Age* (London: Palgrave, 2019), pp. 155-179. They are reprinted here with the permission of Palgrave and the agreement of Ibidem.

need to view uncertainty as a multidimensional concept in a chain process and (2) that we need to consider new types of uncertainty.

Uncertainty in Non-Democracies: A Brief Overview of the Literature

There is relatively little research on uncertainty in non-democratic countries as most of the research in this vein is centred on uncertainty in transitioning or in newly established democracies. Such regimes are said to be infused with "extraordinary uncertainty" (O'Donnell and Schmitter 1986). Transitions, in their view, were a "conjunctural outcome" that resembled Albert Hirschman's use of the term "possibilism" to indicate the domain of the accidental and of unintended consequences (Khachaturian 2015, p. 138). One central hypothesis about uncertainty in transitional regimes is that procedural uncertainty is high and substantive uncertainty is low: "The "discriminating factor" between "efficient" (impartial) and "redistributive" (biased) institutions lies in "the uncertainty of the outcomes they produce" (Tsebelis 1990, p. 117). Authoritarian and democratic actors, for instance, exhibit different attitudes towards uncertainty. While the former attempt to reduce the uncertainty of outcomes, the latter attempt to reduce the uncertainty of institutional rules (Mozaffar and Schedler 2002, p. 11). This is not surprising because political actors in newly established regimes are not used to the rules of the game, so the chance that they reverse back to autocratic rules is high.

But what does the popular saying "rules of the game" mean in relation to uncertainty in transitional countries? Essentially, it presupposes that established regimes operate with one set of rules, and countries moving between various regime types can oscillate between two sets of rules embedded in them. The idea that players will not play by the purported rules of the game means that there is no monopoly over the set of rules. While in established countries the main issue about uncertainty is whether actors will follow the rules or not, in transitional countries, the issues are two: whether the actors will follow the rules, and which rules the actors will follow.

The seminal idea about the "rules of the game" was introduced by Schmitter and O'Donnell (1986), who liken it to a multi-layered chess game, where the chess players can at any point switch between boards. While the authors concede that such "switches" contain surprising turns and twists, they still point out that uncertainty in transitional countries is even greater, because, unlike in a chess game, the number of players is "indeterminate", the players can form shifting alliances, and they can isolate various actors from participating (O'Donnell and Schmitter 1986, p. 76). Thus, a relatively less well considered aspect about the changing rules of the game is social, namely that rules cannot change individually and unilaterally, but there must be a critical number of players who conspire to do so.

If the central issue of transitional countries is how many sets of rules there are, in addition to whether the players follow the rules, and which rules to follow, the central issue in an established authoritarian regime is to what extent the rulers have monopoly over the rules that favour their interests. By implication, in a democracy, there is no group or person who can impose a set of rules that favour their interests. It emerges that the ability to impose the dominant set of rules is the hallmark of an authoritarian regime: "In authoritarian regimes "someone/something" has the capacity to prevent political outcomes adverse to their interests. Power apparatus capable of overturning the outcomes of the institutionalised political process... Crucial moment in the passage to democracy is the threshold beyond which no one can intervene to reverse outcomes in the formal democratic process" (Przeworski 1988, pp. 60-62).

How can we establish empirically that uncertainty has moved from the transitional to the established phase of democratization? Following the above analysis, it seems that procedural uncertainty decreases when there is only one dominant set of rules, and the actors are willing to follow them. As Schedler (2010, p. 3) points out, these perspectives are opposing because one perspective presupposes the internal viewpoints of the actors and is forward looking and intentional, while the other perspective is conducted from the point of view of an external observer and is backward looking and causal. Marrying these two perspectives, and thus ensuring that uncertainty enters a new phase, is extremely difficult because the perspectives usually converge gradually and can fluctuate. Therefore, the boundaries of uncertainty are blurry. The only exception when the internal perspectives of the actors and the external perspectives of the observers converge is when there are "focal events." Such rare and extreme occurrences signal most clearly that procedural uncertainty sharply diminishes or increases.

Moving the analysis from uncertainty in transitional regimes to uncertainty in hybrid or established authoritarian regimes, we are left with relatively scarce wisdom on the subject of uncertainty in non-democracies. The seminal work in this regard is produced by Schedler, who suggests that such regimes suffer from both institutional and informational uncertainty. Strong institutions create procedural certainty because they stabilize actors' expectations. It is considered that "strong institutions create deep certainties, weak institutions much less so" (Schedler 2013, p. 23). Institutional uncertainty in electoral authoritarianism is said to be intermediate. On the one hand, institutional uncertainty is low because the rules of the game are not new, and this familiarity creates an air of certainty. On the other hand, institutional uncertainty is high because institutions are constantly under siege by the threat of rivals, the threat of rebels, the threat of retaliation and the ignorance of the dictators. Although threats from people who comply with institutional rules are not explicitly formulated as such, it is implicit in Schedler's analysis that institutional uncertainty could be threatened by seemingly compliant political actors, if their internal motives are not sincere. It is therefore crucial not only to observe the outward behaviour of obedient citizens in an electoral authoritarianism, but to also inquire whether their obedience is dictated by internal rules or external threats.

To estimate the strength of institutions, it is also important to gauge whether the non-compliant actors are "too few or too powerless to affect the overall institutional equilibrium" (Schedler 2013, p. 30). Informational uncertainties in non-democratic countries are said to originate from three structural factors: repressed subjectivity, which measures whether compliant behaviours are sufficiently internalized, hidden action of state bureaucracies and intelligence agencies, which is a form of self-policing, and unreliable information, which is an obvious byproduct of informational monopolies (Schedler 2013, p. 37).

One original interpretation of substantive uncertainty is to juxtapose it to the "rule of law" variety of uncertainty. According to one interpretation, substantive uncertainty primarily defines outcomes or outputs, but not procedures. In the second type of "rule of law" of uncertainty, "which is increasingly prominent in both scholarly and development-policy circles, a number of theorists argue that the "rule of law" means that democracy offers guarantees regarding substantive outcomes that authoritarian rule does not and cannot" (Alexander 2016, p. 1,146). It seems that institutionalized uncertainty emphasizes ex ante uncertainty over outcomes in democracy far more than the rule of law type of uncertainty, which limits the range of options.

There is no doubt that of all democratic procedures, elections have received by far the most attention in the literature on political uncertainty. The democratizing power of elections is a key mechanism for reducing procedural uncertainty and increasing substantive uncertainty in a democracy. In electoral authoritarianism, where showcase elections replace free and fair elections in an effort to simulate but not to emulate democracy, the relationship between elections and uncertainty is trickier. Elections in an electoral authoritarianism can behave in at least three ways: (1) elections as adornments, where electoral rules reflect existing configurations of power but cannot change them; (2) elections as tools, where elections are instruments that the rulers use to strengthen their power; and (3) elections as arenas, where opponents still get an opportunity to contest power (Schedler 2013, p. 5). It is the uncertainty whether elections are adornments, tools or arenas, that underpins a lot of procedural uncertainty in a façade democracy. The uncertainty around such elections stems from the fact that the elections need to seem competitive enough to imbue legitimacy in the authoritarian regime, but they also need to be closed enough not to allow any substantive opportunities to the rivals to seize power (Bernard, Edgell and Lindberg 2019, p. 466).

A recent study has significantly improved our understanding about the link between façade elections and substantive uncertainty by showing that it is not a dichotomous question whether the relation is positive or negative. Instead, Bernard, Edgell and Lindberg (2019) suggest that the issue is how many elections an electoral authoritarianism can withstand without slipping into a democracy, and what type of elections these are. Their results demonstrate that the uncertainty of reversing a dictatorship disappears after an inflection point, which is usually around the first two or four elections, and that it matters whether these are single party elections, multi-party elections, hegemonic multi-party elections or competitive multi-party elections.

Emulating the electoral procedure in form, while undermining it in substance, is said to work particularly well for Russia. Among other things, emulating elections serves to create a sense of unity in a diverse nation (Krastev and Holmes 2012, p. 38). In addition, simulating elections helps avoid physical intimidation and violence by creating the impression that Putin is in control and is managing the country:

> Fraudulent elections help Putin hold on to power despite chronic thieving by government officials at all levels and the regime's obvious failure to address the country's many developmental challenges. They do this by allowing a regime that cannot control itself or solve its country's basic problems to appear to be more powerful than it is. Fraudulent elections make it unnecessary for Putin to resort to the degree of physical intimidation historically typical of authoritarian regimes but of which his regime is structurally incapable. "Managed democracy," on this account, has been valued by Putin's team not because it simulates democracy but because it simulates management, something that his government otherwise has a very hard time displaying (Krastev and Holmes 2012, p. 40).

Uncertainty in Non-Democracies: The Ambiguity of the New Despotisms

Keane's book The New Despotism (2020) builds upon this core idea about the uncertainty inherent in elections by extending it to a variety of non-electoral procedures, which simulate to be democratic.[4] The originality of Keane's insight comes from revealing the other ambiguities in which institutional uncertainty is embedded. The book shows how the new despotism thrives on ambiguity and what these ambiguities are: combinations of motives, blends of practices, mixtures of economic structures, fluidity in relationships, and duplicity in using the law and the media. All of them increase uncertainty. The first dimension of procedural uncertainty—or what I call ambiguity here—is the new despotism's complicated relationship with democracy. On the one hand, the new despotism derives pleasure from democracy's failures, and loudly points them out. At the same time, it examines democratic achievements and consciously tries to replicate them. Mimicking democratic arrangements, and sometimes actually adopting them, is a key element of 'seducing' the public. Some of the procedures that the new despotisms take from democracy's playbook include: 'e-consultation exercises, online public forums, and small-scale informal consultations conducted by government ministers and known as Tea Sessions, Dialogue Sessions, Policy Feedback Groups, and Policy Study Workshops. The rulers operate Facebook, Instagram, and Twitter accounts' (Keane 2020, p. 95). These innovations make the public more vested in the ruling regime. They make them accomplices.

Whether the new despotism will only mimic democratic procedures or it will occasionally adopt democratic procedures is a key ambiguity, and a source of uncertainty, in non-democracies. The public can never have enough information to figure out to what extent democratic rules extend from local initiatives to a systematic practice. It is also often hard for any single citizen to tell a free and fair election from a manipulated one. All the citizens see are clear signs that the government is listening to the people. This

---

4 This subsection of the chapter fully incorporates the following text: Book review: The New Despotism by John Keane. *LSE Review of Books*. Dimova, G., 2020. Found at: https://blogs.lse.ac.uk/lsereviewofbooks/2020/06/30/book-review-the-new-despotism-by-john-keane/. The book review is reprinted in this chapter with some modifications with the permission of the LSE Review of Books and with the agreement of Ibidem.

impression is heightened by the media, which invariably tells them that the people are important. As is familiar to scholars of populism, the new despotisms 'regularly deploy the rhetoric of "the people" and refer constantly to them as the presumed source of sovereign authority' (Keane 2020, p. 82). To top this ambiguity off, the new despotism makes sure to demonstrate the use of the full power of the law and legal order. The catch — and this is yet another ambiguity — is that leaders use the law selectively to fight opponents, while they subvert the law to shield themselves and their cliques. While the former is plain to see, the latter is often impossible to prove. It seems that the new despotism has planted all these hints, intimations and ambiguities to mislead the public. This uncertainty puts the subjects one step away from willingly surrendering themselves to 'voluntary servitude', as Keane puts it (Keane 2020, p. 108).

But to make that final step to living in ambiguity, embed the ultimate uncertainty, and make citizens utterly and sincerely enjoying it, the public in the new despotisms needs an internal motivating factor. It needs to feel that there is something in it for them. This something needs to be individual and tangible; it needs to be something material. The public needs to be not only cajoled; it also needs to be bribed. Those bribes come in the form of the enjoyment of small material possessions and luxury experiences, such as vacations and hobbies. The middle classes are 'prepared to trade some liberties for comfortable peace and quiet' (Keane 2020, p. 237). Keane tells us that it is quite possible, and even probable, for well-educated, well-travelled and 'well brought up' people to give up their ability to think critically for the opportunity to frequent fancy airport lounges, hotels and shops. Instead of inspiring ideals, driving progress and defending the less fortunate, these middle classes embrace cynical morals and fickle pragmatism. In the best possible scenario, they will forsake morals for professional prestige, not for replicas of Louis Vuitton bags.

The new despotisms' middle classes harbour yet another source of ambiguity, which is a prelude to uncertainty. On the surface, the middle classes seem like opportunistic intellectuals turned ultimate consumerists. But Keane underscores that they lead a comfortable, rather than a luxurious, life. It seems that this ambiguous situation—yet another ambiguity—puts the middle classes at risk. Looking up to the unattainable riches of the elites and looking down upon the insufferable misery of the poor, the survival instinct of the middle classes seems to kick in. It leads them to be satisfied with the small but stable private property they have rather than chase bigger but elusive riches. Thus, the middle classes have consciously or subconsciously become the beacons of the seductively repressive new despotism. And while their numbers are small, the book The New Despotism tells us, their importance is big, because they are visible. Their life is up for show, and it is meant to demonstrate that it is not only the ruling elite that can live a relatively good and stable life. The implication, it seems, is that poverty is a personal failure, not the new despotism's fault.

The responsibility for poverty in a non-democracy is yet another source of uncertainty. The idea that poverty is an individual, rather than the regime's failure, is half-true and half-false in such regimes. By laying this ambiguity out, Keane has masterfully uncovered yet another source of uncertainty. The true part of it is that in a state capitalist economy, which Keane believes the new despotism is based upon, the small business is market-driven and is open to all entrants. Therefore, poverty is the fault of the small business owner. The false part of this account is that big business is entirely under state patronage, which precludes access to people not affiliated with the political elite. Therefore, poverty is not the fault of the business owner.

The half-true and half-false nature of economic relations—yet another cause or a dimension of uncertainty in an authoritarian state—is further complicated by the fact that all economic relations are based on networks of mutual favours. While this system of favours has often been analysed before (e.g. Ledeneva 1998), Keane goes one step further. He writes that the system creates enormous anxiety and uncertainty—and, yes, this is also an ambiguity—as it is never clear whether you would know 'the right person' for every emergency you run into. Instead of feeling repulsed by such a system, the people entangled in these networks feel a sense of solidarity as everyone is an accomplice, and a sense of relief that they have managed to navigate and survive these ambiguities for so long. Thus, uncertainty and ambiguity thrive in non-democracies.

One strength of the new despotism—and another ambiguity—comes from its ability to successfully blend traditional local ways of doing things with an adoption of the most modern practices of democracies. This is an important observation for Keane to make because previous failed attempts at democratization have shown that threading the line between old customs and contemporary Western techniques for governing is a highly precarious balancing act. This combination of local ways and Western practices is very misleading for the new despotism's subjects and no less confusing for outside observers.

A key mechanism sustaining the ambiguity of the new despotism is its quietness. Unlike in Mussolini's Italy, Hitler's Germany and Mao's China, public expressions of celebration and loyalty are discouraged. In the new despotism, 'flesh-and-blood citizens are expected to stay quiet, locked down in private forms of self-celebration' (Keane 2020, p. 97). For example, 'in Tajikistan, which bans lavish private gatherings on the grounds that extravagant parties strain family budgets, a Dushanbe resident was fined for hosting friends at a local restaurant to celebrate his twenty-fifth birthday' (Keane 2020, p. 97). It seems that being quiet is important for the state of ambiguity to perpetuate itself. If people get together, they will compare notes; they will exchange stories. Isolation (here conceived of before the widespread lockdown in response to COVID-19), especially in the company of small material comforts, probably nourishes self-congratulation and self-regard.

Keane is not the alone in shedding light on the utility of ambiguity for despotic regimes, although he does it in the most comprehensive manner. Herd (2019) also argues that Putin maintains his regime by employing a technique of creating an air of uncertainty, where his subordinates always have to guess and interpret what he means. To inject uncertainty, he tends to hint at things, or tell others what they cannot do, as opposed to what they can do. This strategy of ambiguity is also useful as it helps Putin evade responsibility.

Another View of Institutional Uncertainty in Non-Democracies: The Informal Presidentialisation of the Prosecutor-General's Office in Russia

This chapter provides yet another alternative view of uncertainty in non-democracies by showcasing the high degree of institutional uncertainty in Russia. Institutional uncertainty — or the likelihood that people will abide by the formal institutional rules — is present every time there is a factor that informally influences the actors within the institutions. Practically speaking, all corrupt institutions are highly uncertain. It is unknown who will offer a bribe, whom to offer the bribe to, and how much the bribe should be. Equally uncertain are institutions, where advancement is not merit based. The uncertainty comes from the lack of a clear way to calculate the actor's contributions, accomplishments and the respective awards.

In this particular instance in Russia, the informal dependency of the prosecutor on the president means that abiding by the formal rules of the prosecutorial office is uncertain. Thus, institutional uncertainty is high. The fragile democratic tradition in Russia enables the president to bypass the legislature in appointing, and ultimately, controlling the prosecutor. The president has also found an institutional loophole that helps him usurp the accountability channels. Article twelve of the law does not specify what happens if the Federation Council rejects the president's nomination for a prosecutor twice. The personalization of accountability in Russia arises because the formal mode of the dismissal of the prosecutor has not been formalised and because the president has found informal ways to personalize his relationship with the prosecutor.

A quick look at the behaviour of the three Russian prosecutors under Yeltsin testifies to the informal dependency of the prosecutor on the president, and to the degree of institutional uncertainty that it implies. A pattern emerges. First, the prosecutor shows disloyalty to the president, then some compromising material unexpectedly appears in the media, and then the prosecutor is dismissed. Here is one example of the personalization of the presidential-prosecutorial connection: Valentine Stepankov, prosecutor-general between

1991 and 1993, was dismissed by Yeltsin shortly after Stepankov appeared on national TV to condemn Yeltsin's decree to disband the parliament in March 1993 as unconstitutional. In August of the same year, the Russian entrepreneur Dmitriy Yakubovskiy showed a tape containing a conversation in which Stepankov asked him to organize the assassination of the deputy prosecutor Makarov. Stepankov was dismissed two months later.

Here is a second example of the personalization of the presidential-prosecutorial connection: Aleksey Kazannik was prosecutor-general from 1993 to 1994. He disagreed with Yelstin's order to suspend the amnesty of the people imprisoned for the October 1993 rebellion. There was no need for compromising material this time since Kazannik resigned voluntarily shortly thereafter, while defending his judgment (NUPI, 1994). Another example relates to Alexey Ilyushenko, who was prosecutor general from 1994-1996. Before Yeltsin nominated him to the prosecutorial position, he was the president's aide. Ilyushenko was dismissed only days after closing the investigation into the bloody events of October 1993, in which he pinned the blame equally on executive authorities and on the supporters of the Supreme Soviet. Around this time, the media published reports that Ilyushenko was involved in a small car dealership that mysteriously had won a lucrative contract to export oil. It was this news that Yeltsin used as a pretext for his dismissal: "Of course Ilyushenko denies everything but after all the blemish, I cannot formally recommend him again for prosecutor general," said Yeltsin (NUPI, 1994).

A third example of the personalization of the presidential-prosecutorial connection relates to Yuri Skuratov, the prosecutor general from 1997-1999. Skuratov was dismissed when he refused to quit his investigation of the Mabetex scandal, in which Yeltsin and his property advisor Borodin were accused to have accepted bribes from the Swiss company Mabetex. When the Federation council refused to approve the dismissal, a tape surfaced in the media in which a man resembling Skuratov was filmed in bed with two prostitutes. The Council still refused to acquiesce. Skuratov was finally dismissed shortly after Putin assumed the presidency. Currently, after Putin's reforms the president appoints the members of the Federation Council, so it will not be a problem any more to get prosecutors fired and hired. These examples show that institutional uncertainty, as far as it relates to the prosecutorial office at least, is very high because the likelihood that the prosecutor will abide by the formal rules, or the likelihood that the prosecutor will be dismissed by abiding to formal requirements — is slim.

Substantive Uncertainty: The Personalization of Sanctions

In contrast to the previous analysis in this chapter, which focused on institutional uncertainty, this part seeks to provide more empirical data and an alternative theoretical angle to the concept of substantive uncertainty. Substantive uncertainty arises, when it is difficult to predict how the political process will end. In its most standard interpretation, substantive accountability denotes the outcome of an election. This chapter applies the concept of substantive accountability to a new arena, namely the accountability process in Russia. It shows that substantive uncertainty is low because the president's allies, even when they are found guilty, always avoid accountability. There is little doubt as to whether the president's allies will be sanctioned or not. In this sense, the outcome is predetermined and uncertainty is low. But how can we prove that the outcome is predetermined and that the president's allies are always spared a deserving sanction?

One clue is given by the presidentialisation of the sanctioning process in Russia. As figure 3.1. shows, there is a disproportionately big category of demotion of incumbents, which also includes the reappointment of incumbents. The category raises red flags as it indicates that there is a certain trend of recycling of cadres in the political elite. This recycling of incumbents undermines the spirit of accountability. It creates a double reality. It gives the impression that an official is punished for the alleged wrongdoing when in fact he (mostly he) has simply been moved to another position, which is usually just as attractive.

Figure 3.1: Impact of Type of Investigations on the Severity of Sanctions Imposed on the Government[5]

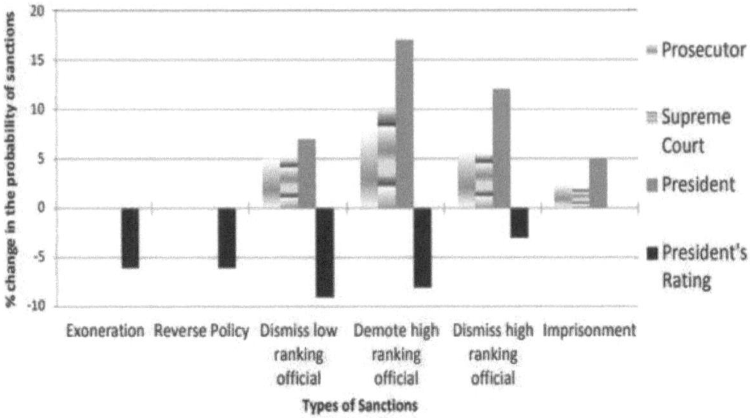

Bar chart showing % change in the probability of sanctions across types of sanctions (Exoneration, Reverse Policy, Dismiss low ranking official, Demote high ranking official, Dismiss high ranking official, Imprisonment) for four categories: Prosecutor, Supreme Court, President, President's Rating.

Why does the reappointment of incumbents indicate a low degree of substantive uncertainty? In this case, the reappointment of disgraced government officials shows that the sanctions are biased in a way that spares the president's allies and punishes the president's enemies. There is no uncertainty as to whether one will be sanctioned if one is in the president's good graces. In principle, the dismissal of government officials means that the government is aware of the incumbents' guilt or that it admits their blame to some extent. The reappointment of such officials, on the other hand, means that the government wants to retain these admittedly guilty officials within positions of power, despite their past record. In this indirect way, corrupt or incompetent officials are rewarded, rather than punished, for their bad record. This trend indicates that high-ranking officials are virtually untouchable, which in turn suggests that political connections transcend notions of the uncertainty related to acting in good faith.

Examples of the Kremlin's revolving door personnel policy are plenty. Sergey Stepashin had been dismissed as an FSB chief in 1995 because of the unsuccessful handling of the Budyonnovsk

---

5   The dependent variable "sanctions" in figure 3.1. has 10 degrees. The coefficients are calculated based on a first differences estimation.

hostage crisis, yet he later became justice minister, interior minister, and briefly a prime minister (NUPI, 2002). Stepashin's reappointment is not nearly as telling as Borodin's. Pavel Borodin, Yeltsin's property chief, came under investigation in 1999 by Swiss authorities for receiving kickbacks and laundering $22.4 million. Borodin was imprisoned by the FBI on 8 January 2001 and sentenced by a Swiss court in 2002 (NUPI, 2002). Although he lost his position as a Kremlin property chief, Borodin was appointed a state secretary of the Union of Russia and Belarus, a comparatively attractive job. The Duma deputy Kozyrev concluded that Russia has in this high-ranking position a convicted criminal according to international standards.

Other cases of reappointments of admittedly corrupt or incompetent officials include the prosecutor Vladimir Ustinov and the governor Nazdradenko. The prosecutor general Ustinov was dismissed in June 2006 because of his improper handling of the corruption case "The Three Whales." Many critics hailed the move as a sign of purging corruption. Several days later this illusion was lifted as Ustinov was appointed justice minister. The former justice minister Yuri Chaika, whose place the former prosecutor Ustinov took, became the new prosecutor general.

A telling example of a person who stays in power despite huge mistakes and low public approval is Anatolii Chubais. Although Chubais was dismissed three times for misconduct or incompetence, he continued to be reappointed to lucrative positions. The first time Chubais was dismissed from the post of chief of the presidential staff for failing to deal with wage arrears. The wage arrears were deemed to have contributed to the poor showing of the pro-government Our Home is Russia party in the December 1995 election. However, Yeltsin reinstated Chubais in the same position only one year later. Chubais's reappointment was met with negative reaction. State Duma Speaker Gennadii Seleznev described the appointment as a mistake. Communist Party leader Gennadii Zyuganov compared the appointment to "spitting in the face of society." Zyuganov claimed that Chubais was almost as hated in Russia as Hitler. Liberal Democratic Party leader Vladimir Zhirinovsky said that a narrow clique of politicians was being reshuffled "like a greasy old pack of cards" (RFE/RL, 1997).

Yeltsin ignored the parliamentarians' anger only to dismiss Chubais later from the post of finance minister because of the "book scandal." Allegedly, Chubais received $100, 000 for a book on privatization he had never written. Although Chubais's public approval rating was only 9,8% in 1998, Yeltsin appointed him a presidential envoy to international financial institutions. Chubais lost this job in August 1998 when the Russian currency collapsed and plunged the country into a financial crisis. Despite being fired three times — for failure to manage wage arrears, for a big corruption scandal, and for the financial crisis, Chubais moved on to assume one of the most coveted positions in the country-head of the United Energy Systems. On May 16, 2002, angry parliamentarians protested and questioned prime-minister Kasyanov about Chubais's $350,000 salary. Although Kasyanov promised the deputies to look into the matter, nothing was done. Chubais continued to reign on the same terms until he failed one more time on 26 May 2005, when blackout struck Moscow.

The State Duma declined to consider a "Motherland"-drafted resolution calling for an emergency shareholders' meeting to discuss Chubais's resignation. "The Motherland party head Rogozin told Ekho Moskvy that Chubais was a "notorious schemer" and a "bad manager." Communist Party leader Zyuganov told the radio station that Chubais "should be fired…the Duma has voted 10 times to sack him, but the party of power [Unified Russia] and [President Vladimir] Putin have always backed him" (RFE/RL, 2005). These examples indicate that people who are favoured by the president are not punished, regardless of what they might have done wrong. Accountability is not based on evidence, merit and rule but on personal connections with the president. Such a presidentialisation of sanctions indicates a low degree of substantive uncertainty.

Inter-Institutional Uncertainty in Non-Democracies is Smaller

At this point, the chapter shifts its focus from (substantive and procedural) institutional uncertainty to inter-institutional uncertainty, which is the new type of uncertainty that the book advances. Inter-institutional uncertainty is hereby operationalized as the uncertainty arising from having multiple institutions acting at the same time and not knowing the rules of which institutions will be applied. In this sense, inter-institutional uncertainty comes prior to the institutional uncertainty outlined in the previous section. Institutional uncertainty is about sticking to the rules of a particular institution, while inter-institutional uncertainty is about choosing which institutional rules will be valid in each instance.

The idea of inter-institutional uncertainty challenges the assumption that there is only one set of rules. This assumption is embedded in previous scholarship on uncertainty, which largely focuses on elections, as discussed earlier in the chapter. Perhaps this dichotomy is valid, when speaking about democratic or non-democratic rules. However, there are many types of non-democratic rules, just as there are many types of democratic rules. It is an obvious fact that there are various institutions, which operate in various spheres of life.

The multiplicity of institutions and of institutional rules is especially valid within the domain of between-elections accountability. Holding the government to account in between elections could embody a wide range of institutions, such as the courts, protests, audit committees, international institutions, etc. There is a decision to be made as to which institution and which institutional rules to use to hold the government to account. This is a consequential decision as each accountability institution embodies its own set of rules with its specific advantages and disadvantages. In the previous chapters, I termed this dimension inter-institutional uncertainty, because it reflects the tension between the institutions.

This chapter argues that inter-institutional uncertainty in non-democracies, and in Russia in this case, is smaller than inter-institutional uncertainty in democracies. There are several ways in which inter-institutional uncertainty is minimized and all of them boil down to the finding that the accountability process is steered by the president. The crux of the argument is that there is no competition between the institutions as to who will investigate and sanction government ministers. In this sense, there is no uncertainty as to which institutional rules will apply, because it is largely the standing of the president and the president's decision that matter. I call this process a monopolization of the accountability channels. Such a monopolization naturally breeds more certainty than a state where there is a free for all competition between the institutions.

Although such a monopolization is hard to prove, it is not impossible. Dimova (2019, pp. 155-179) offers some findings, which can be interpreted as indicators of a highly centralized accountability process, which consequently admits of little inter-institutional uncertainty: (1) the president plays an oversized role in sanctioning the government. This means that presidential investigations consistently produce more sanctions than any other types of investigations of the government; (2) the president has a widely disproportionate role in investigating the government. Taken together, these two indicators point to a very slim contest between the institutions in holding government ministers to account.

Figure 3.2. below provides suggestions as to the substantive, institutional and inter-institutional uncertainty in a democracy and in a non-democracy. It conjectures that democracies contain a higher degree of substantive uncertainty, which denotes the outcomes of a particular process. In non-democracies, specifically in Russia, the outcomes tend to favour the president's allies. As argued above, institutional uncertainty in non-democracies is high because formal rules, while they exist, are continuously undermined by personal relationships, mostly those to the president. By contrast, institutional uncertainty in democracies is low because actors' behaviour closely mimics the expectations of the institutions. Inter-institutional uncertainty in non-democracies is low as it will be detailed below. In democracies, checks and balances make the accountability process a highly contested, and consequently very uncertain, process.

Figure 3.2: Procedural and Substantive Uncertainty in Democracies and Non-Democracies

Procedural and Substantive Uncertainty in Democracies

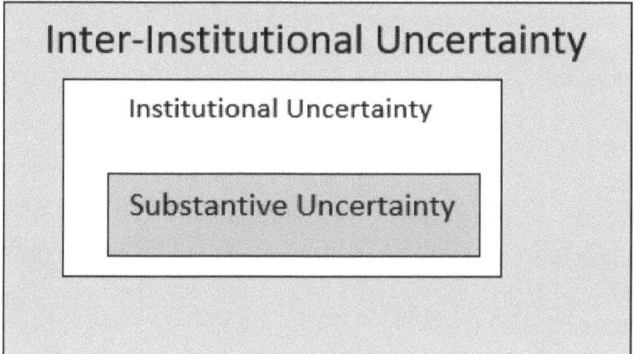

Procedural and Substantive Uncertainty in Non-Democracies

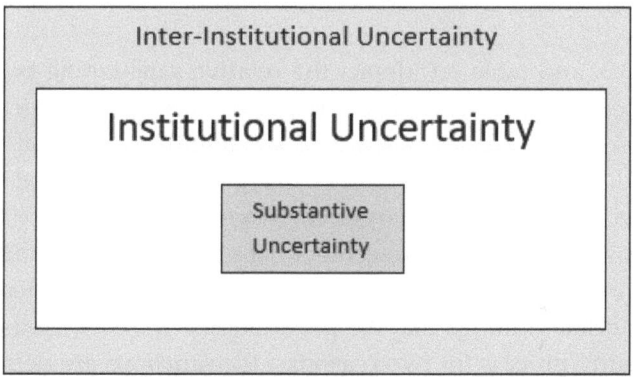

Note: The size of the rectangle reflects the degree of uncertainty. The bigger the rectangle, the bigger the uncertainty.

Smaller Inter-Institutional Uncertainty in Non-Democracies: The President Plays an Oversized Role in Sanctioning the Government

One indicator that inter-institutional uncertainty is low is that there is no uncertainty as to who is going to sanction the government.

Table 3.1: Impact of the Type of Investigation on the Incidence of Government Sanctions for Both Incompetence and Misconduct Charges

Who Conducts the Investigation?	Dependent Variable is: 0= No Sanctions vs. 1=Sanctions		
	Model 1: First Differences	Model 2: Odds Ratios	Model 3: Probit Analysis
President	.43 (.08)**	16.9 (13.92)**	1.40 (.38)**
President's ratings	-.57 (.18)**	.96 (.01)**	-.02 (.007)**
Supreme Court	.29 (.11)**	5.08 (3.8)**	.96 (.44)**
Prosecutor	.19 (.8)**	3.39 (2.13)*	.64 (.36)*

N=205

Figure 3.3. and table 3.1. depict the relative sanctioning power of each accountability forum in Russia. The relative sanctioning power is assessed by regressing all the possible investigations on the resulting sanctions, if any. Those regressions produced the coefficients in the figure. A larger coefficient means that the forum, when investigating the government for media accusations, produces more sanctions that a forum with a lower coefficient. It is clear from the findings that the president has monopolized the accountability process for two reasons—the sanctions are dependent mostly on the president's ratings and on the president's investigations. There may not be any real choice in choosing any other alternatives, because they are very unlikely to produce sanctions. Thus, the whole process about choosing decisions is effectively redundant. This is why inter-institutional uncertainty, which relates to the competition between institutions, is relatively low.

Further bolstering the idea of low inter-institutional uncertainty is the top of the pyramid, which illustrates that the most important determinant of sanctions in light of media accusations is the approval rating of the president. As figure 3.3. and table 3.1 show, if the president's rating decreases from its minimum to its maximum, the likelihood of sanctions of the government increases by 57%. It is notable that it is the president's, rather than the government's ratings, that affect the likelihood of government sanctions. When the approval ratings of the president drop, sanctions of the government are more likely, and vice versa. The element of presidentialisation is obvious in the fact that public opinion matters in the accountability process only insofar it reflects the public attitude to the president. Surprisingly, government approval ratings are inconsequential for government sanctions. By contrast, in Germany, it is the public approval of the opposition parties that matters for imposing sanctions, and in Bulgaria, it is public approval of the government (Dimova 2019, pp. 148; 182).

Another powerful indicator of the presidentialisation of accountability is that presidential investigations of media allegations rank second in importance (after the effect of the approval ratings), which means that the president is the most powerful imposer of sanctions on the government (figure 3.3. and table 3.1). The involvement of the president in the investigation of media accusations of government misconduct or government incompetence increases the chances of sanctions by 43%.

Figure 3.3: The Accountability Pyramid in Russia: Relative Sanctioning Effectiveness of Forums

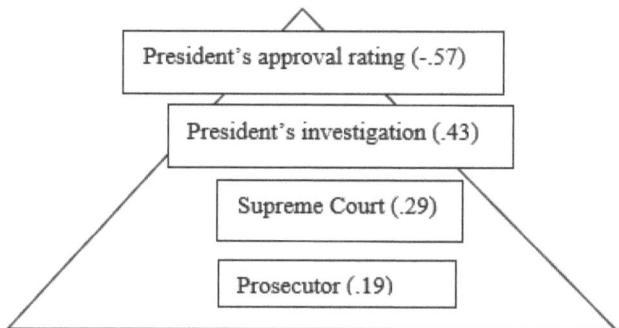

The monopolization of the decision about which forum to choose is also manifested in the fact that there are not many forums, which can contest the presidential power. The base of the pyramid in figure 3.3. is very narrow. The base of the pyramid shows that there is no great variety of effective tools that compete to impose their logic on the accountability process. It consists of just the prosecutor. The Russian Duma is altogether absent from the sanctioning pyramid. The Russian Duma, which is the lower house of the legislature, has an extremely limited impact on the outcome of investigations. Forming a parliamentary committee or putting forward a parliamentary inquiry makes no difference for the likelihood of sanctions. Likewise, international investigations and the involvement of the audit chamber make no difference for the probability of punishing alleged government officials. The height of the accountability pyramid, which measures the difference between the most effective sanctioning forum (presidential ratings) and the least effective sanctioning forum (prosecutorial investigation), is relatively big, which further supports the thesis of the supremacy of the president.

Smaller Inter-Institutional Uncertainty in Non-Democracies: The President Plays an Oversized Role in Investigating the Government

Inter-institutional uncertainty in the accountability process in Russia is also low because there is little doubt who will investigate the government. Presidential investigations far outnumber any other type of investigations of the government. Only in Russia does the president come before the legislature in terms of the number of investigative activity (figure 3.4). This is quite telling and very characteristic of Russia. In democracies, the most widely used legislative tool for imposing investigative accountability are legislative questions. This is the case in Germany, where parliamentary questions are the most widespread tool for investigative the government. The difference is that in Germany, parliamentary questions are not only the most widespread legislative tool for investigation but also the most widespread tool overall. In contrast to Russia, the German legislature also regularly employs legislative committees, which are the second most widely used legislative measure after parliamentary questions (Dimova 2019, p. 143). In addition to the presidential dominance, a unique feature of investigative accountability in Russia is that the Security Forces are involved in investigating the government, which is unusual for either Bulgaria or Germany (figure 3.4).

Figure 3.4: Incidence of Investigations of Media Accusations Levelled at the Government

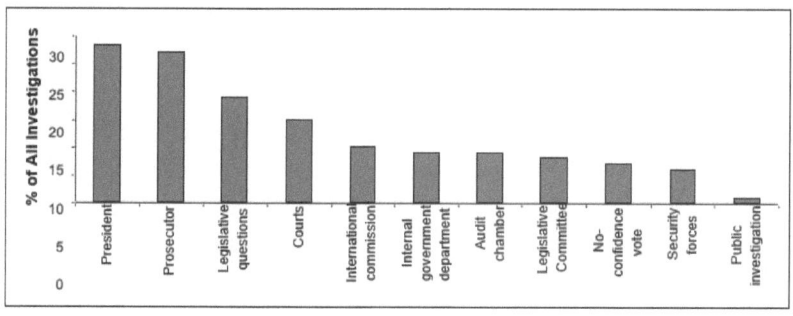

N=205

The presidentialisation of government accountability goes hand in hand with the de-parliamentarisation of government accountability. Effectively, this means that the separation of powers is heavily skewed in favour of the president. This means that as the president usurps power and resources to investigate and sanction the government, the legislature loses a grip on the process. De-parliamentarisation naturally means that parliament is less willing and able to ask the government for clarification, explanation and justification. It also suggests that parliament would punish the government less. In Russia, however, the process of de-parliamentarisation has been taken to a completely new level. The findings indicate that Russia's Duma mechanisms for control, such as public questioning and investigatory committees, do not have a statistically significant impact on the likelihood of sanctioning the government. In fact, in cases when the Duma forms a committee or (threatens) a vote of no-confidence for incompetence allegations, the probability of sanctions strangely decreases; it does not increase.

Parliament's investigations fail mainly because the government does not cooperate. Incumbents simply refuse to respond to

Duma inquiries. Often the ministers ignore Duma requests, or delay answering them until the case is forgotten or more opportune political circumstances arise. One example is the reaction of the first deputy prime minister Oleg Soskovets. He was summoned by the Duma to account for allegations that he abused his office to benefit the presidential campaign. Instead of showing up on the Duma floor, Soskovets sent a letter saying that he thought it is "pointless" for the Duma to examine the issue (RFE/RL, 1996).

Another dimension of the parliament's weakness is that it cannot oblige the government to explain its actions. Officeholders usually avoid divulging information under the pretext of a state secret. In the February 2003 edition of Novaya Gazeta, the journalist and MP Yuri Schechchokin points to yet another failure of the Russian government to rise to the standard of accountability. As a member of the Duma Committee on Public Safety, Schechchokin investigated the 2002 hostage crisis, when Chechen terrorists took 850 people hostages in a Moscow theatre. The Russian special forces raided the building using an unidentified gas. The media widely discussed suspicions that more than 89 hostages died from that gas. Schechchokin wanted to find out whether the authorities used a poisonous substance. His investigation was once again averted by the unresponsiveness of the government, which stated that the Federal Security Bureau could not give information about the gas because it was a "state secret" (Schechchokin 2001).

The executive recourse to the pretext of "national security" is not a unique Russian phenomenon. Noble (1992, p. 539) points out that in the USA "control of classified information is a tool that can potentially be used to circumvent the entire Independent Counsel process, as it puts the Executive Branch in a position of judging whether or not one of its own is prosecuted." However, in Russia, this form of non-cooperation with the Duma is taken to an extreme. Because of several non-appearances of government members, the Duma deputies were so discouraged that they wanted to introduce monetary fines for incumbents who did not attend the required plenary sessions.

In another testament to the legislature's impotence, after parliament refused to pass a resolution to investigate the 1999 Moscow apartment bombings, several deputies formed an independent public committee outside of the Duma (RFE/RL, 2002). Another extreme form of parliamentary control is the MPs' hunger strike. Five delegates from the Motherland party faction went on a hunger strike on 24 January 2004 to protest the government's social benefits reform. This extreme de-parliamentarisation can be explained with the weakness of the political opposition and the short-term time horizons of the Russian deputies who see more benefits from non-co-operating at the present time than in cooperating for the sake of future benefits (Popova 2012). Russian incumbents know that, as long as they are subservient to the president, no other accountability forum can take them to account.

Uncertainty in Non-Democracies

This chapter viewed the accountability process in Russia through the lens of uncertainty. Its purpose was twofold: to introduce new dimensions of uncertainty and to operationalize and test both the new and previously existing dimensions of uncertainty. As far as the existing notions of uncertainty are concerned, it suggested that substantive uncertainty is low because there is an expectation that the president will sanction his opponents. In addition, it suggested that institutional uncertainty is high because the office of the prosecutor general is informally influenced by the president. While these findings are in line with the dominant wisdom in the field, they are novel insofar they provide new insights to the uncertainty applied to the accountability process. In terms of introducing another dimension of uncertainty, the chapter suggested that the inter-institutional uncertainty is low, because both the sanctioning and the investigating of the government depend on the president. As such, there is little ambiguity as to which institution will prevail. Chapters seven and eight add to this puzzle two additional dimensions of uncertainty, namely history-induced uncertainty, which is focused on the ways historical uprisings limit perceptual uncertainty of the office holders, and verbally-induced uncertainty, which is focused on the determinants of the government's blame avoidance techniques. Both can increase doubt and uncertainty.

Having disaggregated uncertainty in its multiple dimensions, the natural question that arises is how to sum up all these types of uncertainty. Accountability is a chain process. At every stage, starting from the accusation, through the verbal defences, to the choosing of accountability forums, to abiding by the institutional rules, to formulating the outcomes of the process—new actors, new constellations of actors and new issues arise. Consequently, new types of uncertainty emerge. What does it mean when substantive, actor-based, verbal and inter-institutional uncertainty is low but institutional uncertainty is high? Does this combination make the process predictable? These questions are taken up in the following chapters.

Table 3.2: Types of Uncertainty in Non-Democracies

Types of Uncertainty	Stage 1	Stage 2	Stage 3	Stage 4	Stage 5
Substantive Uncertainty					LOW: Outcomes/ Sanctions are pre-determined by the president's allegiances
Institutional Uncertainty				HIGH: Informal institutional dependencies	
Inter-Institutional Uncertainty			LOW: Accountability Pyramids show there is no competition between the institutions. The president monopolises the competition.		
Verbal Uncertainty		LOW: Blame Avoidance			
Actor-Level Uncertainty	LOW: Accuser				

Bibliography

Alexander, G. (2016) Institutionalized Uncertainty, The Rule of Law, and The Sources of Democratic Stability. *Comparative Political Studies* 35 (10), pp. 1145–1170. Available at: https://journals.sagepub.com/doi/abs/10.1177/001041402237946?journalCode=cpsa.

Bernhard, M., Edgell, A.B., Lindberg, S.I. (2020) Institutionalising electoral uncertainty and authoritarian regime survival. *European Journal of Political Research* 59 (2), pp. 465-487. Available at: https://ejpr.onlinelibrary.wiley.com/doi/full/10.1111/1475-6765.12355.

Herd, G.P. (2019) Putin's operational code and strategic decision-making in Russia. In *Routledge Handbook of Russian Security*. Abingdon: Routledge. Available at: https://www.routledgehandbooks.com/doi/10.4324/9781351181242-3 [Accessed: January 27, 2023].

Keane, J. (2020) *The New Despotism*. Cambridge: Harvard University Press.

Khachaturian, R. (2015) Uncertain Knowledge and Democratic Transitions: Revisiting O'Donnell and Schmitter's Tentative Conclusions about Uncertain Democracies. *Polity* 47 (1). Available at: https://www.journals.uchicago.edu/doi/abs/10.1057/pol.2014.26.

Krastev, I., Holmes, S. (2012) Putinism Under Siege: An Autopsy of Managed Democracy. *Journal of Democracy* 23 (3), pp. 33-45. Available at: https://www.journalofdemocracy.org/articles/putinism-under-siege-an-autopsy-of-managed-democracy/.

Ledeneva, A.V. (1998) *Russia's Economy of Favours: Blat, Networking and Informal Exchange* (Vol. 102). Cambridge: Cambridge University Press.

Mozaffar, S., Schedler, A. (2002) The Comparative Study of Electoral Governance — Introduction. *International Political Science Review* 23 (1), pp. 5-27. Available at: https://doi.org/10.1177/0192512102023001001.

Noble, R.K. (1992) The Independent Counsel Versus the Attorney General in a Classified Information Procedures Act — Independent Counsel Statute Case. *Boston College Law Review* 33 (3), pp. 585-590. Available at: https://lira.bc.edu/work/ns/d59f998f-80ce-4a40-8e30-791324b9c00e.

NUPI Center for Russian Studies (1994) *Amnesty for Yeltsin's Foes, Resignation of Prosecutor-General*. Available at http://www.nupi.no/cgiwin/Russland/krono.exe?912 [Accessed: March 12, 2006].

NUPI Center for Russian Studies (2002) *Persons: Sergey Vadimovich Stepashin*. Available at: http://www.nupi.no/cgi-win/Russland/personer.exe?81 [Accessed: March 12, 2006].

NUPI Center for Russian Studies (2002) *Chronology of Events: Borodin Found Guilty of Money Laundering*. Available at: http://www.nupi.no/cgi-win/Russland/krono.exe?5099 [Accessed: March 12, 2006].

O'Donnell, G., Schmitter, P.C., Whitehead, L. (1986) *Transitions from Authoritarian Rule: Tentative Conclusions about Uncertain Democracies*. Baltimore: Johns Hopkins University Press.

Popova, M. (2012) *Politicized Justice in Emerging Democracies: A Study of Courts in Russia and Ukraine*. New York: Cambridge University Press.

Przeworski, A. (1988) Democracy as a contingent outcome of conflicts. In- *Constitutionalism and Democracy*. Cambridge: Cambridge University Press. Available at: https://www.cambridge.org/core/books/abs/constitutionalism-and-democracy/democracy-as-a-contingent-outcome-of-conflicts/8CB5719713F4177C1EFB2FAA611C2112 [Accessed: January 27, 2023].

RFE/RL. (1996) *Newsline, February 26*. Available at: http://www.friends-partners.org/friends/news/omri/1996/02/960226I.html [Accessed: December 10, 2006].

RFE/RL (1997) *Newsline, March 10*. Available at: http://www.friends-partners.org/friends/news/omri/1997/03/970310I.html [Accessed: December 14, 2007].

RFE/RL (2002) *Russia: Three Years Later, Moscow Apartment Bombings Remain Unsolved, September 6*. Available at: http://www.rferl.org/content/article/1100714.html [Accessed December 10, 2006].

RFE/RL (2005) *Newsline, May 30*. Available at: http://www.hri.org/news/balkans/rferl/2005/05--30.rferl.html [Accessed: December 14, 2007].

Schechchokin, Y. (2001) Are we Russia or KGB USSR? In Moscow, Russians are caught by foreign special services, while their own are shamelessly lying. *Novaya Gazeta*. Available at: http://ys.novayagazeta.ru/text/2003-01-27.shtml [Accessed: December 11, 2006].

Schedler, A. (2010) Taking Uncertainty Seriously: The Blurred Boundaries of Democratic Transition and Consolidation. *Democratization* 8 (4), pp. 1-22. Available at: https://www.tandfonline.com/doi/abs/10.1080/714000225.

Schedler, A. (2013) *The Politics of Uncertainty: Sustaining and Subverting Electoral Authoritarianism*. Oxford: Oxford University Press.

Tsebelis, G. (1990). *Nested Games: Rational Choice in Comparative Politics*. Berkeley: University of California Press

4 Uncertainty in Democracies

This chapter recasts and re-examines the concept of political uncertainty in democracies. Specifically, it concentrates on the idea of inter-institutional uncertainty and how inter-institutional uncertainty can be reduced or amplified. Similarly to the previous chapter, this chapter applies the concept of inter-institutional uncertainty to the process of accountability. However, it applies the framework to the accountability of the German government to the European Union. It starts from the idea that there is a high level of inter-institutional uncertainty because a myriad of institutions, such as the European Union, the internal governmental investigations, legislature, public opinion, the prosecutor general are in competition as to who will hold the government to account and who will sanction the government.

It suggests that there are two types of factors, which can create certainty or uncertainty as to whether the European Union will prevail in this competition. The factors are typified according to two criteria. The uncertainty inducing factors are relational, relative or aggregative. They pertain to: (1) matters of perception; (2) matters of judgment; (3) matters involving the aggregation of the opinions of more than one person. They are hard to predict. The uncertainty reducing factors are: (1) plainly visible or (2) immutable and cannot be changed. They are easier to estimate, and therefore entail more certainty in calculating the outcomes of the process.

How does this categorization differ from the one introduced in chapters two and three? The previous chapters categorized uncertainty in terms of the milieu in which it is displayed, such as verbal, institutional or inter-institutional uncertainty. This chapter takes a more consequence-oriented approach, which categorizes the factors according to the effect they will have on the possibility to estimate the outcome. In this case, the "outcome" is the European Union having a disproportionately greater impact in the accountability process in Germany than other institutions. The chapter suggests that the uncertainty reducing factors, i.e., the factors that make it easier to estimate the EU's influence, are the nature of the allegations, the identity of the person making the accusations and the ranking of the officials involved. They are categorized as uncertainty reducing because they are not subject to interpretation or calculation. They are what they are perceived to be.

By contrast, the uncertainty-inducing factors, i.e., the factors which make it harder to estimate whether the EU would have more influence than internal governmental investigations or the prosecutor general, are the following: the perception of the legitimacy and independence of the prosecutor, the perception of the allegation that the government is involved in, and the calculus performed by the government. All of them are a matter of judgment rather than an easily observable fact. They imbue the predictability of the outcome with uncertainty because it is hard to estimate them. It is very important to note that this uncertainty is not tied to calculating the magnitude of the impact of the EU in Germany's accountability process. This magnitude, as measured by the coefficients, is estimated via statistical models and presented below. The uncertainty comes from the nature of the factors, such as their observability and subjectivity. It is also important to emphasize that one should not view uncertainty in isolation from substantive debates in political science. In this case, uncertainty is tied to the debate about the democratic deficit in the EU (Follesdal and Hix 2006). Knowledge about the factors, which make it easier to predict whether the EU will prevail in comparison to other institutions, is essential in gauging the certainty of the EU's role in particular occasions.

Inter-Institutional Uncertainty in Democracies

One of the main arguments in this book is that notions of political uncertainty need to consider the uncertainty arising from the interaction between the institutions. In the context of accountability, it has been argued that limiting the study of uncertainty to institutional, substantive or procedural uncertainty, as is usually the case, is unfounded because there are many institutions that can hold the government to account, such as parliament, the courts, the prosecutor, audit chambers, institutional bodies, etc. Inter-institutional uncertainty pertains to the lack of clarity as to which institution will investigate the government and how these multiple investigations will interact (chapter five). Hence, there is a need for an additional dimension of uncertainty, namely inter-institutional uncertainty.

In democracies, which have a robust system of checks and balances and a clear separation of powers, inter-institutional uncertainty should be very high. High levels of inter-institutional uncertainty do not exclude a high level of institutional or procedural certainty. Greater inter-institutional uncertainty is associated with many institutions having roughly equal power. Lower levels of inter-institutional uncertainty are associated with the lack of choice which institution will take over the responsibility of holding the government to account. While the procedures of each institution may be clear, well respected, and predictable, the actual source of uncertainty comes from the difficulty of predicting in which of these multiple accountability forums the accountability process will unfold. For example, the prosecutor may be interested in pursuing a media accusation, but parliament and the EU may not be interested. It is very uncertain which accountability forum will be activated, and to what end. This means that substantive uncertainty will also be high.

Conversely, in managed or less consolidated democracies, institutional uncertainty will be low and substantive uncertainty will be high. It should be noted that substantive uncertainty over outcomes in democracy is considered a blessing. This is so because most actors interpret uncertainty over outcomes as an "opportunity for future winning" (Alexander 2016, p. 1,151). "Di Palma (1984, p. 175) identifies democracy's "best trump card" for attracting support as its "open-endedness, because its game is never final, because nobody loses once and for all and on all arenas." Lake and Rothchild (1996) suggest that democracy's uncertainty "provides many players with an incentive to participate" (p. 60)" (cited in Alexander 2016, p. 1,151). This logic of the relative shares of procedural and substantive uncertainty in established and managed democracies is reflected in figure 4.1, which shows the suggestions of their relative strength.

Limiting the analysis to procedural and substantive uncertainty, however essential both types are, omits the inter-institutional uncertainty, which pervades the process of holding the government to account. For reasons described in this chapter and in chapter three, inter-institutional uncertainty in a managed democracy is usually low, and it is high in an established democracy. This scenario is depicted in figure 4.2, which provides hypothesized guesstimates.

Figure 4.1: Uncertainty in Elections

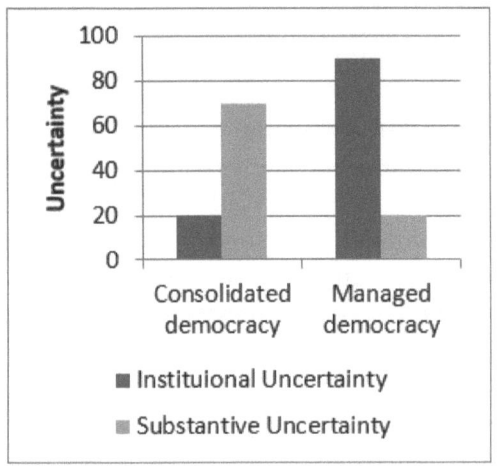

Figure 4.2: Uncertainty in Inter-Electoral Accountability

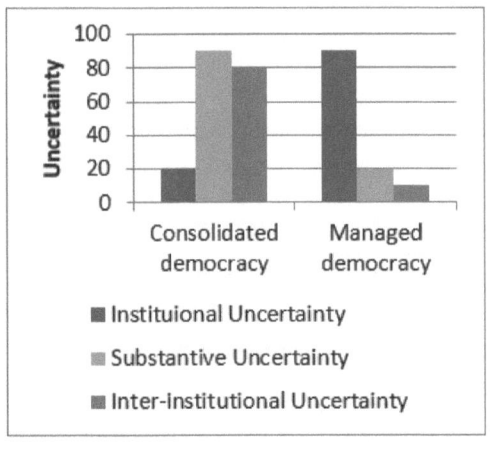

So how can this inter-institutional uncertainty be operationalized? This chapter depicts the relative sanctioning power of various institutions in Germany. These patterns demonstrate that in Germany, inter-institutional uncertainty is high because it is uncertain which accountability forum will sanction the government as there are three bodies with roughly equal sanctioning capacity: inter-governmental bodies, the European Union and the prosecutor. This multiplicity of active investigative institutions creates inter-institutional uncertainty as it is hard to predict which set of rules attached to which institutions will apply in each particular case. This pattern of many effective and competing sanctioning forums is different from the inter-institutional sanctioning pattern revealed in in Russia (chapter three), where the president has monopolized the sanctioning process and inter-institutional uncertainty is comparatively low.

Figure 4.3: High Inter-Institutional Uncertainty: Sanctioning Effectiveness of Forums in Germany

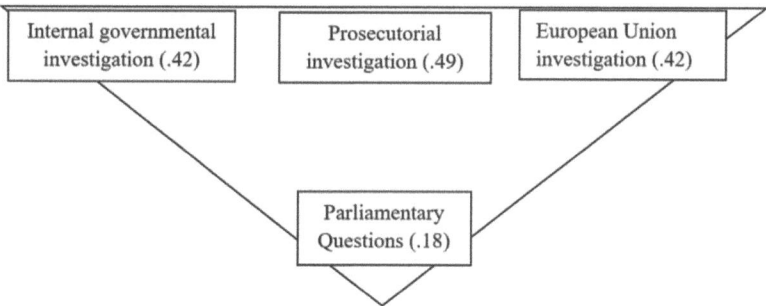

Uncertainty Reducing vs. Uncertainty Inducing Factors

I propose that there are two types of factors that can either reduce or induce inter-institutional uncertainty. The uncertainty inducing factors are relational, relative or aggregative. They pertain to: (1) matters of perception; (2) matters of judgment; (3) matters involving the aggregation of the opinions of more than one person. The uncertainty reducing factors are: (1) plainly visible or (2) immutable and cannot be changed.

The chapter applies these two categories of uncertainty reducing and uncertainty inducing factors to inter-electoral government accountability in Germany. The uncertainty-reducing factors pertain to the nature of the allegations, the identity of the person making the accusations and the ranking of the officials involved. All these categories are not a matter of perception. They are not moral categories. They do not involve an element of aggregation, congregation or other forms of inter-action. As such, they are immutable, irreversible and systemic. Therefore, knowledge about these three factors — the issue, the accuser and the ranking of the alleged official — can reduce uncertainty as to whether the EU, the prosecutor or another accountability body will impose a sanction.

The uncertainty-inducing factors in this case are the perception of the legitimacy and the independence of the prosecutor, the perception of the veracity of the alleged misconduct and the calculus performed by the government. In the first two instances, there is a great level of uncertainty because it is inherently unclear how the perceptions of all people learning about the allegation will stack up. So, there is an element of aggregation as well as there is an element of perception.

Table 4.1: Factors Inducing or Reducing Inter-Institutional Uncertainty

Uncertainty Inducing Factors	Uncertainty Reducing Factors
Prosecutor-related:	**EU-related:**
Public perception of the prosecutor Public perception of the alleged wrongdoing	Identity of Accuser Type of Accusation
Government-related:	**Prosecutor-related:**
Motivation to avoid wider scrutiny	Ranking of the accused official

EU Investigations: Uncertainty Reducing Factors

Inter-institutional uncertainty in Germany, when applied to government accountability, arises because the EU, the prosecutor and the government have a roughly equal sanctioning capacity and it is unclear which of these institutions will prevail in a given situation (figure 4.3.). The first uncertainty reducing factor is the identity of the accuser, which in this case is the EU, as it is not open to interpretation or moral judgment. It is not aggregative. It is not relational. Therefore, this is a factor that creates certainty. My findings show that 60% of the investigations conducted by the EU relate to issues raised by the EU. 30% of the EU investigations follow up accusations made by the opposition. 10% of EU investigations are based on concerns made by the trade unions. Therefore, the EU is not the main sanctioning forum for issues that concern the public, individuals, interest groups, the government or the opposition on a national level. The EU is mainly active in issues that are of concern to the EU itself, and in issues which the EU has raised in the media.

The finding that the EU responds in more than half of the cases to issues that EU representatives have raised shows that the EU makes up its own accountability agenda. Arguably, this result means that the EU accountability deficit is smaller than expected because the EU does not appropriate the agenda of the opposition, the trade unions and other actors in national politics. One of the main criteria for assessing democracy beyond elections is who has the power to set the accountability agenda in the media. The accountability agenda is important because it sets the course of accountability. It determines the issues on which the government will be held accountable. It has the power to channel the interests of some organizations and to block the plans of other organizations. Therefore, the fact that the EU does not sanction the government for issues, which the opposition has raised, means that it does not appropriate issues that are important for national players.

The second finding that reduces the uncertainty about whether the EU controls the accountability process in Germany is this: the EU imposes sanctions mainly in cases of government incompetence, not in cases of government misconduct. As figure 4.4.

demonstrates, there is a functional differentiation between the accountability forums in Germany across incompetence and misconduct issues. The prosecutor deals exclusively with issues of corruption and misconduct, whereas the EU is concerned with policy failures. Why does this factor reduce rather than induce uncertainty? The reason is that cases of incompetence are mostly visible (rather than hidden), they involve evidence, and it is harder to argue against them. As such, they involve more certainty than cases which are subject to moral judgment, such as infidelity, or cases, which involve hard-to-find evidence, such as corruption. Thus, an allegation of incompetence is an uncertainty reducing factor.

Figure 4.4: Specialization of Forums According to Issues

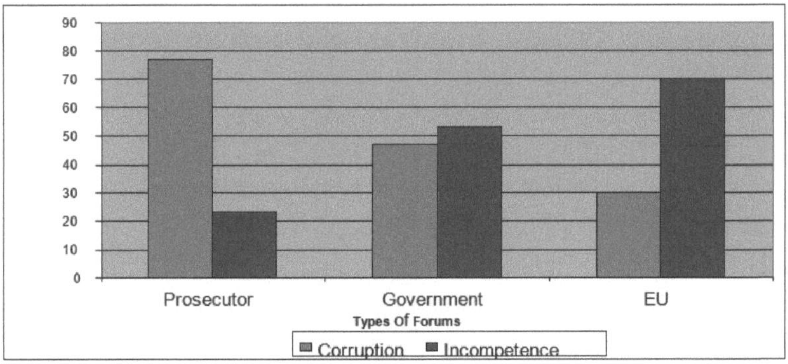

The nature of the accusation and the identity of the accuser are impactful, and these two factors have an uncertainty reducing impact.

Prosecutorial Investigations: Uncertainty Inducing and Uncertainty Reducing Factors

As figure 4.3. shows, prosecutorial investigations of the government are impactful in Germany. The sanctioning power of the prosecutor is roughly equal to that of the EU and the government, and as such it contributes to inter-institutional competition and inter-institutional uncertainty. There is, however, one factor that can make prosecutorial effectiveness less or more certain. This factor is the ranking of the official that is being held to account. In principle, the ranking of an official should be an uncertainty reducing factor, because positions in the government hierarchy are not open to interpretation, moral judgment or aggregation. They are a given. Yet, different rankings open different investigatory paths, which entail different degrees of certainty.

If the accused official is lower ranking, uncertainty that the prosecutor will impose sanctions is lower. The findings reveal that it is easier for the prosecutor to impose sanctions on lower ranking officials than on higher-ranking officials. One example where the prosecutor imposed sanctions on lower-ranking officials was the November 2004 abuse scandal in the army in Cösfelder. High-ranking officers were accused in the media that they had tortured new recruits during training exercises. Immediately after the accusations became public, the minister of defence Struck said that the torture was unacceptable. Several days later, he imposed disciplinary punishment and dismissed twenty-seven soldiers. The prosecutor in Münster started parallel investigations to those of the defence ministry. He charged thirty-one officers, including one captain and four sergeants. Six teams of the prosecutorial office took testimony from 200 witnesses. Policemen searched the private houses of the accused officers and confiscated computers with 162 pictures documenting the tortures (Die Welt, May 9, 2007). In August 2007, the court returned the following verdicts: one probation, one monetary punishment, and two innocent sentences (WDR.de, August 29, 2007). The office of the prosecutor appealed, and increased the punishment to four sentences of probation, one monetary fine and four free sentences (WDR.de, May 12, 2008).

If the accuser is a minister, however, then the uncertainty that the prosecutor will impose sanctions is higher. Uncertainty is higher because prosecutorial investigations work through blemishing the reputation of the politician under investigation, and the resignation or the dismissal of that politician comes as a result of that damaged reputation, not as a direct result of the judicial investigation. The German case shows that prosecutorial success, when the alleged official is a government minister, largely depends on the general political environment and above all on the public condemnation of the incumbent who is under investigation, the government's sensitivity to this condemnation and the relationship between the prosecutor and the legislation. Reputation is a highly uncertainty inducing factor because it involves an element of perception of wrong-doing and it involves an element of aggregating the opinions of multiple of people about this wrong-doing.

The effect of prosecutorial investigations on the dismissals of high-ranking officials is not as direct as the prosecutorial effect on the dismissals of low-ranking officials. Hence, there is a higher degree of uncertainty, when lower ranking officials are involved. It seems that prosecutorial investigations are effective not because they impose outright sanctions. Their effectiveness depends on a combination of the perceived independence of the prosecutor, the critical social reaction to prosecutorial investigations and the government consideration of public reaction. Here is a case in point. The minister of infrastructure Klimmt was accused of having accepted bribes while he was president of the soccer club FC Saarbrücken. The prosecutor started a trial. On November 9, 2000, the court found Klimmt guilty and sentenced him to pay a fine equal to the average salary for ninety workdays. The opposition immediately made calls for his resignation. Klimmt faced a difficult choice. He could agree to pay the monetary fine and acknowledge his guilt. Alternatively, the minister could refuse to admit his guilt but expose himself to scrutiny in a full-blown trial. Klimmt opted to accept the verdict on November 14th. However, on the next day, he reversed his decision. He said that he had changed his opinion because he wanted to prove his innocence and that his decision was made under pressure from the SPD faction in parliament (Die Welt, November 15, 2000). In the end, Klimmt did not follow either course of action. He resigned and the trial ended. It is clear that the prosecutorial investigation facilitated Klimmt's dismissal but it did not cause it directly. The effect of the prosecutor's involvement is thus achieved in stages. In the first stage, the prosecutor manages to impose a relatively mild punishment on a minister, and in the second stage, this mild punishment causes a political crisis or entails political costs, which then lead to the minister's resignation. This process is fraught with uncertainty.

There are cases when the prosecutor actually imposes punishment on high-ranking officials but this happens mainly to former, not current, government officials. For example, the prosecutor directly imposed a monetary fine on the former defence minister Scharping. Minister Scharping was accused of bribery committed before he became minister. He allegedly accepted from the PR agent Moritz Hunzinger clothes worth 27,600 Euro and did not declare them as income. He was also accused of receiving 140,000 German Marks in return for conducting three lectures. In response to accusations of undeclared income, Scharping paid additional 20,000 German Marks in taxes in July 2002, but this move came too late. Chancellor Schröder dismissed Scharping the same month. The prosecutor general started investigations just one month after Schapring's dismissal, and in March 2003 sentenced him to pay 3,000 Euro in penalties. Scharping obliged (Rhein-Zeitung.de, March 13, 2003).

To gauge the role of the prosecutor in the accountability process, it is important that the prosecutor is perceived as independent and legitimate. This perception generates great uncertainty. It is uncertain because it hinges on a multitude of factors. The mode of election of the prosecutor is one: should the prosecutor general be elected by the minister of justice at the approval of parliament and confirmed by the president (as in Germany and Russia), or should the prosecutor be elected by the Supreme Judicial Council, which consists of an equal number of judicial servants and parliamentary representatives (as in Bulgaria)? Another thorny issue is whether the majority of the members of the Supreme Judicial Council, which elects the prosecutor, should be judicial or parliamentary appointees. If they are judicial servants, they are unlikely to challenge the authority of the prosecutor general who appointed them in the first place. If they are parliamentary appointments, the prosecutor would be dependent on the political interests of the majority party in parliament. Another contentious issue is whether the prosecutor should be elected via a secret ballot or in an open election.

Furthermore, uncertainty surrounds the perception of the legitimacy of prosecutorial investigations because there are many additional factors affecting it. They include the following consideration: Should the prosecutor be a member of the judicial or the executive branch? What should the relationship between the prosecutor and the legislature be? Should the prosecutor be answerable to parliament by submitting reports, which will increase his democratic credentials but will decrease his neutrality and independence (Beale2014)? Within the executive branch, should the prosecutor be directly answerable to the minister of justice (as in Germany) or should the prosecutor be answerable to the president (as in the US)? Should local prosecutors be elected (as in the US) or should they be civil non-elected servants (as in France and Germany)? Should there be special training for prosecutors, or should they just have regular juridical education? How hierarchical should the prosecutorial system be? How much power should the prosecutor general have in it? Should the prosecutorial appointment be lifelong or on a fixed term? If there is no certainty about the standing of the prosecutor, there is no certainty how his investigations will be perceived. If there is no certainty how they will be perceived, there is no certainty whether they will entail sanctions. This is mostly the case when high-ranking officials are involved.

Ministerial Investigations: Uncertainty Inducing Factors

My findings show that ministerial investigations of media allegations are, along with EU and prosecutorial investigations, most likely to result in sanctions for the government (figure 4.3). The implications of such a high sanctioning power of the ministerial meetings — or internal governmental investigations — for democracy are not understood well enough. Inherently, these implications are fraught with uncertainty because it is not clear which of the following three scenarios the government will take. In scenario A, the government reverses policies or dismisses officials simply because it wants to be perceived as responsive. It may seek to achieve the impression of being responsive because it is afraid that inaction means that the government will lose popularity. In scenario B, cabinet meetings function as quasi-party meetings, especially when it comes to coalitional governments. They are just a way for representatives of different parties to negotiate their differences under the guise of a governmental meeting.

In scenario C, these internal investigations may be the government's attempt to contain the investigation in its own house. If the investigation spreads to parliament or public committees, more information would be divulged and there are greater reputational hazards. Various investigations presuppose various degrees of public exposure, and the government would naturally prefer the least exposing investigation. Furthermore, various investigations presuppose various political opponents in the accountability forum, and the government would prefer to limit the involvement of the opposition. Thus, when a media allegation surfaces, the government would prefer a governmental meeting, to a parliamentary meeting or a public hearing. The government would also prefer cabinet meetings to party meetings because cabinet meetings are smaller and easier to control. Following the same logic, the government would prefer cabinet meetings to parliamentary investigations because parliamentary meetings include the opposition in the sanctioning process, and the incumbents have no vested interest in having their faith in the hands of the opposition. In the same vein, the government would prefer to be investigated by the parliament than to be sanctioned by public opinion, because negative public opinion means that it will lose votes at the next elections. Ultimately, scenario C is a decisional situation which requires that the government weighs alternative accountability paths, assigns weights to each of them, and chooses one over the other. Because it is unknown which path the government would prefer, and why, scenario C is highly uncertain. Choosing between scenarios A, B and C, adds another element of uncertainty as far as the sanctioning prowess of government investigations is involved.

Inter-Institutional Uncertainty: Implications for the EU Accountability Deficit

Why is inter-institutional uncertainty important? Inter-institutional uncertainty is important because it ultimately allows for the possibility to formulate a credible view about the systematic way in which the EU affects the accountability process in a nation state. Inter-institutional uncertainty is all about the predictability of the outcome of the competition between various institutions. If one institution systematically wins over the others, as it did in Russia (chapter three), then the accountability process has been monopolized and inter-institutional competition is neutralized. This could be especially problematic if an international body, such as the EU, controls the national inter-electoral accountability process.

In an ideal world, we would be able to gauge a clear view of inter-institutional uncertainty when all uncertainty reducing factors obtain, to the exclusion of all uncertainty inducing factors. For example, when inter-institutional uncertainty is very high, as is the case of Germany, it will translate into a relatively low level of substantive uncertainty under the following conditions: the accuser is the EU, the issue is one of incompetence and the ranking of the accused official is low. By contrast, inter-institutional uncertainty translates into a high-level of substantive uncertainty, when the ranking of the accused official is high, and when it is uncertain what the public perception of the prosecutor will be, what the public perception of the wrong doing will be as well as how strong the government's motivation to avoid other investigations will be.

However, the real world is messy. Chains of accountability may meander through uncertainty inducing and uncertainty reducing factors. It is possible that the accuser is not the EU, but the accusation is one of incompetence that concerns the EU, thus making the sanctioning power or the involvement of the EU uncertain. Furthermore, if a high-ranking official is involved, the public perception of the accountability forum and the public judgment of the alleged transgression will induce uncertainty into the accountability equation. However, if the government does not get involved, and no cost-benefit analysis is at play, no uncertainty is induced. In this mix-and-match type of uncertainty inducing and uncertainty reducing factors, the exact impact of inter-institutional uncertainty into substantive uncertainty is unclear.

Figure 4.5: Translating Inter-Institutional Uncertainty into Substantive Uncertainty

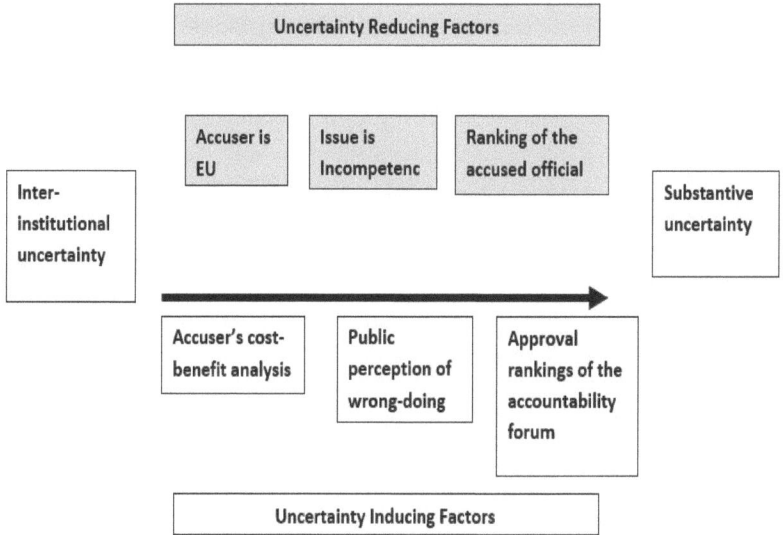

Bibliography

Alexander, G. (2016) Institutionalized Uncertainty, The Rule of Law, and The Sources of Democratic Stability. *Comparative Political Studies* 35, (10), pp. 1145–1170. Available at: https://journals.sagepub.com/doi/abs/10.1177/001041402237946?journalCode=cpsa

Beale, S.S. (2014) Prosecutorial Discretion in Three Systems: Balancing Conflicting Goals and Providing Mechanisms for Control. *SSRN Paper 2433732*. Available at: https://papers.ssrn.com/sol3/papers.cfm?abstract_id=2433732

Bovens, M., Curtin, D., Hart, P. (2010). *The Real World of EU Accountability: What Deficit?* New York: Oxford University Press.

Dimova, G. (2019). *Democracy beyond Elections: Government Accountability in the Media Age*. London: Springer Nature.

Di Palma, G. (1984). Government Performance: An Issue and Three Cases in Search of Theory. *West European Politics* 7 (2), 172-187. Available at:10.1080/01402388408424477

Follesdal, A., Hix, S. (2006). Why There is a Democratic Deficit in the EU: A Response to Majone and Moravcsik. *Journal of Common Market Studies* 44 (3), pp. 533-562. Available at: https://doi.org/10.1111/j.1468-5965.2006.00650.x.

Goodhart, M. (2011) Democratic Accountability in Global Politics: Norms, not Agents. *The Journal of Politics* 73 (1), pp. 45-60. Available at: https://www.researchgate.net/publication/231840737_Democratic_Accountability_in_Global_Politics_Norms_not_Agents.

Grant, R.W., Keohane, R.O. (2005) Accountability and Abuses of Power in World Politics. *American Political Science Review* 99 (1), pp. 29-43. Available at: https://scholar.princeton.edu/sites/default/files/rkeohane/files/apsr_abuses.pdf.

Gustavsson, S., Karlsson, C., Persson, T. (2009) *The Illusion of Accountability in the European Union*. Abingdon: Routledge.

Harlow, C. (2002) *Accountability in the European Union* 11 (3). Oxford: Oxford University Press.

Hobolt, S.B., Tilley, J. (2014) *Blaming Europe? Responsibility without Accountability in the European Union*. Oxford: Oxford University Press.

Koenig-Archibugi, M. (2010) Accountability in Transnational Relations: How Distinctive Is It? *West European Politics* 33 (5), pp. 1,142-1,164. Available at: http://eprints.lse.ac.uk/29564/1/Koenig-Archibugi_Accountability%20transnational%20relations_2017.pdf.

Majone, G. (1996) *Regulating Europe*. London: Routledge.

Menon, A., S. Weatherill. (2008) Transnational Legitimacy in a Globalising World: How the European Union Rescues Its States. *West European Politics* 31 (3), pp. 397–416. Available at: https://www.tandfonline.com/doi/abs/10.1080/01402380801939610.

Moravcsik, A. (2008) The Myth of Europe's 'Democratic Deficit'. *Intereconomics* 43 (6), pp. 331-340. Available at: https://www.econstor.eu/bitstream/10419/42045/1/594752116.pdf.

Schmitter, P.C. (2000) *How to Democratize the European Union – And Why Bother?* Lanham: Rowman and Littlefield.

Vibert, F. (2007) *The Rise of the Unelected: Democracy and the New Separation of Powers*. New York: Cambridge University Press.

Williams, S. (1990) Sovereignty and Accountability in the European Community. *The Political Quarterly* 61 (3), pp. 299-317. Available at: https://onlinelibrary.wiley.com/doi/abs/10.1111/j.1467-923X.1990.tb00820.x.

5 Inter-Institutional Uncertainty
Do Institutions Compete or Cooperate with Each Other?

Inter-institutional uncertainty refers to the fact that it is hard to predict whether institutions will compete or cooperate. Especially when it comes to forums that investigate the government, the dominant wisdom is that institutions will invariably compete with each other, at least as far as democracies are concerned. This chapter shows two cases that prove the opposite scenario, namely that institutions cooperate with each other; they do not compete. The findings are even more compelling because they show cooperative patterns of inter-institutional behaviour in countries with very different democratic credentials. Future research should seek to estimate the dynamics and determinants of the likelihood that institutions will cooperate vs. compete, instead of assuming that they will only compete with each other.

Uncertainty stems from the way institutions interact with each other. Some interactions between institutions may be competitive, other interactions may be cooperative. When it comes to government accountability, conventional wisdom purports that multiple investigations of the government tend to compete with each other, and that this competitive relationship would impede overall accountability because it enables the government to play the investigators against each other. This chapter seeks to rethink this line of thinking by arguing that it is uncertain that institutions will necessarily compete. To come upon either side of the argument, we need to increase the certainty about the proclivity of institutions to systematically behave one way or another. While the chapter does not propose how to increase this certainty, it contributes to the debate by acknowledging the existence of inter-institutional uncertainty and by formulating inter-institutional uncertainty as a type of uncertainty worth studying.

Figure 5.1: Two Examples of Patterns of Inter-Institutional Interactions

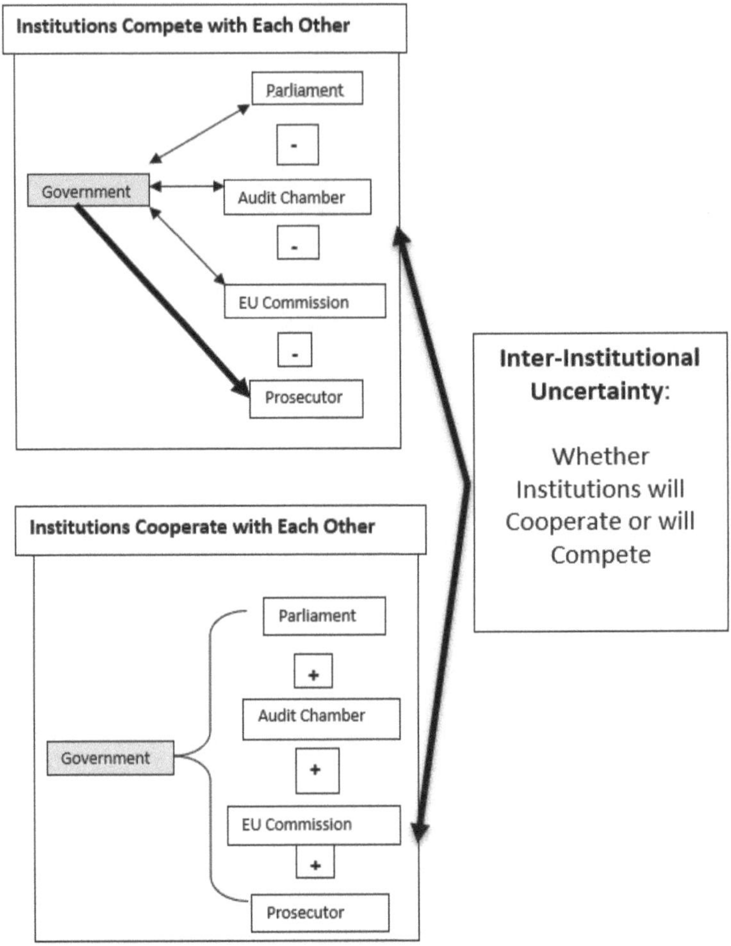

Institutions Compete with Each Other
- Government — Parliament (−)
- Government ↔ Audit Chamber (−)
- Government — EU Commission (−)
- Government → Prosecutor

Inter-Institutional Uncertainty: Whether Institutions will Cooperate or will Compete

Institutions Cooperate with Each Other
- Government — Parliament
- Government — Audit Chamber (+)
- Government — EU Commission (+)
- Government — Prosecutor (+)

Figure 5.1. depicts two scenarios. In the figure on top, institutions compete with each other, and the government sides with the prosecutor (as an example). In the figure in the bottom, institutions cooperate, and the government collaborates with all of them. It is the top-level scenario that corresponds with the dominant thinking in the literature, which is that multiple investigations always start a vicious circle of fault-finding. This perspective is critically reviewed below.

View 1: Institutions Invariably Compete with Each Other

The prevailing wisdom in the literature on accountability is that when there are more than one institution holding the government to account in a democracy, these institutions will compete with each other: "Accountability easily devolves into fault-finding missions that derail into a climate of negativity or in sheer scapegoating. They compete as to which one is going to uncover more "dirt" on the government" (Mulgan 2003, pp. 3-4). Society will become obsessed with "rituals of verification" (Power 1997) where the legitimacy of an investigative body stems from finding flaws with the government. Agents will outbid each other in their race to sanction the government. In this climate of negativity and competition between the forums, the government has more leeway to play the forums against each other. The government could exploit the rivalries between competing investigative agencies by picking sides and cooperating only with the ones that are most favourable to it. Incumbents could form strategic alliances with the ones that are least threatening (Mulgan 2003; Pollitt 2003). In short, multiple accountabilities enable the government to do "forum shopping," which undermines accountability.

The multiplicity of mechanisms is thought to create an "accountability challenge" (Salamon 2002) at best or an "accountability overload" (Halachmi 2014) at worst. "Agency theorists are often quite explicit about the fact that the addition of principals makes it more difficult to control agents" (Schillemans and Bovens 2011, p. 10). Perhaps the most overriding concern of public administration scholars is that the multiplicity of investigations creates a climate of negativity because the forums compete to gain public approval by finding the government's faults. The rivalry between the forums is thought to present an opportunity for the incumbents to pit the investigators against each other and to side with the most favourable investigators. These concerns, along with the fear that there are many conflicting expectations and high coordination, opportunity and transaction costs imposed on the government, create the impression that "everyone will be accountable for everything, but no one will take responsibility for anything" (Bardach and Kagan 1982, p. 323). Overall, the purported "redundant guardianship design" (Braithwaite 1999, p. 98) or "redundant accountability" (Schillemans 2010) is thought to hamper accountability.

The dominant argument is that multiple accountabilities would engage in a vicious race to punish the government. It is this competition or the undefined probability of competition that creates inter-institutional uncertainty. This contention relies on several underlying assumptions, which are not explicitly specified. In my view, these contentions are: (1) that all forums care about their public perception; (2) that all forums seek to create this positive public perception by opposing rather than cooperating with each other and (3) that the public would want the government to be sanctioned.

These three assumptions need not always hold true, and it is imperative to examine the circumstances when they do. There is no compelling reason to assume that all forums will always seek to please public opinion. Despite the mediatisation of many public services and the incessant media coverage (Schillemans 2012), there are many accountability forums, which are unelected, and do not necessarily prioritize the media frenzy. These unelected forums are not inevitably guided by the logic of achieving greater popular appeal. In fact, precisely this is the advantage of the unelected nature of some forums: they curb the popular and sometimes populist impulses of popularly elected forums.

Even if the forums care about public opinion and want to gain its favour by punishing the government, we do not need to assume that they will try to prove themselves only in competition against each other. Proponents of the view that forums will invariably compete assume that the reputation of the accountability forums is a zero-sum game. Reputation, however, could be a positive sum game, where one forum gains public approval, and the other forum is viewed favourably as well. Perhaps another way to gain public approval is to help other accountability forums. This is a very credible scenario when the government opposes the investigations of a highly popular accountability forum. In this case, the best bet of other accountability forums is to defend the more popular forum, not to try to launch a parallel investigation in a competition with it. The winning strategy is for the forums to cooperate, not for the forums to compete. Hence the contours of inter-institutional uncertainty become even blurrier.

Apart from these three unspecified assumptions, there are two assumptions which are well articulated and that supposedly increase the certainty that forums will compete rather than cooperate. The first assumption is that institutions will have diverse and incompatible expectations and competing criteria for assessing the government's behaviour. The second assumption is that the costs of coordinating the interaction between these institutions will far outweigh any costs, which are associated with cooperation. This chapter challenges both assumptions. It argues that the expectations between the investigating institutions may be at odds with each other, but the expectations between the investigating institutions and society may be in sync. Furthermore, it conjectures that while the coordination, opportunity and transaction costs may be high, multiple investigations present lower accessibility costs. Following the revision of the assumptions specified above, one could conjecture that the government could not always play the forums against each other. Cooperation is possible and probable. Inter-institutional uncertainty increases.

Inter-institutional uncertainty stems from the changing and unpredictable incentives of various accountability forums, such as parliaments, committees, audit bodies and courts to cooperate or compete with each other. In the end, the interaction between the institutions and their effect on accountability will depend on their proclivity to coordinate in relation to their proclivity to compete. The relative constellation of competition and coordination can be changing, issue-dependent, context dependent. In other words, it is uncertain. It is uncertain which institutions will compete, and in what configurations. It is also uncertain which institutions will cooperate and in what configurations. Pointing out this multiple-sourced uncertainty is paramount as it produces a more refined view about uncertainty. It will increase clarity as to the advantages and disadvantages of having the incumbents being investigated by the courts, audit chambers, international commissions, public commissions, parliamentary committees at the same time: "having multiplied the number and types of accountability mechanisms in the last decades of the twentieth century, we are left without a good understanding of the interactive and cumulative effect on the thinking and acting of public officials arising from the thick web of laws, rules, guidelines, reporting requirements and oversight bodies" (Thomas 2012, p. 677). If we are to understand inter-institutional uncertainty, we need to study systematically exactly this "interactive and cumulative effect" that Thomas refers to. Rosanvallon (2006, p. 208) summarizes well this new awareness of the cooperating lines of accountabilities: "This perspective affords another new consideration of the relation of law and democracy, judicial and legislative power. Instead of thinking of them as antagonistic or, at best, coexisting forces happily outfitted for mutual containment, it is possible to place them in a single framework."

Scholars arguing that multiple accountabilities generally impede accountability suggest that institutions will have conflicting expectations of the government. While this assumption is likely to obtain, it is far from certain and is rather limited. It is uncertain because it is unclear whether institutions will choose to cooperate or compete. It is limited because it focuses on the conflicting expectations between the institutions but ignores the synergy between governmental policies and institutional expectations, and it ignores the synergy between societal expectations and institutional expectations.

Table 5.1: Sources of Inter-Institutional Uncertainty: One Dominant and Several Alternative Views (see how it relates to figure 5.2.)

Dominant Wisdom: Certainty about institutional conflicting expectations	**Alternative View**: Uncertainty about converging and diverging institutional, societal and governmental expectations
Convergence or Divergence Across and Within Institutions: Institution 1 vs. Institution 2 vs. Institution 3	*Convergence or Divergence within the Government Departments:* Government 1 vs. Government 2 vs. Government 3
	Convergence or Divergence within the Societal Layers: Society 1 vs. Society 2 vs. Society 3
	Convergence or Divergence between the Institutional and the Society Layers: Institution 1 (2,3, etc) & Government 1 (2,3, etc)
	Convergence or Divergence between the Institutional, Society and Government Layers: Society 1 (2,3, etc) vs. Institution 1 (2,3, etc) & Government 1 (2,3, etc)

Figure 5.2: Patterns of Institutional, Societal and Governmental Conflict

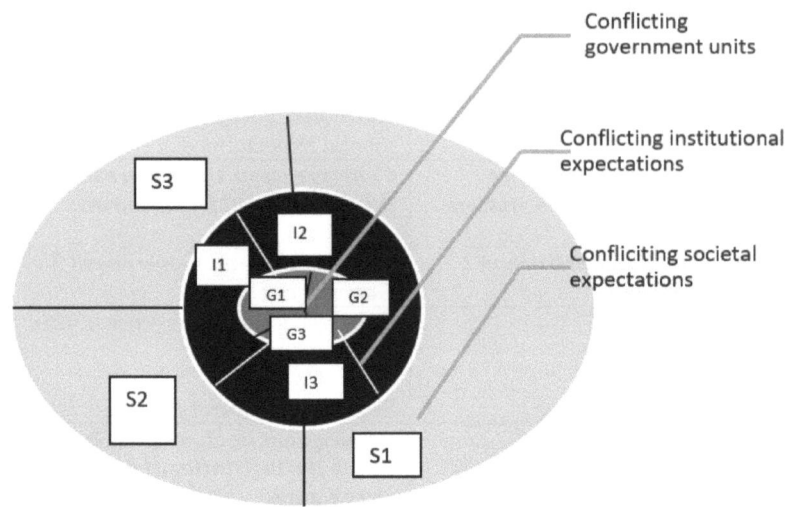

There are some good reasons to believe that institutional expectations of the government will be conflicting (Romzek and Dubnick 1998; Klingner, Nalbandian and Romzek 2002). These concerns form the basis of the fear of a "multiple accountabilities disorder" where conflicting demands for accountability may paralyze the government (Koppell 2005). The chief conflict between the expectations of various forums stems from the contention between elected but non-specialized forums, on the one hand, and non-elected and specialized forums, on the other hand. One type of a conflict of expectations arises between the forums vested in making the government more representative (parliament) and those bodies vested in making it more responsive (e.g., grass-roots public commissions). On another level, international investigative bodies concerned with the spill-over and cross-border effects of a particular government wrong-doing might have different demands from domestic accountability forums, which prioritize the local effects of the wrong-doing.

Political logic may clash with rational-legal logic, when the demands of political and legislative investigators encounter the demands of judges, auditors and others. For example, the government faced colliding demands for accountability in the Iran Contra Affair in the USA. According to the prosecutor general Walsh (1997, p. 49): "Congress had different priorities. Its first responsibility, it believed, was to put the full Iran-Contra story before the public and then to allot blame in political terms, rather than to decide legal guilt or innocence... I recognize in Congress a rival operation that could undo my work before it produced any results. My mandate was to prosecute wrongdoing, not just to uncover it (Walsh 1997, p. 31).

While there are many instances when institutions have conflicting expectations, it is also possible that their expectations converge, as it will be shown below in the case studies. Whether they compete or coordinate is not set in stone, and this is a source of great uncertainty. But there is another source of uncertainty; this is the uncertainty regarding how the institutional expectations will converge not with other institutional expectations, but with government policies and with societal expectations. Schillemans and Bovens (2011) argue that multiple lines of accountability could be in sync because the various forums respond to the greater complexity of governance. The authors contend that there will be new synergies because the government has been splintered into many parts, each of which would benefit from a different investigative forum.

Moreover, not only has the government become more diverse, but society has also become more complex (Dimova 2019, p. 87). Therefore uncertainty arises because it is unclear which societal group will team up with which institutional forum to seek accountability for which government policy. The fragmentation of society is evident in party de-alignment, where traditional parties lose their political base and it is increasingly unclear who holds the government to account (Mair 2011, p. 2; Mair 2013). There is a solid body of literature, mainly in the democratic theory field, which talks about how society has become more diverse (Tormey 2015; Bauman 2000; Stiegler 2011; Slaughter 2004). Considering the increased complexity of society, which is the agent in the accountability process, the multiplication of investigative bodies emerges in a positive light because it allows various fragments of society to find a channel to hold the government to account. "In a complex sovereignty, the multiplication of functional authorities... is a positive means of enlarging the influence of society in politics" (Rosanvallon 2006, p. 203). More specialised accountability forums enable various segments of society to find a fitting forum for pursing their interests. For example, legislative branches deal with the political priorities of the government; international institutions are better suited to target issues, which have cross-border implications; a prosecutor is better fitted to tackle issues of criminal misconduct; public opinion passes judgement on moral issues. Overall, the benefit of functional differentiation is that issues shop for venues, instead of the peculiarity of the venue to determine which aspects of the accusations are relevant. All these synergies will just ensure that the best forum investigates the government, instead of the government "shopping" for the forum that it likes best.

View 2: Institutions Cooperate with Each Other

The main goal of the ensuing empirical part of this chapter is to view uncertainty within the context of multiple investigations of the government, and to embed the consequences of this uncertainty within substantive debates in political science about the democratic value-added of multiple accountabilities. As argued above, uncertainty arises because we assume that multiple investigations of the government always compete, but we are unsure about this because some accountability forums can cooperate. As will be demonstrated below, this dilemma holds both for democratic and non-democratic countries. Specifically, the chapter shows how the forums' cooperation against treacherous incumbents unfolds in two very different types of regimes. It compares the impact of multiple lines of investigations between the judiciary, the legislature and the government in the Mabetex Affair in Russia (1999-2000) and the Visa Affair in Germany (2004-2005). The bottom line is that neither regime is immune from a possible cooperation between the forums, and that hence, inter-institutional uncertainty, while smaller in Russia, is not negligible.

Although the cases look different because they relate to two different types of accusations (policy and corruption), they are similar in some important ways. In the Russian Mabetex scandal, Yeltsin's presidential administration was accused of having accepted considerable kickbacks from the Swiss construction company Mabetex, which had carried out reconstruction work in the Kremlin. The German Visa Affair refers to allegations that the German government has knowingly adopted an immigration policy that eased the smuggling of people from Ukraine and Eastern Europe into Germany (Tagesschau 2005). Yet, the cases are similar in three essential ways. First, they pertain to investigations by multiple organs so we can examine the relation amongst them. Second, in both cases the incumbents try to avoid an investigation by attacking one of the forums. Third, both cases eventually lead to the resignations of the president and the chancellor respectively.

Case Study of Institutional Cooperation in a Non-Democratic Setting: The Russian Mabetex Scandal

Before we review inter-institutional uncertainty in the Mabetex case, it is important to make one important caveat. In chapter three, it was argued that inter-institutional uncertainty in Russia is low because the president has monopolised the accountability process. This subsection argues that inter-institutional uncertainty is low because the institutions have chosen to cooperate with each other. Importantly and extremely rarely, this cooperation opposed the president. The sources of inter-institutional uncertainty differ greatly.

The Mabetex affair showcases at least six instances of interaction between multiple accountability mechanisms, which had a positive effect on imposing accountability on Yeltsin and his property manager Borodin. The first instance, where the diversity of multiple accountabilities enforced accountability, was when the Swiss prosecutor gave evidence to the Russian prosecutor. In August 1999, Carla del Ponte discovered allegedly incriminating evidence that involved the head of the Presidential Administration Office, Mr. Borodin, and the Swiss construction company Mabetex, which had carried out reconstruction work in the Kremlin. The cooperation between the international and domestic accountability bodies was evident as the Russian prosecutor general Skuratov followed the lead of his Swiss colleague and started investigating Pavel Borodin for illegal dealings with the firm Mabetex.

This was a case of a positive interaction, where one court had the evidence and another court had the motivation and the capabilities to carry out the probe. Throughout the probe into Yeltsin's secret accounts, the silent support and approval of the international prosecutor Del Ponte was palpable. In key moments of the ordeal, Skuratov had mentioned that the Swiss Federal Prosecutor Carla Del Ponte had called him to express her "support" and "solidarity." In his turn, Skuratov may have used the support of a foreign official as a key trump card in his own domestic dealings. Del Ponte's support may have increased both the motivation and resilience of Skuratov's probe. There was no doubt that the international and domestic prosecutors cooperated to the advantage of accountability.

The second instance when multiple accountabilities yielded an advantage relates to the moment when the legal accountability channel broke down. On 2 February 1999, the Russian Prosecutor Skuratov resigned under pressure from Kremlin. This could have been the turning point of the entire investigation, if the Federation Council had not refused to approve Skuratov's resignation. This is the first instance when the role of the upper house of the Russian legislature, the Federation Council, was crucial in not dropping the ball. The prosecutor was encouraged by the support of the Federation Council and said that the support from the Federation Council would allow him to "take more resolute action on a number of criminal cases connected with corruption" (Dessert News, March 20, 1999). Throughout the long battle between Yeltsin and Skuratov, the Federation Council refused a total of three times to approve Skuratov's resignation. Instead of competing, the legislature and the prosecutor clearly cooperated with the positive result of enhancing executive accountability.

The third instance of cooperation was when internal governmental accountability sided with the prosecutor. On April 3 1999, the First Deputy Prime Minister Vadim Gustov said that Skuratov's resignation "is not the best option for Russia." Subsequently, both the government's information office and Primakov's press secretary felt it necessary to issue statements saying that Gustov's comment did not reflect the official government view (Novoe Izvestia, April 6, 1999). Just 25 days later, Yeltsin dismissed Gustov. This attempt of cooperation by a presidential aide was punished. Yeltsin was striking down one by one everybody who supported the prosecutor, and by implication, the investigation against him and his property manager Borodin. However, it demonstrated that internal governmental, legal and legislative mechanisms do not have to be at odds.

The fourth instance when the diversity of accountability channels proved helpful was when Yeltsin ordered the Security Council to investigate the prosecutor. The Security Council was more inclined to support rather than to undermine the prosecutor. Once again, Yeltsin tried to undermine the potential cooperation between the Security Council and the prosecutor. He was displeased with the little progress that the head of the Security Council Borduzha was making in incriminating the prosecutor general and replaced him with Putin. Putin was a safe bet for Yeltsin. He had proved his loyalty to Yeltsin and his animosity towards the prosecutor just the month before. In April 1999, Putin and Interior Minister Sergei Stepashin held a televised press conference in which they were critical of a video, which showed a naked man very similar to the Prosecutor General of Russia, Yury Skuratov, in bed with two young women. The video had aired nationwide on March 17, 1999 on the state-controlled Russia TV channel. Yeltsin used this video as a pretext to issue an order for Skuratov's dismissal. Yeltsin argued that Skuratov had damaged the moral authority of the prosecutorial post. In addition, it was said that the prostitutes in the video were paid for by a criminal group that had underhand dealings with the prosecutor. By putting Putin in charge, the Security Council was tamed and neutralized but then another accountability channel sprang up in defence of democratic accountability.

The Constitutional Court was the fifth accountability mechanism that rescued the failing partnership between the Security Council, the prosecutor general and the Federation Council. It was the Federation Council that put the case of Skuratov's resignation before the Constitutional Court. On December 1 1999, the Constitutional Court ruled that the President had the right to suspend Skuratov pending charges in a sex scandal but that Yeltsin could not overrule the Federation Council in its decision not to accept Skuratov's resignation. The support of the Constitutional Court of the prosecutor and the legislature was a pivotal moment in not burying the whole investigation.

From the very beginning of the Mabetex probe, public opinion sided with the investigation of the prosecutor Skuratov. Public opinion was the sixth accountability mechanism that bolstered the accountability network. In the early days of the confrontation between Yeltsin and Skuratov, when Yeltsin dismissed Skuratov because of the sex tape, an opinion poll asked, "What were the reasons for Skuratov's dismissal?" The poll found out that 43% of the respondents believed that the reason is Skuratov's "investigation into Kremlin", and only 8% believed that the sex tape was the real reason behind the dismissal. 49% said that Skuratov should keep his position under the current circumstances, while only 24% backed Yeltsin in his decision to dismiss him.[6] The public encouragement was probably the glue that facilitated the partnership between all accountability forums. It was the informal validation and authentication of all formal probes. It shows that institutional and public types of accountability not always collide.

Many observers may argue that the net effect for the overall accountability was nil because the Mabetex odyssey ended abruptly when Yeltsin unexpectedly announced his resignation on New Year's Eve. On the very same day, his hand-picked acting president Putin signed a decree "On guarantees to the president of the Russian Federation after he leaves office and to the members of his family", which gave Yeltsin lifetime immunity from prosecution. Twenty days later, Putin moved Borodin from the position of Kremlin's property manager and assigned him to another, probably equally prestigious position of the secretary of the Russia-

---

6 The popular backlash from the fallout empowered yet another accountability mechanism to counter Yeltsin. The Duma, the lower house of legislature, tried to impeach Yeltsin. The impeachment was initiated by the communist party but failed.

Belarus Union. In April of the same year, after Putin won the presidency, the Federation Council finally approved Putin's recommendation to dismiss Skuratov. The new prosecutor dropped the case against Borodin. For Russia, the Mabetex case was over. There were no sanctions involved. Nevertheless, perhaps the benefits of the mutual support between the accountability forums could be measured in their impact on Yeltsin's decision to resign.

The international accountability mechanism was activated again when on January 17, 2001 Borodin was arrested at Kennedy Airport in New York on his way to the Bush Inauguration at the request of Swiss authorities. However, Russia bailed Borodin out with a bail in the amount of $3 million. As the Swiss state prosecutor Bernard Bertossa announced that he had found Pavel Borodin guilty of laundering $22.4 million in Switzerland, Borodin refused to pay the fine imposed by the Swiss court. The international accountability mechanism failed to produce sanctions either.

Case Study of Institutional Cooperation in a Democratic Setting: The German Visa Affair

The cooperation between multiple accountability mechanisms proved to be a definite advantage in the Visa Affair in Germany as well. Oppositional politicians claimed that thousands of illegal immigrants — including many from Ukraine and China — were able to enter Germany between 2000 and 2003 after tourist visa criteria were relaxed by the government. This government policy was said to lead to an increase in organized crime, drugs and prostitution on Minister Fischer's watch.

The accountability mechanism that proved vital in starting the investigation was the court in Köln. It first found out that the policy of the German government to issue visas without certain documents has facilitated the trafficking of Ukrainian women into Germany. In a clear case of inter-accountability cooperation, the German parliament picked up the court's accusations just four days after they emerged in the court. On February 11, 2004, the CDU/CSU party began putting written questions and oral inquiries to the government during the session for parliamentary control. For a period of about two months, the judicial and legislative channels investigated the government simultaneously. The prosecutor general in Köln started investigations of employees of the ministry of international affairs because of suspicion of wrongful testimony and facilitation of massive people trafficking. The CDU/CSU fraction in parliament continued to put oral questions to the government. The legislative-judicial cooperation was further bolstered as the prosecutor general in Berlin started investigations against two employees of the German consulate in Tirana with the suspicion of bribes.

However, parliamentary accountability reached its limits and could have been thwarted had the Constitutional Court not intervened. The ruling party in parliament tried to block the creation of the investigative committee and the public hearings of its incumbents. It was the Constitutional Court that made sure that the public inquiries of the legislature continue. The public inquiries were supposedly a very shameful process that exposed the government to a lot of public scrutiny. On April 21, 2000, the Commission of Inquiry heard Ludger Volmer and his predecessor, Günther Pleuger. The hearing lasted more than 12 hours. It was the first such hearing broadcast by television and was watched by more than 400,000 people. The second such hearing was the April 25 hearing of Joschka Fischer in the Commission of Inquiry. It lasted about 14 hours and was viewed by 700,000 viewers alone at the "Phoenix" TV network, which has a 10.5% quota (Wikipedia, April 18, 2015).

The SPD and Green parties, which were coalitional partners in the Schröder government, tried to argue against the creation of the Visa committee. They contended that the committee was a political attempt to put apart the minister of foreign affairs Fischer (Greens) against the minister of the interior Schily (SPD), and to splinter the governing coalition (Deutscher Bundestag, September 2, 2005). The governing parties also tried to postpone the creation of an investigative committee by handing the case for consideration to the Committee for Elections, Immunity and Order. The latter committee suggested modifications that favoured the SPD. One such suggestion was to look for culprits in the period before 1998, when CDU was in power. SPD attempted to block the public hearing of its minister Otto Schily. The committee dissolved itself against the will of the CDU opposition. SPD justified the move with the necessity to issue a report before the mandate of the parliament was over. The opposition, however, insisted that the commission was dissolved to avoid public testimony by the minister of the interior Otto Schily. This testimony was thought to be detrimental for the electoral chances of SPD. Stern magazine comments: "As the chancellor Gerhard Schröder announced on May 29, 2005 early elections, the government saw an opportunity to end the visa-committee, which was damaging its public image… By ending the taking of testimony, the government wanted to avoid, among other things, the testimony of interior minister Otto Schily (SPD), which was originally planned for July 8th" (Der Stern, June 15, 2005).

SPD, using its majority vote, dissolved parliament to prevent the public hearing of Otto Schily. Public hearings are an influential way for the legislature to fulfil its most important institutional objective — disclosing information to the public. At the same time, public hearings of government officials are potentially humiliating experiences for the governing parties. This attempt to dissolve the Visa Committee shows that the political logic of the governing party to protect its minister was stronger than the institutional objective of the legislature to disclose the truth before the public. The dissolution came after the CDU took the case to the Constitutional court, which ruled that the committee must resume work. Of course, the dissolution of parliament was dictated by other objectives as well.[7] However, it provides a good example how the Constitutional Court's intervention was beneficial for the continued work of parliamentary accountability. Overall, the Visa Affair teaches us that even parliaments with disciplined opposition, parliamentary accountability has its limits. The majority decision of the ruling party, which has very little incentive to criticize the government publicly, dictates the accountability process in parliament. Therefore, the intervention of additional forums is a key factor in bolstering parliamentary accountability.

---

7   The official reason was that the government could not fulfil its policy reform with little partisan and popular support.

While the ruling party was trying to find a way out of the investigation, two additional mechanisms, apart from the Constitutional Court, provided a safety net that made sure that the investigation continued. The EU added another dimension to the perception of government wrongdoing. At the beginning of May 2005, a report of the Internal Affairs Committee of the European Union Parliament establishes that the 2000 Volmer decree partly violated the Schengen Agreement. Internal governmental investigations also gave the accountability probe a boost. In July of 2004, the Ministry of International Affairs, the Ministry of Internal Affairs and the State Police send inspectors to investigate the German consulate in Tirana. The results of the mutual investigative efforts of these three accountability channels were quite encouraging. The Ministry of International Affairs dismissed some of its employees, others quit voluntarily, and visa regulations were tightened. Unlike the Russian accountability probe, the German investigations ended up in sanctions. In March 2005, employees of the internal ministry are dismissed. In May of the same year, the people smuggler Anatoli Barg was convicted.

Just as in the Mabetex case, all collaborations between the accountability mechanisms were taking place on the background of an encouraging public opinion. The Foreign Minister Joschka Fischer has long been one of Germany's most popular politicians. But the Visa Affair dented his reputation and threatened to unravel his political future (Deustche Welle, March 3, 2003). For the first time in over six years, in February 2005, opinion polls did not show Joschka Fischer in first place in the popularity vote. Instead, the leading position in the popularity vote went to the Christian Democratic of Lower Saxony, Christian Wulff, with Fischer coming in second (Wikipedia, April 18, 2015). Perhaps in this case public opinion worked hand in hand with the public hearings of the incumbents and bolstered their effect. The interplay of accountability mechanisms was very dynamic. As the public hearings left a disappointed public, another accountability instrument—local elections—materialized. The North Rhine Westphalia elections were held on May 22nd, 2005. The SPD lost to CDU. In yet another instance of interaction between the accountability forums, the governing party in parliament picked up the negative vibe and on the next day, SPD suggested a vote of confidence in parliament, which it eventually lost. New elections were scheduled. On September 8, 2005, the German parliament ended the Visa-Affair with a controversial debate.

The result of the workings and collaborations of parliament, the prosecutor, the court in Köln, the Constitutional Court, the EU Internal Affairs Committee, public opinion and internal governmental investigations was that the big loser of the accountability process was SPD, which lost power. On 18th September 2005, German parliamentary elections were held. Both SPD and CDU won around 36% of the seats. However, it showed that parliament and prosecutor could cooperate in certain cases. The spirit of cooperation between the accountability mechanisms characterized the whole Visa Affair. The cooperation between the prosecutor and the legislature in Germany is evident on several levels. First, the political opposition in parliament got interested in the Visa affair precisely because of a ruling of a court in Köln, which found that the visa policy of the German government had facilitated the trafficking of Ukrainian women into Germany. The ruling came out on February 9, 2004, and the Christian Democratic Union started putting oral and written questions to the government immediately after that (on February 11, 2004).[8] Second, the cooperation between the parliamentary committee and the court in the Visa Affair is also evident in the fact that the judge that reached this verdict was invited to the parliamentary investigative committee. In his testimony, Mr. Höppner and Mr. Bülles used much of the same language that he used in his ruling (Deutscher Bundestag, August 30, 2005).

Third, the courts seemed to reflect the intentions of the parliamentary committee investigating the Visa Affair in yet another way. The court in Köln finished an investigation into the visa affair just 12 days after the parliamentary committee adjourned itself on

---

8   The ruling unfurled a slew of 57 written questions, and dozens of oral questions put forth on March 10th, March 24th, May 5th, June 30, in addition to the regular parliamentary control. There were two big sessions of questions on April 27, 2004 and 21 September, 2004.

June 16, 2005. This development is surprising, not only because it failed to indict again Anatoli Barg, who already had a sentence, but also because it ended the proceedings prematurely, only after six sittings, and cited the vague reason of "economic reasons" (Taggesschau 2005).

The German law regulating the work of investigative committees provides for a broad cooperation between the investigative and judicial investigations. Contrary to the competition for evidence and witnesses in the American case, in Germany evidence is shared. According to the Basic Law, the German courts are entitled to evidence. When there is a disagreement as to whether to call a witness or to use certain piece of evidence in a committee, 25% of the members of the parliamentary committee have the right to decide to ask a judge to resolve the matter. Given that the composition of the committees mirrors the division of parliamentary seats, then it is very easy for the minority parties (unless the governing party has more than 75% of the seats) to remove the question of evidence from the realm of the committee and place it in the hands of the court. In this way, smaller political parties can cooperate with the judicial branch.

The relative strength of the federal courts (Bundesgerichtshof) versus the parliament is enhanced by the courts' power to enforce its decisions by imprisoning those witnesses who refuse to show up before the committee. The compatibility between the courts and parliament is based on the independence of their decisions. According to Article 44 of the Basic law, the decisions of investigative committees shall not be subject to judicial review. The courts shall be free to evaluate and rule upon the facts that were the subject of the investigation. In addition, the investigative Committee is obliged to clarify the following questions: how it is to be ensured the Federal Prosecutor General's powers to direct investigative proceedings are not undermined. Courts and parliament are independent because before the initiation of a lawsuit against a government official, the prosecutor general is obliged to inform the parliament.

Fourth, the Visa Affair teaches us that ministerial accountability in parliaments with disciplined and established parties has its limits. The opposition's most potent tool in parliament is public hearings. The majority party will seek to avoid such public displays of criticism. It will also seek to dissolve investigative committees. When ministerial accountability to parliaments hits its limits, it is the work of other forums, such as the Constitutional Court, to make sure that public hearings and investigative committees proceed. Fifth, the interaction between the forums does not have to be antagonistic. In fact, in both cases forums exchange evidence and start investigations. One forum serves as a fire alarm for another forum. In the German case, the Köln court was the whistle-blower for parliament. In the Russian case, the Italian prosecutor was the fire alarm for the Russian prosecutor. Furthermore, the German prosecutor and parliament exchanged evidence all along the accountability process. Finally, the interaction between multiple accountability mechanisms allows one mechanism to pick cues from another mechanism. For example, public hearing of Fischer in parliament (first mechanism) led to lower approval ratings (second mechanism). This rating was reflected by Federal Elections (third mechanism). The ruling party reacted by suggesting a vote of no-confidence (fourth mechanism). Thus, the interplay between the forums allows them to complement each other, rather than to compete and subvert each other.

Inter-Institutional Uncertainty

As far as institutions are concerned, most of the research on uncertainty is focused on institutional uncertainty. This chapter makes the case for inter-institutional uncertainty, which pertains to the lack of certainty as to whether institutions will cooperate or will compete. The importance of inter-institutional uncertainty is not to be underestimated because it may affect the accountability process significantly.

Bibliography

Bardach, E., Kagan, R.A. (1982). *Going by the Book: The Problem of Regulatory Unreasonableness*. Philadelphia: Temple University Press.

Bardach, E., Kagan, R.A. (1982). *Going by the Book: The Problem of Regulatory Unreasonableness*. Philadelphia: Temple University Press.

Bauman, Z. (2000) *Liquid Modernity*. Cambridge: Polity Press.

Benz, A. (2007) Accountable Multilevel Governance by the Open Method of Coordination? *European Law Journal* 13 (4), PP. 505-522. Available at: https://onlinelibrary.wiley.com/doi/10.1111/j.1468-0386.2007.00381.x.

Braithwaite, J. (1999) Accountability and Governance under the New Regulatory State. *Australian Journal of Public Administration* 58 (1), pp. 90-93. Available at: https://www0.anu.edu.au/fellows/jbraithwaite/_documents/Articles/Accountability_Governance_1999.pdf.

Dimova, G. (2019) *Democracy beyond Elections: Government Accountability in the Media Age*. Cham: Springer Nature.

Gregory, R. (2012) *Accountability in Modern Government*. London: SAGE Publishing.

Halachmi, A. (2002) Performance Measurement: A Look at Some Possible Dysfunctions. *Work Study* 51 (5), pp. 230–239. Available at: http://dx.doi.org/10.1108/00438020210437240.

Halachmi, A. (2014) Accountability Overload. In Mark Bovens, Robert E. Goodin, Thomas Schillemans (eds.). *The Oxford Handbook Public Accountability*. Oxford: Oxford University Press.

Hood, C. (2014) Chapter 37: Accountability and Blame Avoidance. In Mark Bovens, Robert E. Goodin, Thomas Schillemans (eds.), *The Oxford Handbook Public Accountability*.

Hoxby, C.M. (2002) *The Cost of Accountability*. NBER Working Paper, No. 8855. Available at: http://www.nber.org/papers/w8855 (Accessed: February 23 2015).

Klingner, D.E., Nalbandian, J., Romzek, B.S. (2016) Politics, Administration and Markets: Conflicting Expectations of Accountability. *American Review of Public Administration* 32 (2), pp. 117-144. Available at: https://doi.org/10.1177/027740020320020001.

Koppell, J. (2005) Pathologies of Accountability: ICANN and the Challenge of "Multiple Accountabilities Disorder". *Public Administration Review* 65 (1), pp. 94-108. Available at: https://academic.udayton.edu/richardghere/pol%20305/koppell_jonathan_gs.pdf.

Mair, P. (2013) *Ruling the Void: The Hollowing of Western Democracy*. London: Verso.

Mair, P. (2011) *Democracy beyond Parties*. Research Monograph Series, Paper 5 (6). Center for the Study of Democracy. Available at: https://cadmus.eui.eu/bitstream/handle/1814/3291/viewcontent.pdf [Last Accessed: January 30, 2023].

Maravall, J.M., Przeworski, A. (2003) *Democracy and the Rule of Law*. Cambridge: Cambridge University Press.

Mulgan, R. (2003) *Holding Power to Account: Accountability in Modern Democracies.* Basingstoke: Palgrave Macmillan.

Papadopoulos, Y. (2013) *Democracy in Crisis? Politics, Governance and Policy.* London: Bloomsbury Publishing.

Pollitt, C. (2003) *The Essential Public Manager.* London: Open University Press.

Power, M. (1997) *The Audit Society: Rituals of Verification.* Oxford: Oxford University Press.

Romzek, B.S., Dubnick, M.J. (1987) Accountability in the Public Sector: Lessons from the Challenger Tragedy. *Public Administration Review* 47 (3), pp. 227-238. Available at: https://doi.org/10.2307/975901.

Rosanvallon, P. (2006) *Democracy Past and Future.* New York: Columbia University Press.

Salamon, L.M. (2002) *The Tools of Government: A Guide to the New Governance.* New York: Oxford University Press.

Schillemans, T. (2010) Redundant Accountability: The Joint Impact of Horizontal and Vertical Accountability on Autonomous Agencies. *Public Administration Quarterly* 34 (3). Available at: http://dx.doi.org/10.2307/41288351.

Schillemans, T. (2011) Does Horizontal Accountability Work? Evaluating Potential Remedies for the Accountability Deficit of Agencies. *Administration and Society* 43 (4), pp. 387-416. Available at: https://doi.org/10.1177/0095399711412931.

Schillemans, T. (2012) *Mediatization of Public Services: How Organizations Adapt to News Media.* Bern: Peter Lang.

Schillemans, T., & Bovens, M. (2011). The Challenge of Multiple Accountability. In Dubnick MJ, Frederickson HG, editors. *Accountable Governance: Problems and Promises.* New York: Routledge, 3-21.

Scott, C. (2004) Regulation in the Age of Governance: The Rise of the Post-Regulatory State. *Journal of Law and Society* 27 (1), pp. 38-60. Available at: https://dx.doi.org/10.4337/9781845420673.

Shapiro, M. (1988) *Who Guards the Guardians? Judicial Control of Administration.* Athens: University of Georgia Press.

Slaughter, A.M. (2004) Disaggregated Sovereignty: Towards the Public Accountability of Global Government Networks. *Government and Opposition* 31 (2), pp. 159-190. Available at: https://doi.org/10.1111/j.1477-7053.2004.00119.x.

Stiegler, B. (2011) *The Decadence of Industrial Democracies.* Cambridge: Polity Press.

Tagesschau (2005) *Chronology of the Visa Affair*. Available at: http://www.tagesschau.de/inland/meldung174674.html [Accessed: May 27, 2008].

Thomas, Paul. (2012) Accountability in Pierre, J. and Peters, B.G. (editors) *The Sage Handbook of Public Administration*. London: Sage.

Tormey, S. (2015) *The End of Representative Politics*. Cambridge: Polity Press.

Walsh, L. (1997) *Firewall: The Iran-Contra Conspiracy and Cover-Up*. New York: W. W. Norton and Company.

6 Democratic Uncertainty
Fundamental or Processual?

The book has argued that uncertainty manifests itself in various ways. If we focus on the electoral moment, uncertainty has mostly substantive and procedural manifestations. If, however, we view uncertainty in the moments in between elections, uncertainty acquires inter-institutional, verbal, actor-based and other dimensions. The process is multidimensional and embodies various types of uncertainty. This chapter reveals yet another dimension of uncertainty in democracy—fundamental uncertainty. Fundamental uncertainty is based on antagonisms that are deeply seated in a democracy. It emanates from the principle of duality. Duality can relate to the antagonism between the oligarchic dimension and the democratic dimension (Manin 1997, p. 237), between representative government and responsible government (Mair 2013), between doxa and episteme (Urbinati 2014), between democracy in the abstract and democracy in concreto (Schmitt 1988), or between post-election performance and pre-election political rhetoric (Downs 1957). It is discussed with more examples and at a greater depth below.

The fundamental uncertainty revealed in this chapter presents a different aspect of democracy to the uncertainty exposed through viewing democracy through the prism of accountability in between elections. The antagonisms of fundamental uncertainty turn democracy into a zero-sum game. More of one dimension leads to less of the other dimension. They are mutually exclusive. For example, if there is less doxa, there is less episteme; if there is less democracy in the abstract, there is less democracy in concreto, more of an oligarchic dimension leads to less of the democratic dimension. By contrast, democracy through the prism of accountability replaces this mutual exclusivity by a multiple dimensionality and a parallelism. This means that one accountability dimension can have an increase in one aspect, while simultaneously another accountability dimension can have an increase in another aspect.

Electoral democracy is a zero-sum game because the winners and losers are mutually exclusive and relatively predictable. In a democracy beyond elections, which is a G-zero game, winners and losers can coexist in different dimensions and are much less unpredictable. The notion of a G-zero world was popularized by Bremmer (2012), who argued that we live in a G-zero world because "no single country or bloc of countries has the political and economic leverage — or the will — to drive a truly international agenda." Democracy as a G-Zero world reflects a parallel reality.

The Fundamental Sources of Uncertainty in Democracy

This section introduces a new insight into the sources of uncertainty in a democracy. It argues that democracy is fundamentally uncertain and this fundamental uncertainty is different from the substantive uncertainty envisioned by the unpredictability of the outcomes. It is also different from existing sources of uncertainty, which have been summarized in chapter two as perceptual vs. environmental, formal vs. informal, endogenous vs. exogenous. This fundamental uncertainty also differs from the new categorizations of uncertainty introduced in chapters three and four, which have enlarged the existing categorizations by introducing inter-institutional, actor-based and verbal types of uncertainty, as well as uncertainty-reducing and uncertainty-inducing factors. This fundamental uncertainty pertains to an inherent duality underpinning democracy. This duality is the source of uncertainty.

The tradition of perceiving democracy as a duality is long and venerable but it is insufficiently recognized. Below, I review some of the thinking which presents the opposing forces that are inherent in democracy and that are inevitably at odds with each other. This duality takes many names, such as dichotomy, dualism, antinomy, bifurcation, antagonism, schism, dyad, tension (Mouffe 2005, p. 5), polarity (Schmitt 1976, p. 70), diarchy (Urbinati 2014, p.22). Table 6.1. lists several references to the principle of duality. It is important to understand that this duality breeds uncertainty because it is never certain which element will prevail. There is always tension between the elements of democracy. There is a permanent contestation. Democracy is an unsettled state.

Table 6.1: Duality of Representative Democracy[9]

Duality of Representative Democracy		Source
Supply of representation	Demand for representation	Flinders 2012; Hay 2007, p. 39.
Emancipation as individual autonomy	Emancipation as collective power	(Locke) vs. (Rousseau) cited in Rosanvallon 2006, p. 213.
System effectiveness	Citizenship participation	Dahl, 1984
Liberalism	Democracy	Rosanvallon 2006, p. 224.
Individual autonomy	Group empowerment	Rosanvallon 2006, p. 224.
Principle, promise	Reality	Rosanvallon 2006, p. 224.
Law	Politics	Rosanvallon 2006, p. 224.
Institution-civil society	Regulation-nation	Rosanvallon 2006, p. 220.
Justice	Politics	Rosanvallon 2006, p. 281.
Sovereignty	Government	Rousseau 1762
Private will	Public will	Rousseau 1762
Illusion	Reality	Ankersmit 2002
Acceptance	Coercion	Ankersmit 2002
Status Quo	Upheaval	Ankersmit 2002,
Equality	Liberty	Mouffe 2005, p. 5.
Oligarchic dimension	Democratic dimension	Manin 1997, p. 237.
Representative government	Responsible government	Mair 2009
Doxa	Episteme	Urbinati 2014, p. 5.
Ethics	Economics	Schmitt 1976, p. 70.
Democracy in abstract	Democracy in concreto	Schmitt, 1976
State	Civil society	Held 2006, p. 275.
Post-election performance	Pre-election political rhetoric	Downs 1957
Collective action	Conflict of interests or identities	Warren 2009
Political Equality	Economic equality	Przeworski 2009, p. 301.
Ideal of representation	Institutionalization of representation	Pitkin 1964, p. 239.
Abstract solutions	Vivid problems	Pitkin 2004
Substance, purpose, intention	Institutions, behaviour, Performance	Pitkin 1964, p. 238.
Phylogenesis (public maturation)	Ontogenesis (individual maturation)	Hegel 1967
Calculable and manageable actuality	Incalculable (im)possibility	Derrida 1984
Sameness	Oneness	Derrida 1984
Immanent actuality	Transcendent possibility	Derrida 1984
Human incapacity to act	Human capability to act	Derrida 1984
Totality	Infinity	Derrida 1984,
Democratic thought	Political reality	Schmitt 1976, pp. 22-32.
Agent	Principal	Przeworski, Stokes and Manin 1999
Modern freedom of the individual pleasures of private life	Ancient freedom of belonging to a collective	Constant 1819
Head	Heart	Krastev 2013
Individualized, self-interested logic of the market	Community-conscious, altruistic logic of the family	Bilakovics 2012
Triumph of democratic principles	Absence of democratic practice	Bilakovics 2012

To begin with, fundamental uncertainty arises from the lack of clarity how the "democratic dilemma" between system effectiveness versus citizenship participation will be resolved. It is related to "the

---

9 A shorter version of table 6.1. is published in Dimova (2023).

ability of the citizens to exercise democratic control over the decisions of the polity versus the capacity of the system to respond satisfactorily to the collective preferences of its citizens" (Dahl 1984, p. 28). Dahl believes that the democratic revolution has increased the size and scope of the state, but size and scope are incompatible. A small size of the state allows citizens to participate more extensively in decision making but the small scope of government means that the issues in which the citizens take part are relatively inconsequential. Conversely, large states decrease the opportunity for citizens to participate in decision making but large scope ensures that the few decisions that they pronounce themselves on are important. This antagonism is one source of duality, and hence uncertainty.

The fundamental uncertainty of democracy is also centred on the antagonism between the modern freedom of the individual pleasures of private life and the ancient freedom of belonging to a collective (Constant 1819). These two entities are irreconcilable: "the ipseity of the [sovereign] One, the autos of autonomy, symmetry, homogeneity…and even, finally, God" remain entirely "incompatible with, and even clashes with, another truth of the democratic, namely, the truth of the other, heterogeneity, the heteronomic and dissymmetric, disseminal multiplicity …the indeterminate 'each one'" (Derrida cited in Dallmyar 2012, pp. 129-130).Derrida further talks about the incompatibility between the calculable and manageable actuality and the incalculable (im)possibility. Another source of antagonism, and uncertainty, is deduced by Hegel, who distinguishes between phylogenesis (public maturation) and ontogenesis (individual maturation).

In another interpretation, the fundamental uncertainty of liberal democracy stems from the "the recurring polarity of two heterogeneous spheres, namely ethics and economics" (Schmitt 1976, p. 70). Schmitt further notes the breakup point between accepting democracy as a promising goal and accepting democracy as a failing reality. Schmitt wrote in the midst of the two World Wars, and witnessed the collapse of the Weimar Republic. His insight is this: "so long as it [democracy] was essentially a polemical concept (that is, the negation of established monarchy), democratic convictions could be joined to and reconciled with various other political aspirations. But to the extent that it was realized, democracy was seen to serve many masters and not in any way to have a substantial, clear goal. As its most important opponent, the monarchical principle, disappeared, democracy itself lost its substantive precision and shared the fate of every political concept" (Schmitt 1988, p. 24). In short, the duality principle is manifested by the lack of identity between democracy in the abstract and democracy in concreto. Duality gives way to uncertainty.

Uncertainty in democracy is also based on the tension arising from the diarchy of episteme and doxa, or between will and opinion, where the will stands for procedures, rules and institutions and opinion belongs to those who rule indirectly and obey the law (Urbinati 2014, p. 22). The antagonism between the doxa and episteme could be traced in each of Urbinati's three models of the disfigurement of democracy, which are unpolitical, populist and plebiscitarian democracy. In all of them, it is clear that this diarchic set-up of doxa and episteme comes down to a zero-sum game, which means democracy allows for only one winner, either the doxa or the episteme, to prevail. According to Urbinati, "whereas epistemic theory proposes to dislodge doxa from democratic politics and make a diarchy of will and reason, populism takes advantage of the doxa as an active strategy of hegemonic unification of the people that claims to be identical with the will of the sovereign; and plebiscitarianism, while it acknowledges the diarchic system…makes doxa the name of crafted images unfurled by video technicians" (Urbinati 2014, p. 8).

Ankersmit (2002, p. 356) captures the link between uncertainty and democracy by the word "indeterminate": "indeterminacy and indefiniteness now characterize the link between the citizen and the state." He posits that all political representations and representatives are doomed to the indeterminate levitation between antagonistic poles: illusion and reality, sameness and alienation, acceptance and coercion, individual and public interest, domination and compassion, status quo and upheaval (Csigo, 2009). Continuing the theme of duality, Mouffe (2005, p. 3) suggests that modern democracy is premised on two different traditions: "on the one side we have the liberal tradition constituted by the rule of law, the defense of human rights and the respect of individual liberty; on the other hand, the democratic tradition whose main ideas are those of equality, identity between governing and governed, and popular sovereignty."

Another source of fundamental uncertainty is the antinomy between oligarchy and democracy: "representative government includes both democratic and undemocratic features. The duality lies in its very nature, not just in the eye of the beholder... Representative democracy has undeniably a democratic dimension. No less undeniable, however, is its oligarchic dimension" (Manin, 1997, p. 237). Mair (2013) talks about the difference between representative and responsible government. Przeworski, Manin and Stokes (1999) outline the tension between the principal and the agent in a democratic chain of delegation. Downs (1957) conceptualizes of the tension as the difference between pre-election promises and post-electing performance of the government. It seems that uncertainty also comes from the "often-remarked-upon simultaneous triumph of democratic principles and the absence of democratic political practice" (Bilakovics 2012, p. 13), i.e., the fact that democracy is "everywhere preached but nowhere practiced." Furthermore, Bilakovics believes that a growing cynicism arises from the gap between the individualized, self-interested logic of the market and the community-conscious, more altruistic logic of the family.

All these antagonisms intrinsic in democracy create uncertainty because they are incompatible and equally compelling. There is no clear mechanism of adjudicating between them. There is no clear answer which one will prevail. The questions leave a world of possibilities with no predictability: Should democracy be about "abstract solutions" or "about vivid problems" (Pitkin 2004)? Is the purpose of democracy phylogenesis (public maturation) or ontogenesis (individual maturation) (Hegel 1967). How does one marry the calculable and manageable actuality with the incalculable (im)possibility (Derrida 1982)? Should democracy be oriented towards the modern freedom of the individual pleasures of private life or the ancient freedom of belonging to a collective (Constant 1819)?

Processional Uncertainty in Democracy

This section switches from analyzing fundamental uncertainty in democracy to discussing uncertainty in democracy seen through the prism of accountability. I refer to this type of uncertainty as processual, because it is related to the process of holding the government to account. As the previous chapters have argued, democracy through the prism of accountability is highly unpredictable and uncertain because it is multi-dimensional, and each dimension or stage contains various types of uncertainty. It has been presented as a chain process, in which uncertainty arises for a number of reasons: it is unclear which media issues would attract attention, what constellations of the public would organize to address the media allegation, how durable and willing they would be to pursue the allegation in the accountability forums, will there be appropriate and accessible accountability forums to investigate and sanction the government, will the incumbents evade giving verbal explanations, will the investigations fail to result in sanctions and what type of sanctions will be appropriate to address the alleged government offense.

This section seeks to throw light on one aspect of this process, which has not been fully analysed—the uncertainty surrounding political conflict. To begin with, the gauging of political conflict has become more uncertain because of the fragmentation of the public, which has enormously complicated and multiplied the variations of people who can voice their discontent with the government. Instead of having many people choose one representative, now there are many representatives for one person. "The old rule of 'one person, one vote, one representative' – the central demand in the struggle for representative democracy – is replaced with the new principle of monitory democracy: 'one person, many interests, many voices, multiple votes, and multiple representatives'" (Keane 2009). Furthermore, the individual political agents have also become less predictable because of reflexive modernization. Reflexivity is the idea that agents can change their environment and history. For example, agents can change parties and political structures. "They are, at the core, not determined, but indeterminate" (Held 2006, p.

74). The result is a type of a system that is less predictable. It erupts at certain moments and may stay dormant at other moments. Conflict has changed because, while hitherto it has revolved around the will of the majority versus the will of the minority, it now needs to accommodate the will of the vocal minority versus the will of the silent majority. This element of being vocal — which has been introduced by the rise of easily accessible communication technologies — has made it less clear who is pitted against whom in the political struggle.

Furthermore, political conflict has become more de-centralized and less predictable because it substitutes ideological conflicts with issue-based and personality-based conflicts, and such conflicts are harder to foresee. Identities have for a long time been a shortcut to finding one's stance on an issue. With the waning of structural cleavages and the process of de-politicization, issues have triumphed over identities. "Ad-hoc majorities" and "issue-by-issue majorities" (Weale 2019, 73) have emerged. This process is tantamount to the unbundling of bundles of policies. People are less inclined to criticize the government as a whole as opposed to specific ministers and policies. The advent of issue-based and personality-based conflicts randomized the nature and occurrence of political conflict, because it is very hard to predict which issue and which personalities will become most salient. It is also hard to predict whether personalities will triumph over issues or the other way around.

All the changes outlined above — fragmentation of the public, of the reflexivity of political agents, of having one agent have more than one representative, and the substitution of cleavages with issues and personalities — have transformed the modality of political conflict. This change in the make-up of the public is reflected in an alternative dimension of conjuring up the sovereign: unification in difference (Bauman 2000, p. 168). Whereas interest aggregation has been the predominant mode of expressing the public will, which mainly happened during elections, in the present model, the public will is not aggregated, it is diversified, and after it is diversified, it is partially and spontaneously aggregated. Uncertainty arises in "aggregation in difference" because it is less certain how to aggregate a homogenous public rather than how to aggregate (partially) a highly diverse public. Uncertainty is further created by the fact that conflicts based on personalities and issues tend to be resolved in more informal and non-institutionalized ways than conflicts based on cleavages. The contingency of the "unification in difference" also comes from the fact that soft law rather than hard law helps the resolution of conflict. Soft law is less formalized and enforceable than hard law (Papadopolous 2013, p. 230).

There is also uncertainty as to the legitimacy of the resolution of these various political conflicts because several new ways of measuring legitimacy have sprung up. In democracy beyond elections, legitimacy is no longer derived exclusively from the demos. The dominance of procedural legitimacy inherent in elections has waned. Some scholars argue that output legitimacy is the current standard for justifying the legitimacy of non-majoritarian institutions (Thatcher and Sweet 2002). The advent of the European Union posed the question of input, throughput, and output legitimacy (Schmidt, 2013). Other types of legitimacy include respect for evidence, the uncertainties, and positive analysis (Vibert 2007, pp. 121-123). Rosanvallon (2011, pp. 60-71) talks about the breakdown of the dual legitimacy of democracy, which is grounded in substantial and procedural legitimacy: "The dual legitimacy on which democratic institutions depended collapsed in the 1980s." To Rosanvallon, the duality of legitimacy was grounded in a model of generality, which was replaced by a model of particularity. For example, the general category of labour power was replaced by the specialized skills of the workers; the general category of a political class is falling apart and it is harder to aggregate; collective bargaining was replaced by individual bargaining; visible majority was replaced by the invisible people.

Rosanvallon (2011, p. 9) introduces three new types of legitimacy: legitimacy of reflexivity, legitimacy of impartiality and legitimacy of particularity. The legitimacy of impartiality relates to the independent oversight and regulatory authorities. These institutions were created wither by the legislature to check on the executive or by the executive himself to restore his credibility. The legitimacy of reflexivity pertains to constitutional courts, which subject legislation to scrutiny, according to criteria of generality different from those of majority rule. Finally, the legitimacy of particularity expresses the condition where the elites are more accessible and receptive of the people and to particular issues that interest the people (Rosanvallon 2011, p. 172). All these new approaches to legitimacy make us less certain whether to accept an outcome as legitimate or not.

Political conflict has become less predictable and more uncertain because a new mode of participating in politics-monitoring – has occurred (Green 2010). Representative politics offers two basic modes of participation: exit and voice (Hirschman 1990). Another dichotomy of choice in electoral democracy is the choice between delegation and accountability. Electoral accountability itself consists of two modes: retrospective versus prospective voting. In extra-electoral democracy, there is a third way to participate in policy making: non-parliamentary accountability. If we use Hirschman's terminology, non-parliamentary accountability is tantamount to including a "re-entry" option in addition to "voice" and "exit". Rosanvallon (2006, pp. 140-141), basing his writing on Condorcet, best describes this third method of participating in politics through holding the government to account as "a middle ground between politics as usual and politics as insurrection", "a mode of action somewhere between the ballot box and the streets", "a possible alternative to an alteration between passive consent and rebellion". With more options for structuring conflict, it is less certain how it will ultimately pan out. It is uncertain whether, and at what time, people who have chosen to exit the political arena will re-enter it.

Uncertainty in political conflict also arises because conflict in between elections has become more about responsiveness than about responsibility. The government reacting to what the public wants, rather than the government steering the public, is more fraught with contingencies, if one assumes that the public will is fickle. As a result of all characteristics outlined above, extra-electoral democracy is marked by uncertainty. It seems to be at a permanent crossroads. Democracy is also uncertain because it is non-linear. The non-linearity of extra-electoral democracy "moves beyond traditional linear histories of democracy based on the notion of gradual progress toward an ideal type" (Rosanvallon 2006, p. 25).

Table 6.2: Uncertainty in Electoral Democracy and Extra-Electoral Democracy

Uncertainty in Electoral Democracy	Uncertainty in Extra-Electoral Democracy
Homogeneity	Diversity
Homogenous supply	Diversified supply
Homogenous demand	Diversified demand
Delegation	Accountability
Representation	Responsiveness
Voice vs. Exit	Voice vs. Exit vs. Re-entry
Many people-one representative	One person-many representatives
Democratic Legitimacy	Procedural, Input, Throughput, Output Legitimacy
Parliamentary majority	Ad-hoc majority
Silent majority	Vocal minorities
Cleavage based	Issue based or Personality Based
Linear	Contingent
Centralized conflict	De-centralized conflict

Conclusion

The book makes a strong plea for creating a multi-dimensional and integrated model of uncertainty. Therefore, future studies should explore the relationship between processual uncertainty, inherent in the accountability process, and fundamental uncertainty, which is embedded in the philosophical construct of democracy. On the surface, the two types of uncertainty seem incompatible, because the former depicts democracy as a parallel reality, and the latter describes it as a zero-sum game. However, it would be fair to argue that processual uncertainty is a manifestation of fundamental uncertainty. In processual uncertainty, different constellations of actors take precedence, and depending on their relative domination, fundamental uncertainty looks different. For example, if during the process of accountability some business interests prevail, then it is the oligarchic dimension of fundamental uncertainty that is manifested. However, if the vocal majority steers the accountability process, then it is the collective action aspect of fundamental antagonism that takes precedence, not the conflict of interests and identities. It is precisely because processual uncertainty is so fickle that fundamental uncertainty can be so antagonistic.

Bibliography

Ankersmit, F. (2002) *Political Representation*. Stanford: Stanford University Press.

Bauman, Z. (2000) *Liquid Modernity*. Cambridge: Polity Press.

Bilakovics, S. (2012) *Democracy without Politics*. Cambridge: Harvard University Press.

Bremmer, I. (2012) *Every Nation for Itself: Winners and Losers in a G-Zero World*. London: Portfolio Penguin.

Colwell, A. (2020) "I Genuinely Think 2020 is scary": David Runciman on Trump, Young People, and the Future of Democracy. UCL PI Media. Available at: https://uclpimedia.com/online/i-genuinely-think-2020-is-scary-david-runciman-on-trump-young-people-and-the-future-of-democracy[Accessed: February 2 2023].

Constant, B. (1819) *The Liberty of Ancients Compared with that of Moderns*. Rev edn. Publisher unknown.

Csigo, P. (2009) *Book Review: Political Representation*. Available at http://politicsandculture.org/2009/11/09/review-political-representation/ [Accessed: March 27, 2017].

Dahl, R.A. (1984) Polyarchy, Pluralism, and Scale. *Scandinavian Political Studies 7* (4), p. 225-240. Available at: https://tidsskrift.dk/scandinavian_political_studies/article/download/32492/30434.

Dallmayr, F. (2012) Jacques Derrida's Legacy: Democracy to Come. In *Theory after Derrida*. 2nd edn. Abingdon: Routledge India. Available at: https://www.taylorfrancis.com/chapters/edit/10.4324/9780429485954-2/jacques-derrida-legacy-democracy-come-fred-dallmayr [Accessed: February 2, 2023].

Dimova, G. (2023). *A Rigorous debate on Inter-Disciplinary Boundaries and Democracy*, ECPR: https://theloop.ecpr.eu/a-rigorous-debate-on-intra-disciplinary-boundaries-and-democracy/

Derrida, J. (1984) *Margins of Philosophy*. Chicago: University of Chicago Press.

Downs, A. (1957) *An Economic Theory of Democracy*. New York: Harper and Row.

Flinders, M. (2012) *Defending Politics: Why Democracy Matters in the 21st Century*. Oxford: Oxford University Press.

Gagnon, P. (2014) *Democratic Theorists in Conversation: Turns in Contemporary Thought*. Basingstoke: Palgrave Macmillan.

Green, J. (2010) *The Eyes of the People: Democracy in an Age of Spectatorship*. New York: Oxford University Press.

Hay, C. (2007) *Why We Hate Politics*. Cambridge: Polity Press.

Hegel, G.W.F. (1967) *The Phenomenology of Mind*. 2nd edn. Mineola: Dover Publications.

Held, D. (2006) *Models of Democracy*. 3rd edn. Cambridge: Polity Press.

Hirschman, A. (1990) *Exit, Voice, and Loyalty: Responses to Decline in Firms, Organizations and States*. Cambridge: Harvard University Press.

Keane, J. (2009) *Monitory Democracy and Media-Saturated Societies. Griffith Review, Edition 24: Participation Society*. Available at: https://core.ac.uk/download/pdf/30685323.pdf [Accessed: November 20, 2013].

Krastev, I. (2013). *In Mistrust We Trust. Can Democracy Survive When We Don't Trust Our Leaders?* TED Conferences.

Mair, P. (2013) *Ruling the Void: The Hollowing of Western Democracy*. London: Verso.

Manin, B. (1997) *The Principles of Representative Government*. Rev edn. Cambridge: Cambridge University Press.

Mouffe, C. (2005) *The Return of the Political*. London: Verso Books.

Papadopoulos, Y. (2013) *Democracy in Crisis? Politics, Governance and Policy*. London: Bloomsbury Publishing.

Pitkin, H. (1964) Hobbes's Concept of Representation. *American Political Science Review* 58 (2), pp. 328-340.

Pitkin, H.F. (2004) Representation and Democracy: Uneasy Alliance. *Scandinavian Political Studies* 27 (3), pp. 335–342. Available at: https://onlinelibrary.wiley.com/doi/abs/10.1111/j.1467-9477.2004.00109.x.

Przeworski, A. (2009) *Democracy, equality, and redistribution. In Political Judgement: Essays in Honour of John Dunn*. Cambridge: Cambridge University Press. Available at: https://doi.org/10.1017/CBO9780511605468.011 [Accessed: February 2, 2023].

Przeworski, A., Stokes, S.C., Manin, B. (1999) *Democracy, Accountability, and Representation*. Cambridge: Cambridge University Press.

Rosanvallon, P. (2006) *Democracy Past and Future*. New York: Columbia University Press.

Rosanvallon, P. (2011) *Democratic Legitimacy: Impartiality, Reflexivity, Proximity*. Princeton: Princeton University Press.

Rousseau, J.J. (1998) *The Social Contract*. Ware: Wordsworth Editions.

Runciman, D. (2013) *The Confidence Trap: A History of Democracy in Crisis from World War I to the Present*. Princeton: Princeton University Press.

Schmidt, V. (2013) Democracy and Legitimacy in the European Union Revisited: Input, Output and 'Throughput'. *Political Studies 61* (1), pp. 2–22. Available at: https://doi.org/10.1111/j.1467-9248.2012.00962.x.

Schmitt, C. (1976) *The Concept of the Political*. New Brunswick: Rutgers University Press.

Schmitt, C. (1988) The Crisis of Parliamentary Democracy (*Studies in Contemporary German Social Thought*). Cambridge: MIT Press.

Thatcher, M., Sweet, A.S. (2002) Theory and Practice of Delegation to Non-majoritarian Institutions. *West European Politics 25* (1), pp. 1–22. Available at: https://doi.org/10.1080/713601583.

Urbinati, N. (2014) *Democracy Disfigured: Opinion, Truth and the People*. Cambridge: Harvard University Press.

Vibert, F. (2007) *The Rise of the Unelected: Democracy and the New Separation of Powers*. New York: Cambridge University Press.

Warren, M. (2009) *A Second Transformation of Democracy? In Democracy Transformed? Expanding Political Opportunities in Advanced Industrial Democracies*. Oxford: Oxford University Press.

Weale, A. (2019) Three Types of Majority Rule. *The Political Quarterly 90* (1), pp. 62-76. Available at: https://doi.org/10.1111/1467-923X.12570.

7 Historically Induced Uncertainty[10]

This chapter explores how incumbents form their preferences when regime types change. It juxtaposes the perceptions of the Hungarian and the Soviet Communist Party hard-liners during the transition from Communism in 1989-91. It is argued that, during this time, the memory of a historical uprising reduced the incumbents' misperceptions about their popular legitimacy via two mechanisms. First, historical memory functioned as a "public tolerance indicator" because it brought the opposition together and demonstrated the true distribution of political support. Second, the memory of a past uprising served as a "conservative reformer" when it sparked internal party debate about the legitimacy of the regime. This line of reasoning contributes to the scarce literature on actors' preferences formation under conditions of transitional uncertainty. It also provides a useful analytical bridge between actor-oriented and system-centred approaches to democratization.

Political actors form their preferences based on their perceptions about their public support. As the Soviet Union began to dissolve in 1989, however, the true extent of the public support for the Communist incumbents in satellite states such as Hungary was unknown because Communist regimes did not hold contested elections. Transitional uncertainty also arose from the undefined institutional rules, the fluid party structure and the unknown reaction of the Soviet Union.

Incumbents dealt with uncertainty in different ways. Some party members underestimated the importance and extent of their political legitimacy. These hard-liners stubbornly clung to the old order. Other Communist leaders appreciated the true scale of societal changes, along with the limitations of their power, early on. These politicians took timely steps to democratize and compromise

---

[10] This chapter appeared originally as Yankova, G., 2008. Can the Memory of a Historical Uprising Reduce Transitional Uncertainty?: A Comparative Study of Hungary and the Former Soviet Union. *Demokratizatsiya* 16 (2). It has been slightly modified here. It is reprinted here with the permission of *Demokratizatsiya*.

with the opposition. The variance of the incumbents' preferences constitutes a puzzle. Earlier scholarship on democratic transitions has generally treated perceptions as exogenous, leaving the reasons for the disaccord largely unexamined. This study elucidates the development of actors' preferences during transitional periods.

The chapter argues that the historical memory of a failed antiregime uprising can reduce the incumbents' uncertainty about their political legitimacy by providing those in power with a barometer of public dissatisfaction. Two mechanisms are at work. First, the historical memory of a popular insurrection opens a debate about the party's legitimacy. During the debate, the more progressive party members criticize the conservative members for their role in defeating the popular uprising. The conservative members then resign, and the party reforms and democratizes. Second, commemorations of past uprisings reveal the strength of the opposition and show the regime's limited public support. The rulers realize that the likelihood of preserving the status quo has decreased and that the only way to preserve power is to associate with the popular historical symbols. As the demonstrations commemorating historical heroes increase, the hard-liners who hoped to embrace the progressive ideas only in words discover they need to back their new image with reforms and compromises.

This chapter revisits the theoretical discussion about the nature of transitional uncertainty and the process of preference formation. It specifies how historical memory can impact the incumbents' perceptions about their legitimacy under conditions of uncertainty. Next, it positions the argument within the scholarship of democratic transition and suggests that the proposition connects structural and actor-oriented explanations of regime change. In the first empirical part, the chapter distinguishes five episodes in which the memory of the 1956 uprising informed and moderated the incumbents' perceptions in Hungary: the fall of Janos Kadar, the rise of Karoly Grosz, the interview of Imre Poszgay, the demonstrations of March 15, 1989 and the reburial of Imre Nagy. The second empirical part examines the factors that motivated the Soviet hard-liners to stage the 1991 coup. It is hypothesized that the incumbents' misperception in the Soviet Union can partly be attributed to the lack of a memory of a popular anti-regime uprising.

The Argument: The Memory of a Popular Uprising Can Reduce the Incumbents' Misperception of Their Legitimacy

What was the incumbents' decision calculus during the period of transition from Communism? With hindsight, many signs predicted the regime's demise in 1989. At the time of the transition, however, these were open to various interpretations.

> The surprised included the leaders of the incumbent communist regimes... What is it that can keep even the most astute and best-informed members of a society unaware of imminent political changes of epochal significance? ... If signs of change are now so clear, why were they not noticed prior to late 1989? Why has our hindsight with respect to the collapse of East European communism proved vastly superior to our foresight? (Kuran 1995, p. 1,528)

Transitions are uncertain because they are "unusually full of information, and confusing information at that, given the deregulation of politics and economics . . . and the absence of such filters as class, institutions, roles, and interests to sort out environmental clues... The environment, in short, lacks correctives and makes clear judgments impossible and this encourages quite idiosyncratic interpretations" (Bunce and Csanadi 1993, p. 70).11 Of all the uncertainties during transition. The most important unknown variable is public support for the regime. The early transitional democracies, however, did not have precise indicators of public support.

---

11 It is important to distinguish between uncertainty in established and transitional democracies. In countries with democratic traditions, politicians easily recognize possible and probable choices. Actors do not know whether they will lose or win because final outcomes depend on the actions of the others. In transitional democracies, political actors are not only unsure what will happen but also which developments are possible and probable. In this sense, democracy is a system of organized uncertainty while transitions are periods of disorganized uncertainty. In a system of organized uncertainty, the likelihood of misperceiving one's chances for success is much higher than in a disorganized system. See Adam Przeworski, "Democracy as a Contingent Outcome of Conflicts." in Constitutionalism and Democracy, ed. Jon Elster and Rune Slagstad, pp. 59-78 (Cambridge: Cambridge University Press, 1988).

Some surveys were conducted, but their accuracy was marred by the complex relations between opinion polling and political circumstances under Communism (Kwiatkowski 1992). In addition, political parties were in flux and citizens were often unaware of their existence. Therefore, transitional actors must accept proxies for public support.

Kernell (2000, p. 571) suggests there are three methods of estimating public opinion in the absence of accurate polling techniques: extrapolation from the results of previous elections, reading newspaper endorsements, reconsidering the "prognostications of intelligent men acquainted the politics of the district." All three indicators were very imprecise instruments for deciphering public support in the post-Communist countries in 1989. Previous elections did not gauge political legitimacy because they were uncontested. Media endorsements were a bad proxy for the degree of public support because the Communist Party controlled most newspapers and television. Insightful and knowledgeable men were rarely given the floor if their predictions did not favour the regime.

The memory of a past uprising, however, can be a good approximation of public support, when the standard means of assessing political legitimacy are lacking. Historical memory can serve as a "public tolerance indicator" by bringing the oppositional forces together and professing their strength. According to Kuran (1995, p. 1,532), people express their private preferences publicly only when the cost of doing so is low:

> [One] determinant of the person's private preference is the set of benefits and costs associated with alternative public preference options. If the likely cost of joining the rally, and thus revealing a preference for political change, is a stint in jail or ostracism by one's peers, the prudent course of action may be to remain on the side-lines... The external benefits and costs associated with a public-preference choice generally depend on the choices of others. If only a few people are demonstrating against the regime, the possible external cost of participation is likely to be much higher, and the expected benefit much lower, than if the streets are packed with demonstrators.

Historical memory lowers the cost of public expression of a political preference because its official focus is not to protest directly against the regime but to celebrate a past uprising. Because the demonstrations only indirectly subvert the incumbents' authority, the likelihood of punishment is lower. Consequently, people are more daring in expressing their preferences. The idea that past historical repertoires can mobilize oppositional forces is not new, but these demonstrations can also serve to inform the incumbents of their limited public support and this information potentially changes their willingness to compromise (Bunce 2003, p. 79).[12]

In its role of a "conservative reformer", the interpretation of a failed anti-regime uprising opens a debate about the legitimacy of the Communist regime. The party members are reminded that public opinion is important and that it does not favour them. The historical discussion sets the party reformists and conservatives apart and ultimately prompts the conservatives to soften their political stance. If they were involved in defeating the protesters, they may even leave the party. This process leads to the gradual reformation of the Communist Party.

The general argument is the likelihood of political outcomes depends on the distribution of political power. Actors will rationally calculate the likelihood of realizing their most preferred outcome, but transitions from Communism lack reliable "reference points," such as elections and polls, to indicate the power distribution between the Communist hard-liners, the Communist reformists, and the opposition. In the absence of such data, actors will overestimate or underestimate popular sentiment.

Demonstrations related to the historical memory of popular uprisings, however, can be used to accurately determine the unpopularity of a regime because it allows the public to voice its opposition in a relatively low-risk environment. Such events can expose the strength of popular opposition and remind the incumbents that popular legitimacy is important and that they lack it.

---

12 Bunce (2003, p. 170) comes closest to perceiving mobilizations as a "public tolerance indicator": "Mass mobilization can reduce uncertainty, thereby influencing the preferences of the Communists, and the division of power between them and the opposition."

Where in the Literature is the Proposition Situated?

Theories of democratization can be roughly categorized as system-oriented or actor-oriented (Merkel 1999; Kitschelt 2003, p. 413; Welsh 1994, p. 379). Initial scholarship underscored structural factors, such as economic development, social class, education levels, property rights, cultural norms, or the timing of industrialization (Moore 1993; Lipset 1981). The advent of the second and third waves of democratization questioned the centrality of the environment and bolstered actor-oriented theories that explained democratic outcomes with the strategic interactions of politicians (O'Donnell, Schmitter and Whitehead 1986; Di Palma 1990; Kitschelt 1993). According to this second theory, political actors choose their strategy based on their perception of the utility of the transitional outcomes and the corresponding chances for realizing them (Colomar 1995, p. 74).

The proposed argument provides an analytical bridge between structural-historical and actor-centred approaches to democratization. The proposition is related to actor-oriented theories because only political actors can recollect a historical memory. The Polish transition is one case where a past anti-regime uprising existed and yet the memory of it was unimportant because the actors did not take advantage of it. Kubik and Linch (2006, pp. 11-12) point out that "solidarity ... seems to offer an abundant reservoir of 'symbolic material' out of which skilful political-cultural entrepreneurs should be able to fashion a compelling symbolic/mythical foundation for the new, post-Communist democratic Polish republic. This has not happened, however." The Polish political leaders deliberately avoided talking about historic memories at the roundtable. As one participant stales, a major condition of the negotiations "was the principle of not discussing symbolic problems. We were to solve the future and avoid arguing about the past. We believed, and I think most of us agreed here, that if we started getting into discussions about the past wrongs, we wouldn't accomplish anything"

(Kubik and Linch 2006, p. 17).[13] The memory of a past uprising in Poland was not important because the political actors chose not to refer to it.

The proposition is also related to system-oriented theories because historical memory affects the incumbents' perceptions only in conjunction with other structural "reference points," such as the fall of Communism in neighbouring countries, economic liberalization, the federal structure of the state, and the development of civil society. The impact of historical memory varies with the importance and availability of these conditions. Some serve to reinforce it; others lessen it. The negotiators at the Hungarian roundtable in September 1989, for example, learned from the defeat of the Communist Party in the Polish elections in June 1989 (Starr 1991). This reinforced the impact of historical memory. In another example, the memory of a past uprising in Germany was less influential for the transition than the fact that the country was artificially divided after World War II and people who spoke the same language wanted to come together. The country's structural division lessened the effect of historical memory.

The proposed argument about historical memory can easily be confused with path dependent explanations. It differs, however, along five dimensions (Mahoney 2000). First, the independent causal factor in path-dependent analysis is a popular uprising, while I focus on the memory of a popular uprising. Second, path-dependent analyses are interested in the impact of successful uprisings, while I examine the consequences of unsuccessful revolutions. Third, path-dependent studies posit an uninterrupted course of events following an uprising, while the proposed analysis connects two distant points in time — that of the revolution and its interpretation during democratization. Fourth, path-dependent analyses

---

13 Scholars note that it was only after the first elections when "everybody realized that the negotiations at the roundtable were misinformed about the real bargaining power of each party and accepted agreements that overestimated the strength and popular support of the communists. When the public was allowed to express its preferences ... the established lie which underpinned communist-dominated official life quickly disappeared. The actors changed their priorities." See Josep Colomar and Margot Pascual. "The Polish Games of Transition." *Communist and Post-Communist Studies* 27, no. 3 (1994): 290.

are deterministic, whereas I suggest the impact of historical memory is a function of the agency of politicians. Finally, I suggest that history is an instrument rather than an independent causal factor.

This argument also challenges some aspects of rational choice theory. Rational choice approaches stipulate that political preferences are based on knowledge of one's political legitimacy. They fail to specify, however, how actors gauge their popular support. Most studies assume that preferences are exogenous. As Renwick (2006, p. 52) points out, "Rational choice analyses ... typically take the overall definition of choice situation and the options that actors perceive as given: they cannot account for the frames within which rational choices are made." Politicians are "cognitively rational in the sense that they change their beliefs about the world as a function of information they get" (Przeworski 1988, p. 44). The question of how remains unanswered, however.

Hungary: More Flexible Incumbents and the Memory of a Popular Anti-Regime Uprising

I propose two mechanisms, labelled here as "conservative reformer" and "public tolerance indicator," that updated the preferences of some members of the Communist Party in Hungary. The gradual shift in the use of 1956-related rhetoric within the Communist Party—from the conservative leaders to the reformist leaders—acted as the "conservative reformer" in Hungary. Historical memory, acting as a "public tolerance indicator." inspired two massive anti regime demonstrations and became a major indicator of the strength of the opposition.

The Memory of the 1956 Uprising as a "Conservative Reformer"

The memory of the 1956 uprising was closely related to the process of reforming the Hungarian Communist Party. Table 7.1. outlines the political developments and the role the historical memory of the uprising played in the events.

The memory of the 1956 uprising facilitated the process of bringing down the Hungarian Communist Party Secretary General Janos Kadar and increasing the popularity of Kardy Grosz. Kadar realized his role in crushing the 1956 revolution constituted a major political liability for him. His decision to cede power was connected to the legacy of 1956. Although the deteriorating economy and his ill health were concomitant factors, Kadar's decision was mainly dictated by his "deep-seated fear for having to account for his personal record"(Tokes 1996, p. 304). Tokes points out that: "Kadar could ill-afford the laying bare of his record. It is only in the last months of his life that he owed up to the crushing burden of his role in the deaths of Laszlo Rajk and Imre Nagy—he called it my personal tragedy—and of his error in summarily labelling the events of October 1956 as a counter-revolution" (Tokes 1996, p. 303). The New York Times (Reuters, 1989) reported that "the exhumation in March of the body of the leader of the 1956 rebellion, Imre Nagy, was a severe blow to Mr. Kadar" and implied that this event was responsible for the sudden deterioration of Kadar's mental and physical state. Ironically, Kadar died on the day when the Hungarian Supreme Court announced Nagy's full legal rehabilitation.

Table 7.1: The Impact of the Historical Uprisings and Corresponding Developments During the 1989 Transition in Hungary

Date	Political developments	Role of the 1956 events
May 22, 1988	General Secretary Janos Kádár is effectively removed from power. Kádár fears the legacy of his role in crushing the 1956 uprising.	Conservative reformer
January 1, 1988	Kádár's successor, Károly Grósz, publicly underscores his role as a Communist dissident in 1956.	Conservative reformer
February 10, 1989	Imre Pozsgay's interpretation that the 1956 revolt was a popular uprising leads to an extraordinary Central Committee meeting in which members agree to introduce a multi-party system.	Conservative reformer
March 15, 1989	The demonstration celebrating the anniversary of the 1848 revolution brings the opposition together.	Public tolerance indicator
June 16, 1989	The reburial of the 1956 revolutionary hero, Imre Nagy, demonstrates the opposition's strength. Many Communist Party members join the parade.	Public tolerance indicator and consevative reformer
June 23, 1989	The Central Committee Plenum topples Károly Grósz in the face of the massive turnout at the Nagy reburial.	Conservative reformer
June 13– September 19, 1989	As a result of the mass demonstrations commemorating the 1956 and 1848 revolutions, the Communist Party decides to make actual concessions to the opposition at the roundtable.	Conservative reformer
October 23, 1989	People turn up in great numbers to celebrate the thirty-third anniversary of the outbreak of the 1956 revolution.	Public tolerance indicator
March 25, 1990	Hungary holds its first free election.	Public tolerance indicator

The political career of Grosz, Kadar's successor, was also connected with the memory of 1956. Very early in the pre-transition period, Grosz made an effort to associate himself with the 1956 uprising. He used the occasion of a televised New Year's interview on January 1, 1988, to emphasize how he had been reprimanded for collaborating with radical university students in October 1956.[14] Grosz's

---

14 His narrative was correct but incomplete. While Grosz portrayed himself as a victim, he failed to acknowledge that his involvement with the insurgents was accidental at best. At the time of the uprising, he was an emissary of Rudolf

association with 1956 seems out of character, because he later opposed the rehabilitation of Imre Nagy and refused to interpret the 1956 events as an uprising, but rather as a counterrevolution. It is reasonable to conclude that Grosz used the 1956 rhetoric to sell his image to the public. A perceptive politician with a substantial experience in the public relations sector, he must have realized that a favourable attitude toward the 1956 events would increase his popularity. Charles Gati (1990, p. 131) observed: "The past may assist those who seek to escape from complex and often painful realities ... the silent [people], haunted by the memory of their passivity during the Communist era, may try to blot out that experience by identifying with the best and the bravest their history can offer."[15]

The memory of the 1956 events also facilitated the reformation of the Communist Party because it unleashed a rigorous debate about the regime's legitimacy. This was the third important manifestation of historical memory as a "conservative reformer." Imre Pozsgay, who made a shocking revelation in his January 28, 1989, interview with the popular radio program 168 Hours, started the discussion. Pozsgay reported on behalf of the Historical Subcommittee that the October 1956 rebellion was a popular uprising. The statement defied the official version, which held that the 1956 uprising had been a counterrevolution organized by a foreign country.

Foldvari, the first secretary of the Borsod County party committee. Foldvari, not Grosz, authorized the printing of a radical manifesto supporting the insurgents in the county's newspaper. When the revolution was crushed, Foldvari used Grosz as a scapegoat to avoid a life sentence in prison and accused him of publishing the manifesto. Having accidentally become an anti-regime activist, Grosz was expelled from the party. His alleged repression was short-lived as his party membership was subsequently restored and he was appointed a political supervisor of the Hungarian radio and TV programming.

15 Grosz's subsequent career downfall demonstrates that association with historical symbols brings popularity only when it is accompanied by actual commitments. Once Grosz started acting at variance with his pro-1956 rhetoric, he lost favor with the public. His resignation as prime minister in November 1988 was caused by the revelation that he wanted to introduce martial law in Hungary. Istvan Horvath, a distinct party reformist, revealed to his fellow Central Committee members that Grosz had asked him whether he would authorize the use of firearms by the police against environmental demonstrators in front of the parliamentary building (Tokes 1996, p. 296). When it became clear that Grosz preached peace but ordered violence and when his deeds started defying his interpretation of the 1956 uprising. Grosz lost his post.

According to the new interpretation, the 1956 protests expressed the Hungarian people's discontent with the system. The regime that forcefully crushed the uprising was therefore illegitimate. One Communist Party member observed: "The vast majority is dumbfounded, and not because they have heard the results of an academic research from the Historical Subcommittee, but because they feel that a pillar of the institutionalized political system is somehow based on 1956. And now they have the impression that this foundation is being removed from underneath" (Mihaly Jasso cited in Benziger 1989).

Pozsgay's historical interpretation was an open challenge to the Communist Party. The old Communist elite were at pains to gauge the right response. Signs of popular support for Pozsgay were ambiguous. 3,000 people withdrew from the party immediately after the broadcast. At the same time, 470 local organizations of the Communist party wrote letters to support Grosz (Dienstag 1996, p. 57). The conservative Communists did not want to expel a potentially popular politician, so they had to agree to Pozsgay's interpretation of the 1956 events. But an agreement that 1956 was a "popular uprising" meant the regime had crushed the will of its people. If it wanted to keep a popular politician in the party and preserve an air of legitimacy, the Communist Party had to compromise. The hard-liners took a middle-of-the-road view and stated that the events started as an uprising but ended as a counterrevolution. They decided not to punish Pozsgay and to introduce a multiparty system. A negotiating team was appointed to work with the opposition. These decisions indicated that the conservatives had made progress in "updating" their views.

Was historical memory coincidentally or causally related to the democratization of the Communist Party? Scholars agree that Pozsgay's interpretation facilitated the party's reformation because it amplified the gap between progressives and conservatives: "Some groups in the Party became more and more estranged from the core. A dividing issue was created during the re-evaluation of 1956" (Sajo 1996, p. 70). Several factors indicate the interview had an impact. First, the Central Committee session, where the decision to introduce a multiple-party system was made, was specifically convened to address Pozsgay's interview. Therefore, one can establish a causal connection insofar as the interpretation of the 1956 uprising opened a discussion forum. Second. Pozsgay explicitly associated the uprising with popular opinion. He stated that the committee's evaluation "approaches those of historians and public opinion and expresses the feeling of public opinion" (Reuters 1989). Third, according to the minutes of the Central Committee meeting, all members dealt simultaneously with "1956" and the question of a multiparty system (Nyyssönen 1999, p. 163).

The Memory of the 1956 and 1848 Uprisings as a "Public Tolerance Indicator"

The extraordinary meeting convened to discuss Pozsgay's interview was a necessary but insufficient step toward updating the incumbents' perceptions. Although the Communist members invited the opposition to roundtable negotiations, they were not planning to make meaningful concessions. A large segment of the Politburo believed the negotiations were a way to legitimize their decisions. Most Politburo members were still not aware of how limited their popular support was: "No one knew at that point what kind of change the masses would support. At that point, the three public power contests were still ahead. Perhaps, in those days, the possibility of a forceful reversal still existed and some day we may learn whether secret plans were made to liquidate the opposition and pacify the opposition by force, if needed" (Bruszt 1990, p. 368).

The memory of historical uprisings moderated the options of the Communist hard-liners by demonstrating the opposition's strength. Historical memory helped the opposition display its strength because it lowered the barriers to demonstrating. The cost of demonstrating at a historical rally was lower than the cost of demonstrating against the Communist government. People were less fearful of reprisal and turned up in greater numbers because of the demonstration's nature. In the face of the mass demonstrations, the Communists realized their most preferred outcome—preserving political power—was less probable than they had initially anticipated. The realization of the regime's limited support induced the hard-liners to make substantial political concessions.

The rally on March 15, 1989, was the first to impact the hardliners' willingness to compromise with the opposition. It commemorated the failed 1848 revolution against Habsburg rule. Apprehending the opposition's strength, the government wanted to celebrate the occasion with a unified demonstration. The opposition, however, invited the population to their own demonstration. The results were both surprising and categorical. The government's rally summoned only 20,000 to 30,000 people, while the opposition convened about 100,000 demonstrators. The parallel and competing demonstrations became institutionalized as "tests of strength" and, lacking parliamentary representation, a public manifestation of the popular will (Hofer 1991, p. 7).

Without official measurements of public support, such as elections, the historical rallies became the most accurate measurement. During the March 15, 1989 demonstration, people realized there were two different political alternatives and started asking, "Are you going to their demonstration or to ours?" The opposition also realized it had many followers and became aware of its new identity. The memory of 1848 outlined a space for contestation where the opposition took precedence. "It is precisely in the ritual's ability to hold both sides with their irreducible tension together that a key to its legitimacy can be found... It provided a space for contestation and contained the rivalry" (Ittzés 2005, p. 1).

The rally to rebury Nagy was the second manifestation of historical memory in its role as a "public tolerance indicator." Nagy was the 1956 revolutionary hero. He was briefly a prime minister during the 1956 revolution and is credited for announcing Hungary's withdrawal from the Warsaw Pact. When Soviet troops crushed the revolution, Nagy was arrested. His trial was ended and he was hanged by the Kadar regime. The 1989 reburial was a public negation of the regime's negation of Nagy. By the time of the rally, the hardliners had exhausted all means of marginalizing, criminalizing, or co-opting the opposition. They had only one option left — to incorporate themselves in the political space defined by the opposition. Many of them placed wreaths in front of Nagy's coffin.

Because it was clear this symbolic gesture did not suffice to gain credibility with the electorate, they also signed an agreement with the Opposition Roundtable (EKA), an umbrella of oppositional formations, to enter the trilateral negotiations. In this way, the public support that became clear through the demonstrations informed and updated the preferences of the incumbents.

> For the party's reform Communist leaders, it was now a race against time... Hundreds of thousands were likely to be in Heroes' Square on June 16, and a national audience would watch the funeral on television... So as to not blast the castle, they moved with uncharacteristic speed and solicitousness to reach agreement with the united opposition for direct and almost unconditional negotiations (Bruszt and Stark 1991, p. 227).

Most scholars agree the Nagy reburial affected the incumbents' preferences. Laszlo Kurti (1990, p. 8) writes: "The funeral ritual at Heroes' Square brought about not only the significance of historical symbols and dead heroes, but, equally important, the state's admission of failure... In the absence of a Hungarian Lech Walesa or Vaclav Havel to lead the opposition, the Hungarian elite turned to its historical roots. These 'undead' culture heroes, in particular Imre Nagy, were set against the living Communist foes, namely Janos Kadar and his follower Karoly Grosz." Timothy Garton Ash (1990, p. 47) wrote that historical memory functioned as a substitute for elections: "In Poland it was an election. In Hungary, it was a funeral: the funeral of Imre Nagy."

A host of other interpretations underscore the importance of historical memory as a "public tolerance indicator." Mass-mobilization theories argue that past uprisings provide the repertoire for mass demonstrations: "Hungary has a well-established tradition of street demonstrations and struggles (1956 in particular), which played a significant role during the power transfer of 1988-90" (Ekiert and Kubrik 1998, p. 575). An anthropological perspective connects the act of exhumation of revolutionary heroes with uncertainty and political power struggles: "I see dead bodies as one of the many vehicles through which people in post-socialist societies reconfigure their worlds of meaning, in the wake of... a profoundly disorienting change in their surroundings" (Verdery 1999, p. 50).

Karl Benziger (1989, p. 144) stated that the Imre Nagy funeral "reaffirmed the strength and solidarity of the community itself." Ash (1990, p. 55) reported that some observers of the funeral thought the "longer term impact of the event, and above all the nationwide televising of the event, could not be overstated... The most optimistic assessment came from the controversial Young Democrat Victor Orban. Imre Nagy's funeral would be to Hungary, he said, what the first visit of Pope John Paul II had been to Poland."

The only study that defies the utility of historical symbols is an analysis of the first post-Communist elections. "This study correctly points out that elections are a more reliable indicator of political legitimacy than historical memory: both the conservatives and the liberals failed to express the interests of the electorate, and instead played the game of politics of symbols that featured starkly drawn ideological contrasts" (Szelényi, Szelényi and Poster 1996, p. 466). However, it fails to consider that historical discourses were a necessary if imperfect substitute for electoral rhetoric during the transitional period.[16]

The Soviet Union: Greater Uncertainty of Perceptions and More Resilient Hard-Liners

While the Hungarian Communists continually readjusted their positions, some Soviet hard-liners failed to update their views. The conservatives' unwillingness to compromise was most evident in their decision to stage a coup d'état. On Sunday, August 19, 1991, eight high-ranking officials put General Secretary Mikhail Gorbachev under house arrest in his summer home in Foros in Crimea. They demanded that he sign a decree turning power over to Vice President Gennady Yanayev. Gorbachev refused to cooperate. The hard-liners announced a six-month state-of-emergency rule by

---

[16] Historical memory continues to play an important role in electoral campaigns in Hungary. The fiftieth anniversary of the 1956 revolution coincided with the 2006 parliamentary elections and the meaning of uprising once again became a primary campaign issue. All major political contenders, including the Hungarian Civic Union and the Hungarian Socialist Party, claimed to be heirs to the 1956 spirit.

decree. They ordered about 750 armoured vehicles on the streets of Moscow. The next day, Russian President Boris Yeltsin clambered atop an armoured truck outside the Russian White House to announce he would assume command. Yeltsin's appearance inspired protests throughout the country. On Tuesday, thousands of people built barricades and urged the military commanders to turn back. Troops started defending the protesters. On Tuesday afternoon, Yeltsin announced to the Russian parliament that some of the conspirators were fleeing to Vnukovo Airport. The conspirators were arrested and imprisoned. The coup ended after two days.

Many explanations of why the coup failed exist. Some claim the conspirators underestimated the probability that Gorbachev would not cooperate (Knight 2003; Taylor 2003). A second possible cause is the conspirators underestimated Yeltsin as a foe: "Betting that Yeltsin's authoritarian leanings and the animosity he nursed toward Gorbachev would be enough to make him putty in their hands. Kryuchkov said approximately the following: 'we will reach an agreement with Yeltsin, we will fix this problem without any measures beforetime" (Colton 2008, p. 46). A third explanation is that the plotters were disturbed by imminent signing of the Union Treaty. Other factors for the failed coup are the limited popular acceptance for the Communist regime, critical economic conditions, a no longer submissive army, and the lack of a determined leadership (Kramer 2003, p. 6).

Given that the coup's success was unlikely, the real puzzle is not so much why the conspiracy floundered but why the Communist hard-liners believed it would succeed. I suggest the plotters failed to correctly read four major reference points. First, the plotters did not interpret the massive demonstrations as indications of limited popular legitimacy. They believed instead that people were cither manipulated into protesting by cunning politicians or that the protesters constituted a non-representative part of the population. Second, the conspirators failed to update their perceptions in light of the unfavourable outcomes of elections and opinion polls. They perceived all indicators of limited popular legitimacy as a conspiracy meant to discredit them. Third, despite their recognition of the economically destitute, the conspirators insisted the planned economy model was remediable. Finally, the conspirators ignored the lessons generated by the fall of Communism in Eastern and Central Europe in 1989. They chose to concentrate on distant historical episodes when Communism thrived. Table 7.2. illustrates the differences between the reformists' and the hard-liners' perceptions. Communism thrived.

Table 7.2. Juxtaposition of the Communist Party Reformers' and Hard-liners' Perceptions of Various "Reference Points"

Reference points	Hard-liners' perception	Reformists' perception
Demonstrations	Manipulative politicians trick people into demonstrating.	Demonstrations are an expression of the public will.
	The protestors represent a minority of the population.	The demonstrations were massive.
Elections	Yeltsin won two elections because they were rigged.	The election of Yeltsin and Gorbachev proved that people supported democratic changes.
Army	The Soviet army is historically the guardian of national values. It can decide better than the people what is best for the country.	The army is demoralized and unprofessional. It should serve the people, not vice versa.
Economy	The economy is floundering because Gorbachev is an unapt leader.	The economy is floundering because Communism failed.
History	The three uprisings in the ex-Communist block (Hungary 1956, Czechoslovakia 1968, Poland 1981) show that people gradually learn to abide by the army.	The fall of Communism in Central Europe showed that regimes that are not backed by the people are doomed.
	The October Revolution was glorious.	It is wrong to adhere to the ideology of Communism's founders, because the world has changed.

Among the misperceptions that led to the coup, the biggest was the overestimation of the regime's legitimacy (Balzer 2005, p. 193). Gorbachev stated: "If the coup had happened a year and a half or two years earlier it might, presumably, have succeeded. But now society was completely changed... This is the plotters' biggest mistake — they did not realize that society was no longer what it used to be a few years before. The new democratic achievements of perestroika ... predetermined the plotters' defeat" (Gorbachev 1991, pp. 19-20). Gorbachev's advisor Anatoly Chernyaev (2000, p. 385) similarly believed "a fundamental change has occurred in society's attitude, the people themselves have changed. And this was the putschists' main miscalculation."

It is puzzling why the incumbents overestimated their public support, given that there were many signs of public discontent. According to Mark Beissinger (1998, p. 403), there were 2,177 violent and 6,644 nonviolent protest demonstrations in the Soviet Union between 1987 and 1992. In the wake of the August coup, the warning signs were even more distinct as there was a quantum leap in protests.[17] The plotters had several misconceptions that helped them misinterpret the extent of public support for their regime. They believed a handful of self-interested populists initiated the demonstrations, the discontented protesters were not representative of the population as a whole, and elections and opinion polls that favoured the opposition were rigged.

The Soviet hard-liners did not interpret the massive demonstrations as a "reference point"; they believed that self-interested authorities inspired the protests. Valentin Pavlov (1993, p. 23) wrote that "[central, republic, and local activists] took to isolation, separatism and nationalism as the main way to save themselves and their power." Vladimir Kryuchkov (1996, p. 6) agreed with Pavlov: "The separatist moods did not originate from the masses, they were initiated by nationalist and for some reasons anti-Soviet groups... Apart from the outbursts of nationalism and the fruitful ground for its manifestation created by the propagandistic efforts of antisocialist powers, the situation in the Baltics was relatively stable."

The hard-liners also believed the protesters represented only a tiny minority of the population. Kryuchkov wrote in his memoirs that "there were three groups in the regions of political tension. First, a group of about 5-10 percent actively expressed a negative

---

17 Here are a few pointers that, theoretically, should have made the plotters beware of the public discontent: The Soviet army cracked down on Azeri protesters in Baku on January 20, 1990, leaving sixty casualties. In April 1989 Soviet troops killed nineteen pro-independence demonstrators in Tbilisi, Georgia. In March 1990, the Lithuanian parliament passed unilaterally a declaration of independence. Ten months later, Soviet troops broke through a human cordon of about 1,000 protesters protecting the Lithuanian television center and killed fourteen people. Similar events occurred in Latvia, where the military took five casualties after usurping the Interior Ministry.

attitude to the Union and the socialist state. This part of the population... actively defended its positions, organized demonstrations. A second group of about 15-20 percent firmly defended the Union and the choice of socialism...The third group of approximately 70 percent behaved passively. ... A deeper analysis showed that this passive part of the population, without a doubt, in its bigger part tended to support the preservation of the Union" (Kryuchkov 1996, p. 6).

In other cases, hard-liners concentrated on the more favourable signals from the population. Dmitry Yazov, for example, believed Gorbachev's reelection as Soviet president with 71% of an uncontested ballot proved that he was unpopular: "The people, tired of bickering and extremely disappointed with their leader, would never rise in his [Gorbachev's] defence. The results of the first election of the Russian president spoke of the distrust in Gorbachev" (Ivashov 1992, p. 69). Other conservative incumbents avoided drawing conclusions from unfavourable opinion polls by insisting that they were manipulated. Pavlov (1993, p. 27) argued that Yeltsin won the Russian presidency because Gorbachev sabotaged the election. Similarly. Pavlov believed Yeltsin's election to the post of chairman of the Supreme Soviet at the congress of national deputies was rigged. He states in his memoirs that the support for Yeltsin's opponent, Ivan Polozkov, was greater, but Gorbachev forced him to withdraw his candidacy at the last minute (Pavlov 1993, pp. 25-26).

Why did the hard-liners consistently disregard otherwise obvious signs of a lack of popular support? One hypothesis is the success of crushing previous uprisings instilled confidence in the coup plotters. Ted Gurr (1988, p. 49) argues that the "successful use of coercion enhances leaders' assessment of its future utility." Another view purports that the conspirators were intrinsically immune to considerations of public opinion because they had the mentality of party bureaucrats:

> [The Politburo members] did not listen to anything, did not understand. Just horrid. . . Our Party leaders were absolutely innocent babies with respect to public opinion. They were brought up on propaganda. They read the newspapers Pravda and Izvestiya. They believed that the entire Soviet people, as

> one people, support them and so on. This was deeply implanted. So, knowing what people think about you. as general secretary, and if you aren't accepted by everyone — and moreover, sometimes it happens that more people don't accept you than those who do — a first reaction is that everything is a lie, some underhand practices (Arias-King 2005, p. 309).

A further factor underlying the hard-liners' misperceptions is that they have not experienced a local anti-regime popular uprising. The author's counterfactual hypothesis is the memory of a Soviet past anti-regime uprising could have fulfilled the same functions it did in Hungary — demonstrating the power of the opposition and starting the process of reforming the Communist Party. The Soviet hard-liners remembered the past uprisings in foreign countries, but rebellions in neighbouring countries do not have the same effect as local rebellions. At the same time, very few local Soviet protests rebelled against Communism per se. The struggle against the Soviet regime was subordinate to the struggle for national independence: "In spite of the widespread belief that the breakup of the USSR would evoke a violent struggle between supporters and opponents of the Soviet regime, violence over the issue of secession from the USSR was minimal" (Beissinger 1998, p. 406). In the absence of clearer reference points, the conservative politicians had difficulties assessing the distribution of power. Historical memory of an anti-regime uprising is not a necessary or sufficient condition of democratizing the regime's hard-liners. It can, however, underscore the impact of a debilitated army, nationalist sentiments, and other historical reference points.

Can the Memory of a Failed Uprising Affect the Perceptions of the Communist Incumbents during Transition?

The process of actors' preference formation during the transition from Communism has already been examined. Incumbents had difficulty estimating their popular legitimacy for two reasons. First, power holders in authoritarian regimes do not value public support, and second, the distribution of political power during transitions is uncertain. One factor that can increase the certainty of power distribution during transition is the memory of a past anti-regime uprising through the observation of two mechanisms. Historical memory functions as a "public tolerance indicator" by increasing the visibility of the oppositional strength. It provides a low-cost opportunity to demonstrate against the regime because the protest is indirect and the punishment less likely. This aspect of historical memory is especially important in young democracies where the opposition has been relatively inactive. The second mechanism through which historical memory affects the hard-liners' preferences is the "conservative reformer." Here the evolving interpretation of the past event fosters a process of self-examination within the Communist Party. This context enables the advancement of progressive members.

Historical memory's potential to democratize the perceptions of the Communist incumbents connects structural and actor-centred theories of democratization. Historical memory is important only if political actors choose to reminisce about it. The impact of historical memory varies according to the relative significance and availability of various structural reference points, however. Such reference points are the economic situation, the situation in neighbouring countries, the nature of civil protests, or the federal and ethnic composition of the state. In this sense, historical memory is a facilitating factor that, in conjunction with other conditions, can have important implications for updating and moderating the incumbents' stance.

Bibliography

Arias-King, F. (2005) The Correlation between Healthy and Ill Forces Is Not in Our Favour. Interview with Tatyana Zaslavskaya. *Demokratizatsiya* 13 (2), pp. 297-317. Available at: http://ariasking.com/files/DemZaslavskaya.pdf

Ash, T.G. (1990) *We the People: The Revolution of '89 Witnessed in Warsaw, Budapest, Berlin and Prague.* Cambridge: Penguin Books.

Balzer, H. (2005) Ordinary Russians? Rethinking August 1991. *Demokratizatsiya* 13 (2), pp. 193-218. Available at: https://doi.org/10.3200/DEMO.13.2.193-218.

Beissinger, M. (1998) Nationalist Violence and the State: Political Authority and Contentious Repertoires in the Former USSR. *Comparative Politics* 30 (4), pp. 401-422. Available at: https://doi.org/10.2307/422331.

Benziger, K.P. (1989) *Imre Nagy and the Unsettled Past: The Politics of Memory in Contemporary Hungary*. Available at: https://www.yumpu.com/en/document/view/7233026/imre-nagy-and-the-unsettled-past-the-politics-of-the-new-school [Accessed: November 22, 2022].

Bruszt, L. (1990) 1989: The Negotiated Revolution in Hungary. *Social Research* 57 (2), pp. 365-387. Available at: https://www.researchgate.net/publication/283694694_1989_The_Negotiated_Revolution_in_Hungary.

Bruszt, L., Stark, D. (1991) Remaking the Political Field in Hungary: From the Politics of Confrontation to the Politics of Competition. *Journal of International Affairs* 45 (1), pp. 201-245. Available at: https://www.jstor.org/stable/24357065.

Bunce, V. (2003) Rethinking Recent Democratization: Lessons from the Postcommunist Experience. *World Politics* 55 (2), pp. 167-192. Available at: http://www.jstor.org/stable/25054217.

Bunce, V., Csanadi, M. (1993) Uncertainty in the Transition: Post-Communism in Hungary. *East European Politics and Societies* 7 (2), pp. 240-275. Available at: https://doi.org/10.1177/0888325493007002003.

Chernyaev, A. (2000) *My Six Years with Gorbachev*. University Park: Pennsylvania State Press.

Colomar, J. (1995) Strategies and Outcomes in Eastern Europe. *Journal of Democracy* 6 (2), pp. 74-85. Available at: http://dx.doi.org/10.1353/jod.1995.0026.

Colomar, J., Pascual, M. (1994) The Polish Games of Transition. *Communist and Post-Communist Studies* 27 (3), pp. 275-294. Available at: http://dx.doi.org/10.1016/0967-067X(94)90015-9.

Colton, T.J. (2008) *Yeltsin: A Life*. New York: Basic Books.

Dienstag, J. (1996) "'The Pozsgay Affair": Historical Memory and Political Legitimacy. *History and Memory* 8 (1), pp. 51-66. Available at: http://www.jstor.org/stable/25618697.

Di Palma, G. (1990) *To Craft Democracies: An Essay on Democratic Transitions*. Berkeley: University of California Press.

Ekiert, G., Kubrik, J. (1998) Contentious Politics in New Democracies: East Germany, Hungary, Poland, and Slovakia, 1989-93. *World Politics* 50 (4), pp. 547-581. Available at: https://doi.org/10.1017/S004388710000736X.

Elster, J. (1996) *The Roundtable Talks and the Breakdown of Communism*. Chicago: University of Chicago Press.

Gati, C. (1990) East-Central Europe: The Morning After. *Foreign Affairs* 69 (5), pp. 129-145. Available at: https://doi.org/10.2307/20044605.

Gorbachev, M. (1991). *The August Coup: The Truth and the Lessons.* New York: HarperCollins.

Gurr, T. (1988) War, Revolution, and the Growth of the Coercive Stale. *Comparative Political Studies* 21 (1), pp. 45-65. Available at: https://doi.org/10.1177/0010414088021001003.

Hofer, T. (1991). *The Demonstration of March 15, 1989, in Budapest: A Struggle for Public Memory.* Program on Central and Eastern European Working Paper Series, No. 16. Centre for European Studies. Available at: https://fdocuments.net/document/the-demonstration-of-march-15-1989-in-budapest-a-struggle-for-public-memory.html [Accessed: February 2, 2023].

Ittzés, G. (2005) Ritual and National Self-Interpretation: The Nagy Imre Funeral. *Religion and Society in Central and Eastern Europe* 1 (1), pp. 1-19. Available at: https://rascee.net/index.php/rascee/article/view/5/6.

Ivashov, L and Marshal Yazov. (1992) *Rokovoi Avgust 1991*. Moscow: Mujestvo.

Kamm, H. (1988) Hungarian Party Replaces Kadar with his Premier. *The New York Times*. Available at: https://www.nytimes.com/1988/05/23/world/hungarian-party-replaces-kadar-with-his-premier.html [Accessed: February 2, 2023].

Kernell, S.I. (2000) Life Before Polls: Ohio Politicians Predict the 1828 Presidential Vote. *PS: Political Science and Politics* 33 (3), pp. 569-574. Available at: https://doi.org/10.2307/420860.

Kitschelt, H. (1993) Review: Comparative Historical Research and Rational Choice Theory: The Case of Transitions to Democracy. *Theory and Society* 22 (3), pp. 413-427. Available at: http://www.jstor.org/stable/657740.

Kitschelt, H.P (2003) Accounting for Post-Communist Regime Diversity: What Counts as a Good Cause? In Ekiert, G., Hanson, S. (eds), *Capitalism and Democracy in Central and Eastern Europe: Assessing the Legacy of Communist Rule.* Cambridge: Cambridge University Press. Available at: https://scholars.duke.edu/display/pub1021979 [Accessed: February 2, 2023].

Knight, A. (2003) The KGB, Perestroika, and the Collapse of the Soviet Union. *Journal of Cold War Studies* 5 (1), pp. 67-93. Available at: https://www.jstor.org/stable/26925261.

Kramer, M. (2003) Special Issue: The Collapse of the Soviet Union (Part 1). *Journal of Cold War Studies* 5 (1), pp. 3-16. Available at: https://www.jstor.org/stable/26925259.

Kryuchkov, V. (1996) *Lichnoe Delo*. Moscow: Olymp.

Kubik, J. Linch, A. (2006) The Original Sin of Poland's Third Republic: Discounting "Solidarity" and its Consequences for Political Reconciliation. *Polish Sociological Review* 153, pp. 9-38. Available at: http://www.jstor.org/stable/41274951.

Kuran, T. (1995) The Inevitability of Future Revolutionary Surprises. *American Journal of Sociology* 100 (6), pp. 1,528-1,532. Available at: https://doi.org/10.1086/230671.

Kurti, L. (1990) People vs the State: Political Rituals in Contemporary Hungary. *Anthropology Today* 6 (2), pp. 9-38. Available at: http://dx.doi.org/10.2307/3033002.

Kwiatkowski, P. (1992) Opinion Research and the Fall of Communism: Poland 1981-1990. *International Journal of Public Opinion Research* 4 (4), pp. 358-374. Available at: https://doi.org/10.1093/ijpor/4.4.358.

Lipset, S.M. (1981) *Political Man: The Social Basis of Politics*. Baltimore: Johns Hopkins University Press.

Mahoney, J. (2000). Path Dependence in Historical Sociology. *Theory and Society* 29 (4), pp. 507-548. Available at: http://www.jstor.org/stable/3108585.

Merkel, W. (1999) *System transformation: An Introduction to the Theory and Empiricism of Transformation Research*. Opladen: Leske und Budrich.

Moore, B. (1993) *Social Origins of Dictatorship and Democracy: Lord and Peasant in the Making of the Modern World*. Boston: Beacon Press.

Nyyssönen, H, (1999) *The Presence of the Past in Politics: "1956" after 1956 in Hungary*. Laukaa: Sophi Press.

O'Donnell, G., Schmitter, P.C., Whitehead, L. (1986) *Transitions from Authoritarian Rule: Tentative Conclusions about Uncertain Democracies*. Baltimore: Johns Hopkins University Press.

Pavlov, V. (1993) *Avgust Iznutri: Gorbachev Putch*. Moscow: Delovoimir.

Przeworski, A. (1988) Democracy as a Contingent Outcome of Conflicts. In Elster, I., Slagstad, R. (eds), *Constitutionalism and Democracy*. Cambridge: Cambridge University Press.

Renwick, A. (2006) Why Hungary and Poland differed in 1989: The role of medium-term frames in explaining the outcomes of democratic transition. *Democratization* 13 (1), pp. 15-36. Available at: https://doi.org/10.1080/13510340500378233.

Reuters (1989). Hungary, in Turnabout, Declares '56 Rebellion a Popular Uprising. *The New York Times*. Available at: https://www.nytimes.com/1989/01/29/world/hungary-in-turnabout-declares-56-rebellion-a-popular-uprising.html [Accessed: February 2, 2023].

Sajó A.(1996) The Roundtable Talks in Hungary. In: Elster J, editor. *The Roundtable Talks and the Breakdown of Communism.* Chicago: University of Chicago Press, pp. 69-98.

Starr, H. (1991) Democratic Dominoes: Diffusion Approaches to the Spread of Democracy in the International System. *Journal of Conflict Resolution* 35 (2), pp. 356-81. Available at: https://doi.org/10.1177/0022002791035002010.

Szelényi, S., Szelényi, I., Poster, W.R. (1996) Interests and Symbols in Post-Communist Political Culture: The Case of Hungary. *American Sociological Review* 61 (3), pp. 466-477. Available at: https://doi.org/10.2307/2096359.

Taylor, B.D. (2003) The Soviet Military and the Disintegration of the USSR. *Journal of Cold War Studies* 5 (1), pp. 17-66. Available at: https://www.jstor.org/stable/26925260.

Tokes, R. (1996) *Hungary's Negotiated Revolution: Economic Reform, Social Change, and Political Succession.* Cambridge: Cambridge University Press.

Przeworski, A. (1991) *Democracy and the Market: Political and Economic Reforms in Eastern Europe and Latin America.* London: Cambridge University Press.

Verdery, K. (1999) *The Political Lives of Dead Bodies: Reburial and Post-Socialist Change.* New York: Columbia University Press.

Welsh, H. (1994) Political Transition Processes in Central and Eastern Europe. *Comparative Politics* 26 (4), pp. 379-394. Available at: http://dx.doi.org/10.2307/422022.

8 Verbally Induced Uncertainty[18]

The book has so far contended that what politicians say can largely impact the perceptual uncertainty experienced by the public. In the example given in the introduction, it was suggested that the media allegation that the former Bulgarian prime minister has kept money, guns and gold bars, would have gone two separate ways if the alleged Prime minister had denied the allegations, as he did, and if he had not denied them. Denials infuse the public space with uncertainty, or at least they make it more likely that the observers, who by default do not have access to complete information, are more prone to wonder about the veracity of the allegations. Verbal uncertainty affects perceptual uncertainty.

Figure 8.1: Relations between Constraints of Blame Avoidance Strategies, Verbal Uncertainty and Perceptual Uncertainty

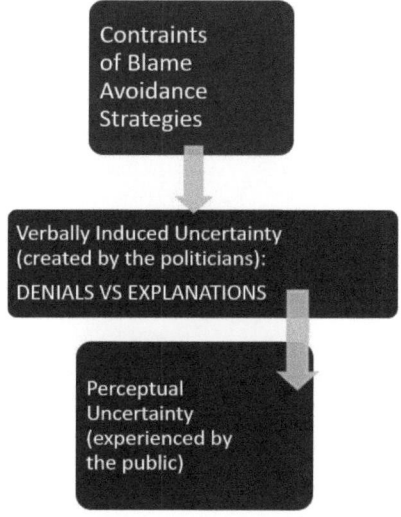

---

[18] This chapter appeared originally as Dimova, Gergana. 2019. *Government Responses to Media Allegations: Comparison between an Established and a Managed Democracy.* Global Media Journal (Russian Edition) 9 (2). It has been partially modified and complemented here. It is reprinted here with the permission of Global Media Journal and the agreement of Ibidem.

If verbally induced uncertainty is arguably so impactful in terms of perceptual uncertainty, as it indeed has the power to force the public to be in two minds, what are the determinants of verbal uncertainty? Are politicians constrained by the degree to which they can deny alleged wrongdoing, and if they are, what are the parameters of these constraints? This is the central inquiry of this chapter. Based on a dataset of 692 accusations containing 1,890 articles published between 1995 and 2005 in Germany and Russia, the chapter establishes that the verbal creation of uncertainty is constrained by the nature of the wrongdoing (misconduct versus incompetence), the identity of the accuser (media or the political opposition), as well as the existence of a formal investigation.

The specific "puzzle" that this chapter seeks to resolve is what is the nature of the constraints and the causes of the very different blame avoidance responses of government officials, who have been alleged of wrongdoing, in Germany and Russia.

Figure 8.2: Government Responses to Public Allegations in Germany and Russia (as a percentage of all allegations)

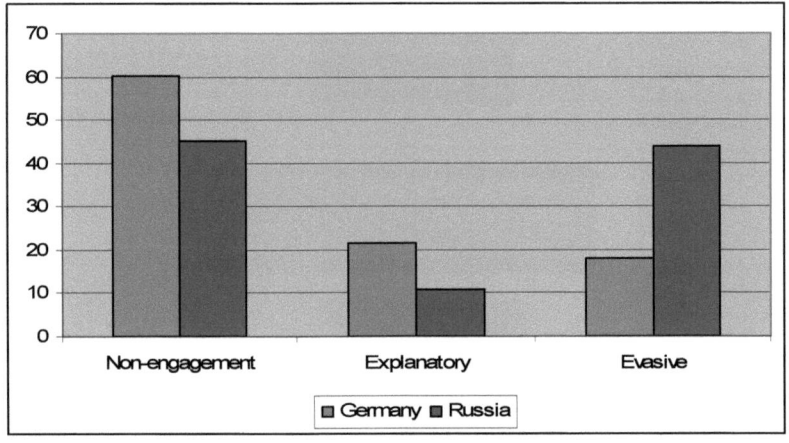

N=692

How is Blame Avoidance Linked to Uncertainty?

Verbal responses can significantly increase and decrease uncertainty in any political situation. Politicians' spin and blame avoidance techniques may not be able to change reality, but they can change the perception of reality. Even the most outrageous claims, when repeated a few times, can start creating doubts. It takes time for claims to be fact-checked, and even when they are fact-checked, the fact-checking itself can be perceived as biased. As the proverb goes, "Throw enough mud at the wall, and some of it will stick." The most obvious example of misleading information is the so-called fake news. Although the fake news is created by the media, and journalists carry the main responsibility for it, politicians can peddle fake news, or they can create them by making misleading statements. Psychologists have long recognised the "correspondence of general measures of perceived uncertainty to levels of message quality" (Gifford, Bobbitt and Slocum 1979, p. 458).

Given the huge power of verbal statements to create uncertainty in the minds of the public, it is befuddling that the relationship between verbal responses and uncertainty has not been systematically theorised. The limited scholarship on the subject mainly analyses how people perceive verbal information under uncertainty, but it does not target the opposite link, namely how verbal information creates uncertainty. For example, it is believed that people are more likely to believe misinformation about the coronavirus, when they are uncertain (De Witte 2020). Some scholars hypothesize that politicians are deliberately ambiguous on policy issues so as to attract more voters (Shepsle 1972). Scarcity of information can also contribute to uncertainty. Wedeen (2018) argues that Facebook's decision in 2014 to shut down pages connected to the Syria uprising may have caused a lot of uncertainty about the situation in the country.

Understanding government responses to public allegations is crucial because the executive spin game could increase public uncertainty about any issue significantly. Mikhail Khodorkovsky, one of Russia's wealthiest oligarchs and a prisoner for 10 years, cited as an example Putin's blame game after the Malaysia Airlines flight MH17 was downed over Ukraine in 2014. [19] According to Khodorkovsky, the presidential administration first denied that the

---

19 Khodorkovsky shared this observation at a talk in the UK Parliament in 2018.

plane was brought down, then it said that it was brought down but not by a missile; then it said that it was brought down by a missile but that the missile was not Russian; then it said that it was a Russian missile, but the Russians did not launch it. It is important to understand that the stakes behind this verbal equilibristic could be instrumental for creating or maintaining doubt, uncertainty and misinformation.

The logic of this chapter reinforces Beck's (1992) idea that there is a very large social and interpretative element in recognising, accepting and managing modernisation. Specifically, it argues that some dangers, misconduct and blunders are inherently open to interpretation. According to Beck, the nature of uncertainty arises because: (1) modernisation creates dangers in that it severs the equation between the people who produces dangers, such as pollution, atomic bombs and deforestation, and the people who may be affected by them. Because of this "distance" between the dangers themselves and the people who stand to be exposed to them, it is very hard to ascertain the precise degree of danger. Here is where the second factor comes in: (2) science is no longer perceived as "value neutral" and not directly related to the people producing the dangers. It no longer delivers the "so-called 'neutral' figures, information, or explanations which are to serve as the 'unbiased' basis for decisions on the broadest variety of interests. Which interests they select, however, on whom or what they project the causes, how they interpret the problems of society, what sort of potential solutions they bring into view — these are anything but neutral decisions" (Beck 1992, p. 174). Discrediting the objectivity of science opens a space for contestation of values, such as how the side effects of pollution should be managed across classes and localities. This space for contestation in turn opens the leeway for blame games. Although Beck's study of risks and uncertainty does not explicitly outline the importance of blame games, blame avoidance is implicit:

> Everywhere the spotlight in search of a cause [for deforestation] falls, fire breaks out, so to speak, and the hastily assembled and poorly equipped "argumentation fire company" must try to put it out with a powerful stream of counterarguments, and save whatever can still be saved. Those who find

themselves in the public pillory as risk producers refute the charges as well as they can, with the aid of a 'counter-science' gradually becoming institutionalized in industry, and attempt to bring in other causes and thus other originators. The picture reproduces itself. Access to the media becomes crucial. The insecurity within industry intensifies: no one knows who will be struck next by the anathema of ecological morality. Good arguments, or at least arguments capable of convincing the public, become a condition of business success. Publicity people, the 'argumentation craftsmen', get their opportunity in the organization (Beck 1992, p. 32 -italics are mine).

It is this "argumentation fire company" and these "argumentation craftsmen" that this chapter seeks to throw light on. But it takes this argument to a new level by quantifying and systematizing the work of the "argumentation craftsman." Specifically, it inquires whether the argumentation has any limits to it. Can anybody say anything about any type of danger? Or is this "argumentation", or blame game, constrained by other forces. In Beck's book, the very nature of modernization and its side effects are unclear, and because of this lack of clarity, blame games ensue. He gives the example of Brazil inviting many polluting enterprises to produce environmentally harmful products in the Brazilian coastal marsh. Yet when the deleterious consequences of this move became apparent, the government and the manufacturers blamed it all on the people who were getting sick, not on the industries they have ushered in: "The main causes of disease are malnutrition, alcohol and cigarettes', the spokesman for Pegropras says. "The people are already ill when they come from Copatao," agrees Paulo Figueiredo, boss of Union Carbide, "and if they get worse, they blame it on us. That's simply illogical" (Beck 1992, p. 43).

It is important to understand that risks and uncertainties can be socially embedded and verbally characterized. But is there a link between the uncertainties, the conditions under which they arise, and the verbal responses, which characterize them? The chapter sets out to discover what factors affect executive responses in the media. Do government officials formulate their responses in a vacuum? Or are they constrained by certain factors? In other words, if someone wants to obfuscate muddle an issue, or create counter- arguments that do so, and eventually create uncertainty, are these verbal techniques delimited? While Beck talks about the facts that the subjectivity of science and the lack of clear side effects of the dangers of modernisation give leeway to seemingly unlimited scope for blame avoidance and blame shifting, this chapter analyzes the precise relationship between the nature of the misconduct and the type of blame avoidance.

Research on this subject has initially underscored the importance of "negativity bias," a notion that incumbents prefer to keep silent rather than address an allegation (Weaver1986). It has also revolved around the question whether the nature of the allegation — policy failure or a moral misconduct — could open avenues for different spinning strategies (Boin et al 2010). This early research has been criticised for its implicit linearity, being too static and for ignoring contextual factors (Hinterleitner 2017). These criticisms have been addressed by an interdisciplinary mix of literatures, such as situational crisis communication, contingency theory, public relations, blame-avoidance (Hood 2014; Boin, Hart and McConnell 2009; Weaver 1986), crisis management (Boin et al 2010) and even deliberative theory (Habermas 2006). As the sheer number of theoretical approaches indicates, the contextual factors vary widely. They most generally range from the historical context to the institutional context to the personal context. These three types of factors are expected to shape the way incumbents make a case for themselves in the media and react to various phenomena.

The chapter analyses the various techniques for blame avoidance. In the context of studying the perceptual uncertainty of the public, these techniques are important because various spinning blames create various degrees of uncertainty. Various blame strategies have the potential to create uncertainty to a different degree. While future research should explore which verbal responses create more confusion and uncertainty in the public, studying the types of responses constitutes worthwhile first step in that regard.

This question "what are the government responses in the media?" has suffered from an abundance of typologies. The multiple coding schemes of government blame avoidance strategies ranges from coding anticipatory versus reactive (Sulitzeanu-Kenan and Hood 2006), presentational versus agency-related responses (Hood, Jennings and Copeland 2016), or strategies related to managing blame versus managing information (McGraw 1991). These formulations of government responses have existed in parallel but not in conversation with each other. Thus, multiple coding schemes have made comparison across countries or across studies very difficult. In essence, they have obscured the "puzzle" of government responses. In the last two decades, however, the literature has forged a fragile but significant consensus to keep sight of the main inquiry, namely whether the responses that the incumbents provide make them more accountable to the public or not (Hood, Jennings and Copeland 2016). The present article continues this trend of narrowing the criteria according to the answerability dimension by reducing government responses to three main types: keep silent, accept blame and deny blame.

What Factors Constrain Verbally Induced Uncertainty?

Primary Causal Variables Affecting Government Responses: "volume of allegations" and "type of allegation"

Two primary causal variables affecting blame avoidance strategies are the "volume" (Weaver 1986) or "negativity" of news coverage (Hood 2010; Sulitzeanu-Kenan 2010) and the "nature of the allegation." The notion of negativity bias constitutes a central premise and posits that the government's chief priority is to avoid blame rather than claim credit. The rationale is that the public rewards success four times less than it punishes wrongdoing (Weaver 1986).

The importance of the "nature of the allegation" as a factor influencing government responses has increased. In earlier writings, the nature of the allegation is deemed less consequential because incumbents' strategies were thought to be entirely the verbal making of the incumbents themselves. Edelman (1988, p. 31) argued that "a policy failure, like all news developments, is a creation of the language used to depict it" and Boin et al (2010) view crisis responses as "framing contests." In contrast, Brändström and Kuipers (2003) take a more evidence-based approach to allegations and suggest that the choice of strategies depends on the failures themselves.

More specifically, government strategies are affected by considerations whether the fiasco violates crucial norms, relates to high-level officials, and whether the failure is on systematic or an individual level. Bolstering the importance of the nature of the crisis further, Bovenset et al (1999, p. 145) argue that the "observability" of the alleged wrongdoing is important. The authors distinguish between policy fiascos, such as natural disasters, which are observed, and political fiascos, which are construed. Furthermore, policy fiascos put the blame on the government as it was not misfortune but mismanagement that has brought on the bad consequences. Further research on the type of allegation distinguishes between the subjective and objective dimensions of the crisis, and crises with endogenous versus exogenous causes (Boin, Hart and McConnell 2009, p. 100). McConnell (2003) differentiates between the level of secrecy, the threat, the time horizons and the imminence of the crisis (sudden, creeping, chronic crisis). Djerf-Pierre, Ekström and Johansson (2013) discern between a moral scandal and a policy failure.

Context-Specific Variables Affecting Verbal Uncertainty

Early research on government responses has been criticised for being "widely acknowledged" to be "scattered and unconcentrated, and that, for the most part, it neglects both contextual factors and comparative research" (Hinterleitner and Sager 2015, p. 140). More specifically, communication scholarship has been faulted for disregarding institutional constraints and interactional factors. It has also come under attack for following a linear logic of sequence. A few critics have lamented the absence of comparative research, which only exacerbates the above shortcomings. These criticisms have been addressed fully or partially by a second generation of research, which has fully embraced the value of contextualising the causal factors. This second wave of research has evolved by contextualising the actor-specific and environment-specific factors exerting an influence on government responses (Hinterleitner and Sager 2015; Hinterleitner 2017).

Zooming in on the contextual factors, we note that actor-specific factors consider the leadership style of the actors (Boin et al

2010) and the ordering of the agents' preferences (Sulitzeanu-Kenan and Hood 2005). Game-theoretical insights explain how government ministers weigh in the trade-off between the benefits of appearing responsive in dismissing an alleged minister versus the benefits of appearing loyal to the prime-minister's appointees (Berlinski, Dewan and Dowding 2012). Some theorists have shifted attention from the government to the accuser. Hood et al (2009) incorporate the identity of the accuser by pointing out that if the incumbent is alleged by the government's own party or by a member of the government, then the allegation is perceived as a less legitimate and credible threat. In this vein of research, Dimova (2012; 2013) discusses the costs and benefits of making accusations for alleged incumbents. The benefits could be symbolic or monetary, while the costs are shaped by a myriad of factors, such as informal media practices, defamation laws, the strength of journalistic associations, and relations with the Secret Services, which possess compromising materials.

Research on context-specific (rather than actor-specific) drivers of government responses has proliferated in several directions. Earlier writings highlight the impact of causality, responsibility or blameworthiness (Shaver and Drown 1986). Further context-specific factors pertain to the networks within which actors are situated (Moynihan 2012) and the institutional advantages some actors enjoy in dispersing blame (Brändström and Kuipers 2003). Habermas's (2006) theory of communicative action adds to that research agenda by underscoring the interactive character of crisis responses. Situational crisis management contributes to context-specific factors by evaluating intensifying factors, such as a history of similar past crises or a negative prior reputation, because they are likely to "intensify" attributions of the organization's crisis responsibility (Coombs 2004). Insights from the field of public relations contextualises the causes of incumbents' strategies by integrating the impact of public perceptions (Jin and Hong 2010) and the type of the medium on which the allegations and the responses are delivered (Schultz, Utzand and Göritz 2011; Liu and Fraustino 2014). Contingency theory demonstrates how the timing of responses affects their public perception (Jin and Cameron 2007).

Of particular interest here are the institutional conditions under which blame avoidance unfolds. The literature posits three types of connections between blame avoidance strategies and institutional factors. The first argument suggests that the institutional setting structures the way that blame is perceived by the public. This rationale dates to Powell and Whitten's (1993) insight that voters are not going to blame all governments equally for bad economic performance. The authors designed the "clarity of responsibility" index, which posits that voters will attribute responsibility differently, depending on whether there is a coalitional government, presidential regime, divided government, etc. This insight about the institutional context of attributing blame has been largely corroborated (Anderson 2000; Lewis-Beck, Nadeau and Elias 2008). A second connection posits that the executives can avoid some of the blame for unpopular welfare policies if they frame these policies in a particular way, which is constrained by institutional factors. The third type of relationship between institutions and blame avoidance is posited by Brändström and Kuipers (2003), who suggest that the type of institutions provide various opportunities for government officials alleged in media scandals to disperse blame.

Formulating the Hypotheses Linking Contextual and Primary Constraints and Verbal Uncertainty

Out of the many possible variables that could possibly impact on verbally induced uncertainty, the chapter focuses on comparing the relative explanatory power of the "nature of the allegation," the "type of accuser" and "the presence of an investigation into the media allegation" as drivers of evasive versus explanatory responses. It is hypothesized that the relative significance of the nature of the accusation and the identity of the accuser would differ in Germany and Russia. In Germany, the nature of the accusation would be a more important factor impacting government responses because attacking journalists or members of the opposition is not a sustainable option. The strategy of counterattacks is risky and costly. It could backfire because both the opposition and the media in an established democracy are credible institutions with long history. Thus, the only "wriggle room" for the incumbents is to make use of the "elasticity" and hidden character of misconduct allegations. The German officeholders would be more likely to be evasive when accused of misconduct rather than corruption because misconduct charges are less observable and harder to prove. We propose the following hypothesis:

H2: *The "nature of the allegation" is a more impactful factor for government responses in an established democracy, while the "identity of the accuser" is more impactful in a managed democracy.*

As argued above, the variation in the observability and consequences of various types of allegations open the allegation to politicisation and therefore to various responses (Bovens et al 1999). Building on these advances in theoretical research, which consider the nature of the allegation, we distinguish between incompetence charges and misconduct charges. This distinction structures and solicits specific government responses by defining the room for blame avoidance. Incompetence charges are harder to deny than misconduct charges for three main reasons: (1) evidence of incompetence or a policy failure is easier to find; (2) the consequences of incompetence charges are more visible to the public than the consequences of corruption or personal misconduct and (3) the consequences of incompetence are easier to evaluate because they are less subject to moral judgement. For example, incompetence charges, such as failed government's attempt to stop a terrorist incident, are easier to prove than a minister's marital infidelity. In another instance, the misconduct allegation that German chancellor Kohl accepted illegal party financing for the CDU is more liable to contention than the allegation that there was infected meat on the market shelves. Furthermore, the negative effects of illegal party financing are more open to moral judgement than the negative effects of eating infected meat. Based on these ruminations, we suggest the following hypothesis:

H3: *Corruption allegations, rather than charges of incompetence, are more likely to elicit evasive responses in an established democracy.*

Unlike in Germany, in Russia, the identity of the accuser would be a powerful causal factor. We suggest that the opposition and the media constitute two major categories of accusers. They have a different status and operate on the basis of a quite different political constituency, which is likely to be relevant to government responses. First, the media and the opposition differ in regard to the mechanisms they have at their disposal to elicit responses from the government. Their claims have various degrees of institutional "embeddedness." The media are an informal accuser and the weight of their accusation hinges on the approval of the public and the propensity of other institutions to take the claim seriously. By contrast, the opposition has a formalised and institutionalised way to assert their claims in parliament. It can use parliamentary inquiry or parliamentary committees to follow up on their criticism. Consequently, the government may be more inclined to discard media allegations and take oppositional allegations seriously.

Second, the media and the opposition have different legitimacy as makers of the accusations. The opposition is elected, the media are not. The opposition is considered to be representative. By contrast, the criticisms of the media represent the views of the editorial staff or the owners of the media outlet. Furthermore, the media are not accountable, whereas the opposition is accountable to the electorate at the next elections. In addition, it is not clear what motivates the media and the opposition to criticise the government publicly. The opposition's job is to watch for the public interest and monitor the government. The media, on the other hand, seek to make monetary profits as well. Because of their differing status in terms of legitimacy, accountability, representativeness and motivation, media and oppositional allegations are poised to create different leeway for government strategies. The following hypothesis is proposed:

H4: *Allegations made by journalists rather than the opposition are more likely to elicit evasive responses in a managed democracy.*

The chapter builds upon the literature arguing that institutional factors matter for the blame avoidance game. However, it adds a fourth rationale to the existing three connections between institutional settings and blame avoidance outlined above. It argues that the presence of an investigation affects the leeway for denying wrong-doing. The motivation behind it is that formal investigations have more authority and power to prove crimes, such as subpoena witnesses and demand written documentation than any other channel. Knowing that their misconduct or corruption is more likely to be found out through an official outlet, it would be harder for incumbents to deny the wrong-doing. Of course, the impact of the type of investigation on government responses would differ across regime types. In authoritarian regimes, the legislative body is largely impotent, which means that a parliamentary investigation is less likely to find any wrong-doing and thus the authorities would be less likely to be scared into admitting blame. The prosecutor general in Russia, on the other hand, is sometimes an extended arm of the executive, and the incumbents are more likely to be affected. The direction of the effect of a prosecutorial investigation on the likelihood of denying blame would differ, depending on which arm of the government the prosecutor favours and which arm is alleged in the behaviour. Conversely, in a democratic regime, the opposition is stronger, parliamentary investigations into media allegations would have more legitimacy and power, and consequently, the executive members would be less likely to deny the blame. These ruminations result in the following hypothesis:

H5: *Incumbents are less likely to engage in evasive tactics if there is institutional investigation of the media allegation.*

Results

General Observations

In regard to the first causal variable, the type of allegation, Germany and Russia differ because incompetence allegations dominate in Germany (86%) whereas both types of allegations feature in fairly equal measures in Russia (56% vs. 44%) (figure 8.3).

Figure 8.3: Distribution of Incompetence and Misconduct Charges in Russia and Germany

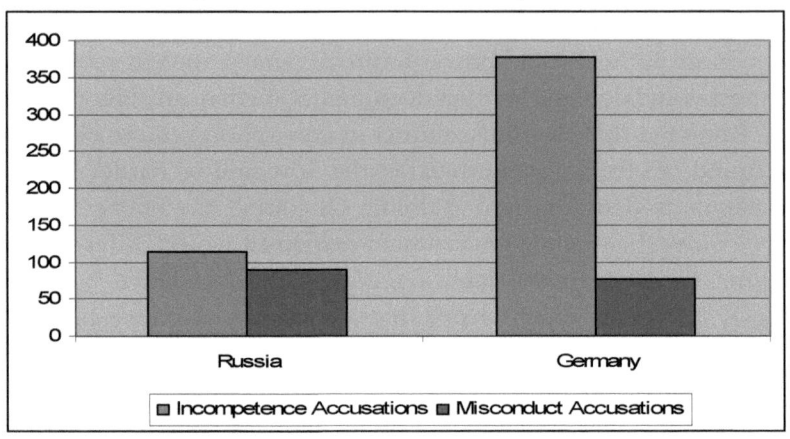

N=692

Germany and Russia also show variation on the second causal factor, i.e., the identity of the accuser. In Germany, the most active critic of the government in the media is the opposition. In Russia, the most active critic of the government in the media is the media (figure 8.4).

Figure 8.4: Distribution of the Types of Accusers in Russia and Germany

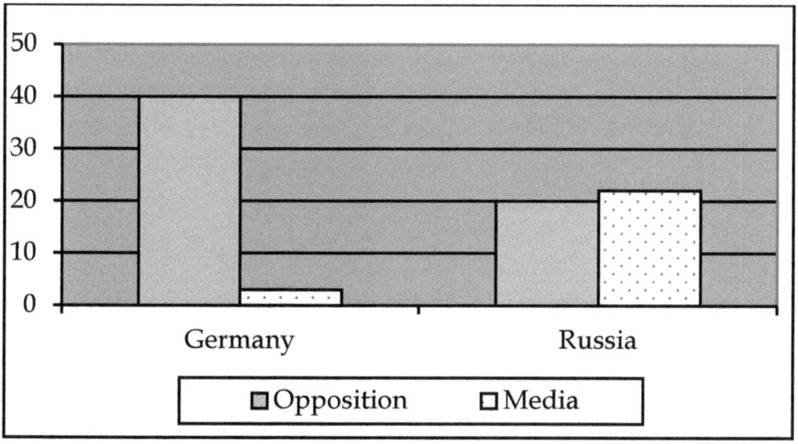

[Bar chart showing Opposition and Media accusers for Germany and Russia]

N=692

The first hypothesis, which proposed that government officials are more likely to give explanatory responses to media allegations in an established rather than in a managed democracy, is supported. The findings show that the Russian government is indeed more likely to adopt evasive, sometimes even quite aggressive, responses to media allegations, whereas the German government is more likely to adopt defensive, explanatory strategies. Defensive strategies that are prevalent in Germany are supposedly more conducive to democratic accountability because they provide the public with useful information. By contrast, the Russian government is significantly less inclined to defend its positions and explain its actions in response to public allegations. We find no examples where the Russian government confessed or apologized, as their German counterparts did on occasion.

The relation between the country, on the one hand, and the three categories of responses (evasive, explanatory and non-engagement) was significant, as Pearson X2 (2, N = 655) = 50.77, p < .0001. The association between the type of the country and the type of responses is strong as Cramér's V equals .27 (Cohen 1998). Evasive strategies are more closely associated with Russia, while explanatory responses are more strongly associated with Germany.

There is almost no probability that the association is accidental as Pearson X2 (2, N = 655) = 1118.82, p < .00001.

Moving to the statistical analysis, a brief look at the overall findings lends credence to hypothesis two, namely that the "nature of the allegation" is a more impactful factor for government responses in an established democracy, while the "identity of the accuser" is more impactful in a managed democracy. Unlike German strategies, Russian responses are affected by the identity of the accuser rather than by the nature of the allegation. The identity of the accuser, when the accuser is a journalist, is statistically significant while the nature of the allegation is not. This picture of varying causal patterns reveals that the comparison across regime types is useful as it provides important keys to the variation of factors affecting government blame avoidance strategies.

Hypothesis 3, which states that corruption allegations, rather than charges of incompetence, are more likely to elicit evasive responses in an established democracy, in this case Germany, is supported. The government usually provides explanatory responses to claims of incompetence while it uses evasive tactics in response to claims of misconduct. Table 8.1. shows how responses in Germany are predicated on the nature of the accusation, not on the accuser. Table 8.1. reports on the model for government responses in Germany, listing the regression coefficient, standard error, odds ratio, and the ratio's 95% confidence interval for each predictor. A test of the full model with all predictors was statistically significant at χ^2 (16, N = 166) = 21.59, p < .10, indicating that the predictors, as a set, relatively significantly distinguished between incumbents' explanatory tactics versus those instances in which officials opted for evasive tactics. The model explained 24.6% (Nagelkerke R^2) of the variance. Classification correctly predicted 69.9% of explanatory and evasive responses.

Table 8.1. Logistic Regression: Predictive Model of Government Responses in Germany

	b (SE)	95% CI for odds ratio Lower	Odds ratio	Upper
Intercept	-1.80 (1.00)			
Type of accusation	1.04 (.51)*	.91	2.55	7.11
Number of Articles	-.01 (.01)*	.95	.98	1.00
Investigation: Parliamentary questions after the accusation	-.99* (.55)*	.10	.35	1.15
Investigation: Lower court reviews the emerged allegation	4.04 (1.80)*	1.58	44.07	1224.60
Investigation: The accusation is part of a prior lawsuit	.94 (1.64)	.08	2.22	57.20
Opposition is the accuser	-.04 (.35)	.54	1.13	2.35
Media is the accuser	.37 (.94)	.17	1.17	7.69
Position of the accused incumbent	-.01 (.03)	.92	.98	1.05
The alleged incumbent is threatened with a suit	-1.46 (1.07)	.03	.24	2.00
Investigation: International commission	-1.19 (1.35)	.01	.26	3.86
Investigation: Internal department	-.31 (.81)	.18	1.01	5.59
Investigation: Parliamentary Committee	.07 (.62)	.21	.73	2.52
Investigation: Parliamentary questions prior to allegation	-.28 (1.08)	.09	.82	7.06
Investigation: Party meeting	.68 (.87)	.37	2.07	11.56
Government popularity	.05 (.21)	.67	1.04	1.60
Opposition popularity	-.24 (.48)	.32	.89	2.45
N	166			
Nagelkerke R^2	.246			

Note 1: Odds ratio = exp(b). Model χ^2 (16, N = 166) = 21.59, p< .10. * p< .05. ** p< .01. ***p < .001.
Note 2: Condition: binary dependent variable=1 if government gives evasive responses; =0 if government gives explanatory responses.

According to the Wald χ2 statistic, the following individual conditions predict a change in the odds of giving evasive versus explanatory answers. The statistically significant categorical predictor variables were as follows: members of parliament question the government in parliament, b = -.99, Wald χ2 (1) = 2.96, p < .10; being accused in the media of corruption compared to being accused in the media of incompetence, b = 1.04, Wald χ2 (1) = 3,21, p < .10; the allegation is reviewed in a lower court of justice, b = 4.004, Wald χ2 (1) = 4,92, p < .05; the number of articles covering the allegation, b = -.01, Wald χ2 (1) = 1.80, p < .10.

The findings confirm the conventional wisdom that the intensity of critical coverage matters for blame avoidance strategies. An increase of 1 article covering a certain allegation decreases the likelihood of an evasive response. Furthermore, making an allegation of corruption or misconduct rather than one of incompetence increases the chances of the government giving an evasive (rather than an explanatory) response. Why are the German incumbents more likely to deny charges of corruption than charges of incompetence? Corruption allegations, as argued above, are easier to rebuff because they are harder to prove, observe and judge. Hence, claims of misconduct only rarely trigger substantive and explanatory responses. Rather, those claims are discredited, and the German government seems to be inclined to cast allegations of misconduct and corruption as attacks rather than to give information about them. For example, in 2001 the chancellor Gerhard Schröder was accused of taking part in money laundering through the privatisation of the Leuna refinery. This was alleged to have happened during Schröder's mandate in Lower Saxony. The government's response was to accuse the accuser by stating that the Leuna affair was misused to stage a campaign against the government. The government also gauged accusations as calumny and black smear ("Diffamierungen") (Die Welt, 2001).

Table 8.2. reports on the model testing factors impacting on government responses in Russia, listing the regression coefficient, standard error, odds ratio, and the ratio's 95% confidence interval for each predictor. A test of the full model with all predictors was statistically significant at χ2 (14, N = 122) = 26.42, p < .10, indicating that the predictors, as a set, significantly distinguished between evasive and explanatory responses to media allegations. The power of the model was relatively strong, with R2 = .43 (Nagelkerke), meaning that 43% of the variance was explained. Classification was relatively impressive, correctly predicting 88.52% of evasive and explanatory responses.

Table 8.2: Logistic Regression: Predictive Model of Government Responses in Russia

Intercept	-3.51 (1.95)			
Type of accusation	-.64 (.71)	.16	.62	2.40
Accuser: Opposition	.76 (.74)	.57	1.72	5.17
Accuser: Journalists	2.05 (1.22)*	.67	4.29	27.26
Number of Articles	.06 (.04)*	.99	1.08	1.17
Yeltsin vs. Putin	.97 (1.60)	.10	2.26	49.56
Investigation: Parliamentary Committee	-.22 (.81)	.27	1.14	4.77
Investigation: Parliamentary questions prior to allegation	-.39 (.97)	.13	.74	4.07
Investigation: Prosecutor	-2.06 (1.32)*	.009	.11	1.47
Investigation: Supreme Court	-.57 (1.37)	.03	.48	7.05
Investigation: President	-.54 (.76)	.14	.63	2.74
Investigation: Governmental Department	-1.44 (1.30)	.01	.19	2.54
Investigation: Security Services	-.78 (1.58)	.01	.41	9.32
Investigation: International Commission	1.22 (1.54)	.14	2.53	43.94
President's popularity	.005 (.024)	.95	1.00	1.05
N	122			
Nagelkerke R^2	.43			

Note 1: Odds ratio = exp(b). Model $\chi 2$ (14, N = 122) = 26.42, p < .10. * p< .05. ** p< .01. *** p< .001.
Note 2: Condition: binary dependent variable=1 if government gives evasive responses; =0 if government gives explanatory responses.

According to the Wald χ2 statistic, the following individual conditions predict a change in the odds of giving explanatory versus giving evasive answers in Russia. The statistically significant categorical predictor variables were as follows: the accusation being made by a journalist, $b = 2.05$, Wald χ2 (1) = 2.82, $p < .10$; the number of articles covering the allegation, $b = .06$, Wald χ2 (1) = 2.29, $p < .10$; the accusation being reviewed by the prosecutor-general, $b = -2.06$, Wald χ2 (1) = 2.42, $p < .10$.

As shown in table 8.2., once again, our findings are in line with mainstream research that has established that the intensity of critical coverage matters in established democracy. The chapter demonstrates that this finding applies to Russia's managed democracy. As hypothesis four proposed, the identity of the accuser matters in Russia. If the accusation is made by a journalist (rather than anybody else, who is not a media representative, be it an incumbent, the opposition, or the public), the chances that the incumbent would give an evasive rather than an explanatory response increase. Russian incumbents may be more likely to give evasive responses to journalistic claims because journalistic associations are weak, and some media outlets have little credibility as they are thought to be the mouthpieces of wealthy tycoons. Another reason could be that the government selects the most outrageous or the most impotent critics to impart the impression that there are active critics of the government but that they are too outrageous or too unconvincing. It is much easier for the state to deny egregious accusations (that the state has enabled). For example, Zasursky (1999) suggests that the state allows the nationalist Zhirinovsky to appear in the media because they make the state appear moderate in comparison. If the accuser is an oppositional member, there is no effect on the blame game. Attacking the opposition is less of a priority for Russian incumbents as the opposition poses little serious threats to the elites.

The findings offer some enlightening results regarding hypothesis 5, namely that "incumbents are less likely to deny blame if there is an institutional investigation into the media allegation." The results reaffirm the purported connection between institutional design and government responses. Both in Germany and Russia, various types of investigations turn out to have a significant effect on blame avoidance strategies. The intriguing part of this result is that, while incumbents tend to take stock of various investigations, their strategies differ, depending on the source of investigation. Thus, parliamentary questions in Germany decrease the likelihood of denying blame, while investigations by lower courts tend to increase the likelihood of denying blame. This finding engenders the speculation that democratic governments are very sensitive to the legitimacy, authority and power of various investigations. They will engage in explanatory tactics only if the body investigating them is powerful enough to produce evidence and witnesses in due time. The most important difference between the lower courts and parliamentary questions, however, is their public exposure. Thus, incumbents in a democracy would be most likely to switch from evasive to explanatory strategies, not only when there is proof of wrongdoing, but also when the public can witness it.

As for Russia, as expected, the Russian legislative body is too weak to exert any type of influence and change the blame game. A prosecutorial investigation is the only one that matters as it decreases the odds of evasive responses by 11%. If it is true that the prosecutor-general in Russia is mostly under the influence of the powerful president (Greenberg 2009), then engaging in evasive tactics when investigated by the prosecutor would be a costly option.

Conclusion: Is Verbal Uncertainty a Free for All?

The chapter argued that the creation of verbal uncertainty is not a free for all. Politicians can deny media allegations, but their denials are constrained by several factors. Specifically, denials in an established democracy and a transitional or non-democratic country are restricted by a different set of causal factors. Russian governments tend to deny allegations more often than the German incumbents, which means that verbally induced uncertainty is greater in Russia than in Germany. Notably, the most common response to public allegations was 'silence' in both countries. Regardless of the regime type, incumbents hope that the media storm will die a natural death by ignoring the allegations. As far as the constraints of verbally induced uncertainty are concerned, government responses are restricted by two main factors: the identity of the accuser and the nature of the allegation. In Germany, government strategies are mostly dependent on the type of accusation. Government responses are more evasive in cases of misconduct than in cases of incompetence. The account-giving and account-holding revolves around the issues, the evidence and its interpretation. The additional finding is that German ministers are more likely to explain themselves in the media, if there is a formal investigation of the government. By contrast, the likelihood of issuing denials in Russia is affected by the identity of the accuser rather than the type of accusation. Interestingly, out knowledge of verbally induced uncertainty is shrouded in uncertainty itself. The model for Germany explains only 24.6% of evasive and explanatory responses, and the model for Russia explains 43% of the data.

Bibliography

Anderson, C.J. (2000). Economic voting and political context: a comparative perspective. *Electoral Studies* 19 (2), pp. 151–170. Available at: https://doi.org/10.1016/S0261-3794(99)00045-1.

Beck, U. (1992) *Risk Society: Towards a New Modernity*. Frankfurt: Sage Publications.

Berlinski, S., Dewan, T., Dowding, K. (2012) *Accounting for ministers: Scandal and survival in British government 1945-2007*. New York: Cambridge University Press.

Boin, A., Hart, P., McConnell, A. (2009) Crisis exploitation: political and policy impacts of framing contests. *Journal of European Public Policy* 16 (1), pp. 106-181. Available at: https://doi.org/10.1080/13501760802453221.

Boin, A., Hart, P., McConell, A., Preston, T. (2010) Leadership Style, Crisis Response and Blame Management: The Case of Hurricane Katrina. *Public Administration* 88 (3), pp. 706-725. Available at: https://doi.org/10.1111/j.1467-9299.2010.01836.x.

Bovens, M.,Hart, P., Dekker, S., Verheuvel, G. (1999) The politics of blame avoidance: defensive tactics in a Dutch crime-fighting fiasco. In Anheier, H.K. (ed.), *When Things Go Wrong: Failures and Breakdowns in Organizational Settings*. Available at: https://www.semanticscholar.org/paper/The-politics-of-blaim-avoidance%3A-defensive-tactics-Bovens-Hart/3e5fe4e7310ff234013ea0bd9e63839904526495 [Accessed: February 3, 2023].

Brändström, A., Kuipers, S. (2003) From 'Normal Incidents' to Political Crises: Understanding the Selective Politicization of Policy Failures. *Government and Opposition* 38 (3), 279-305. Available at: http://www.jstor.org/stable/44483032.

Cohen, J. (1988) *Statistical Power Analysis for the Behavioral Sciences*. 2nd edn. Hillsdale: Lawrence Erlbaum Associates.

Coombs, W.T. (1998) An Analytic Framework for Crisis Situations: Better Responses from a Better Understanding of the Situation. *Journal of Public Relations Research* 10 (3), pp. 177-191. Available at: http://dx.doi.org/10.1207/s1532754xjprr1003_02.

Coombs, W. T. (2004) Impact of Past Crises on Current Crisis Communication: Insights from Situational Crisis Communication Theory. *The Journal of Business Communication (1973)* 41 (3), pp. 265-289. Available at: https://doi.org/10.1177/0021943604265607.

Coombs, W. T., Holladay, S. J. (1996) Communication and Attributions in a Crisis: An Experimental Study in Crisis Communication. *Journal of Public Relations Research* 8 (4), pp. 279-295. Available at: https://doi.org/10.1207/s1532754xjprr0804_04.

Corbett, E.P.J. (1988) Foreword. In Ryan, H.R. (ed.), *Oratorical Encounters: Selected Studies and Sources of Twentieth-Century Political Accusations and Apologies*. Westport: Greenwood. Available at: https://doi.org/10.2307/2078443 [Accessed: February 3, 2023].

Die Welt (2001) *Schmidt: Swiss Leuna Files are Misused for Campaigns*. Available at: https://www.welt.de/print-welt/article472425/Schmidt-Schweizer-Leuna-Akten-werden-zu-Kampagne-missbraucht.html [Accessed: February 3 2023].

Dimova, G. (2012) Who Criticizes the Government in the Media? The Symbolic Power Model. *Observatorio* 6 (1), pp. 63-85. Available at: https://doi.org/10.15847/OBSOBS612012550.

Djerf-Pierre, M., Ekström, M., Johansson, B. (2013) Policy failure or moral scandal? Political accountability, journalism and new public management. *Media, Culture and Society November* 35 (8), pp. 960-976. Available at: https://doi.org/10.1177/0163443713501932.

Edelman, M. (1988) *Constructing the Political Spectacle*. Chicago: University of Chicago Press.

Gifford, W.E., Bobbitt, H.R., Slocum J.R. (1979) Message Characteristics and Perceptions of Uncertainty by Organizational Decision Makers. *Academy of Management Journal* 22 (3), pp. 458-481. Available at: https://doi.org/10.5465/255738.

Greenberg, J. D. (2009) The Kremlin's Eye: The 21st Century Prokuratura in the Russian Authoritarian Tradition. *Stanford Journal of International Law* 45 (1). Available at: https://www.semanticscholar.org/paper/The-Kremlin%27s-Eye%3A-The-21st-Century-Prokuratura-in-Greenberg/e6c5d68e0dff2a3f2591cb41edbf0dc397bf3729.

Habermas, J. (2006) Political Communication in Media Society: Does Democracy Still Enjoy an Epistemic Dimension? The Impact of Normative Theory on Empirical Research. *Communication Theory* 16 (4), pp. 411-426. Available at: https://doi.org/10.1111/j.1468-2885.2006.00280.x.

Hinterleitner, M. (2017) Reconciling Perspectives on Blame Avoidance Behaviour. *Political Studies Review* 15 (2), pp.243-254. Available at: https://doi.org/10.1111/1478-9302.12099.

Hinterleitner, M., Sager, F. (2015) Avoiding Blame—A Comprehensive Framework and the Australian Home Insulation Program Fiasco. *Policy Studies Journal* 43 (1), pp. 139-161. Available at: https://doi.org/10.1111/psj.12088.

Hood, C. (2014) Accountability and Blame Avoidance. In Bovens, M., Goodin, R.E., Schillemans, T. (eds.), *The Oxford Handbook of Public Accountability*. Oxford: Oxford University Press. Available at: https://doi.org/10.1093/oxfordhb/9780199641253.013.0007 [Accessed: February 3, 2023].

Hood, C., Jennings, W., Copeland, P. (2016) Blame avoidance in comparative perspective: reactivity, staged retreat and efficacy. *Public Administration* 94 (2), pp. 542-562. Available at: https://doi.org/10.1111/PADM.12235.

Hood, C., Jennings, W., Dixon, R., Hogwood, B., Beeston, C. (2009) Testing times: Exploring staged responses and the impact of blame management strategies in two examination fiasco cases. *European Journal of Political Research* 48 (6), pp. 695-722. Available at: https://doi.org/10.1111/J.1475-6765.2009.01830.X.

Hood, C., Jennings, W., Hogwood, B., Beeston, C. (2007) *Fighting fires in testing times: exploring a staged response hypothesis for blame management in two exam fiasco cases*. CARR Discussion Papers (DP 42). Centre for Analysis of Risk and Regulation. Available at: http://eprints.lse.ac.uk/36122/1/Disspaper42.pdf [Accessed: February 3, 2023].

Hood, C. (2010) *The Blame Game: Spin, Bureaucracy, and Self-Preservation in Government*. Princeton: Princeton University Press.

Jacobs, S., Schillemans, T. (2016) Media and Accountability. Typology and Exploration. *Policy & Politics* 44 (1), pp. 23-40. Available at: http://dx.doi.org/10.1332/030557315X14431855320366.

Jin, Y., Cameron, G.T. (2007) The Effects of Threat Type and Duration on Public Relations Practitioner's Cognitive, Affective, and Conative Responses in Crisis Situations. *Journal of Public Relations Research* 19 (3), pp. 255-281. Available at: https://doi.org/10.1080/10627260701331762.

Jin, Y., Hong, S.Y. (2010) Explicating crisis coping in crisis communication. *Public Relations Review* 36 (4), pp. 352-360. Available at: https://doi.org/10.1016/j.pubrev.2010.06.002.

Lewis-Beck, M.S., Nadeau, R., Elias, A. (2008) Economics, Party, and the Vote: Causality Issues and Panel Data. *American Journal of Political Science* 52 (1), pp. 84-95. Available at: https://doi.org/10.1111/j.1540-5907.2007.00300.x.

Liu, B.F., Fraustino, J.D. (2014) Beyond Image Repair: Suggestions for Crisis Communication Theory Development. *Public Relations Review* 40 (3), pp. 543-546. Available at: http://www.sciencedirect.com/science/article/pii/S0363811114000812.

Mancini, P. (2018) Political Scandals as a Democratic Challenge | "Assassination Campaigns": Corruption Scandals and News Media Instrumentalization. *International Journal of Communication* 12, p. 20. Available at: https://ijoc.org/index.php/ijoc/article/view/7098.

Markovits, A., Silverstein, M. (1991) *The Politics of Scandal: Power and Process in Liberal Democracies*. Boulder: Lynne Rienner Publishers.

Mazzoleni, G., Schultz, W. (1999) "Mediatization" of Politics: A Challenge for Democracy?' *Political Communication* 16 (3), pp. 247-261. Available at: https://doi.org/10.1080/105846099198613.

McConnell, A. (2003) Overview: Crisis Management, Influences, Responses and Evaluation. *Parliamentary Affairs* 56 (3), pp. 393-409. Available at: https://doi.org/10.1093/parlij/gsg096.

McGraw, K. (1991) Managing Blame: An Experimental Test of the Effects of Political Accounts. *American Political Science Review* 85 (4), pp. 1,133-1,157. Available at: https://doi.org/10.2307/1963939.

Moynihan, D.P. (2012) Extra-Network Organizational Reputation and Blame Avoidance in Networks: The Hurricane Katrina Example. *Governance* 25 (4), pp. 567-588. Available at: https://doi.org/10.1111/j.1468-0491.2012.01593.x.

Oates, S. (2003) Television, Voters and the Development of the 'Broadcast Party'. In Hesli, V., Reisinger, B. (eds.), *The 1999–2000 Elections in Russia: Their Impact and Legacy*. Cambridge: Cambridge University Press. Available at: http://10.1017/CBO9780511550355.002 [Accessed: February 3, 2023].

Oates, S. (2006) *Television, Democracy and Elections in Russia*. London: Routledge.

Powell, G.B. and Whitten, G.D. (1993) A Cross-National Analysis of Economic Voting: Taking Account of the Political Context. *American Journal of Political Science* 37 (2), pp. 391-414.

Schultz, F., Utz, S., Göritz, A. (2011) Is the medium the message? Perceptions of and reactions to crisis communication via twitter, blogs and traditional media. *Public Relations Review* 37 (1), pp. 20-27. Available at: https://doi.org/10.1016/j.pubrev.2010.12.001.

Shaver, K.G., Drown, D. (1986) On causality, responsibility, and self-blame: A theoretical note. *Journal of Personality and Social Psychology* 50 (4), pp. 697-702. Available at: https://psycnet.apa.org/doi/10.1037/0022-3514.50.4.697.

Shepsle, K.A. (1972) The Strategy of Ambiguity: Uncertainty and Electoral Competition. *American Political Science Review* 66 (2), pp. 555-568. Available at: https://10.2307/1957799.

Sikorski, C.V. (2018) Political Scandals as a Democratic Challenge. The Aftermath of Political Scandals: A Meta-Analysis. *International Journal of Communication*, 12. Available at: https://ijoc.org/index.php/ijoc/article/view/7100.

Sulitzeanu-Kenan, R. (2010) Reflection in the Shadow of Blame: When Do Politicians Appoint Commissions of Inquiry? *British Journal of Political Science* 40 (3), pp. 613–634. Available at: https://10.1017/S0007123410000049.

Sulitzeanu-Kenan, R., Hood, C. (2005) *Blame Avoidance with Adjectives? Motivation, Opportunity, Activity and Outcome*. ECPR Joint Sessions. Available at: http://dx.doi.org/10.13140/2.1.2945.1204 [Accessed: February 3, 2023].

Weaver, R.K. (1986) The Politics of Blame Avoidance. *Journal of Public Policy* 6 (4), pp. 371–398. Available at: https://doi.org/10.1017/S0143814X00004219.

Wedeen, L. (2008) *On Uncertainty: Fake News, Post-Truth and the Question of Judgment in Syria*. Available at: https://www.uchicago.in/events/on-uncertainty-fake-news-post-truth-and-the-question-of-judgment-in-syria/ [Accessed: February 3, 2023].

Yankova, G. (2006) Political Accountability and Media Scandals: A Comparative Exploration. *CEU Political Science Journal* 1 (3), pp. 50-71. Available at: http://epa.niif.hu/02300/02341/00003/pdf/EPA02341_ceu_2006_03_50-71.pdf.

Yankova-Dimova, G. (2013) *Issue 3, Volume 1, Spring 2013. Module 5: Legal Issues and Mass Media. Media Scandals: How Political Scandals Arise.* Available at: https://www.pglu.ru/upload/iblock/6ed/gergana.pdf [Accessed: February 3, 2023].

Appendices to Chapter Eight

Appendix 8.1: Description of the Number of Articles and Accusations

Data Characteristics	Germany	Russia
Total articles	1,397	493
Total accusations	488	204
Highest number of Articles per accusation	163	59
Mean number of Articles per accusation	5.9	6.1
Minimum number of Articles per accusations	1	1

Appendix 8.2: Measurement of Key Variables

Information about each accusation includes: the number of articles related to the accusation, the type of accusation, who made the allegation, which government minister was accused, whether there was an investigation of the allegation and how the government responded. A detailed description of each variable is found in appendix 8.3.

Type of Allegation

The allegations were grouped into two main categories: incompetence and misconduct. Incompetence allegations include mishandling of natural disasters, fires, terrorist attacks, bad policy decisions. Misconduct charges include cases of corruption, marital infidelity, being gay, paedophilia, acts of illegality. The variable "type of allegation" equals 1 in case of misconduct allegations and 0 in case of incompetence allegations.

We have incorporated the logic used in the blame barometer, which is the most detailed coding method for grading the "media heat coming onto the government from the media" (Hood et al 2009). However, we have modified the blame barometer to be both more precise and more comprehensive. According to the blame barometer, the three most important indicators of the degree of media negativity contained in an allegation are: the volume of articles, the position of the accuser and the presence of various calls to investigate/sanction the government. Out method codes the volume of the articles and the position of the accuser as separate independent variables. The advantage of this process of essentially disaggregate the measure of media negativity (which is otherwise collapsed into one measure) is that it allows the investigator to determine which of the two causes the variation in government responses. In addition, our measure of a media allegation is much broader than the barometer's "calls for investigations or resignation." The latter constitute just a small part of all media criticism as it is entirely possible to criticise the government without necessarily demanding its resignation or an investigation. Our measures take stock of such additional factors.

Specifically, the allegations are coded according to three comprehensive criteria, such as: (1) explicit description of the act of accusing: use of verbs such as allege, accuse, charge, attack; (2) Indirect description of the act of accusing: Person A says the government's policy tests his/her patience; Person B is angry at the government's policy; Person C expresses dissatisfaction; People are gathered to protest against a policy; Person D threatens or initiates a lawsuit against the government; Person E calls for the government resignation; Person F calls for investigating the government.; (3) Media articles which were coded as accusations also include references to a policy or behaviour of an incumbent as morally wrong, unacceptable, harmful, illegal, corrupt, inappropriate, dishonest, untrustworthy. This is indicative list of all the words the coders found to express unfavourable attitude to the behaviour or the policies of the incumbents.

The identity of the accuser

The identity of the accuser consists of nine categories: government member, opposition, journalist, individual person, businessman, international organization, judicial representative, NGO, trade unions.

From all these accusers, the two most prominent and important ones are the media and the opposition. The variable the 'media as an accuser' is coded 1 if a journalist makes the accusation and 0 if any other person or organisation makes it. The variable 'the opposition is an accuser' is coded 1 if a member of the opposition makes the accusation and 0 if any other person or organisation makes it.

Government Responses

The responses that the incumbents gave to public allegations are classified in three broader categories of "no comment", "evasive response" and "explanatory response". In the regressions, only cases using evasive and explanatory responses were analysed. Government responses were coded as 1 if the government gave evasive responses, and were coded 0 if the government gave explanatory responses. Evasive responses include the categories of "deny charges", "attack accuser verbally", "file libel suit", and "attack accuser non-verbally." Explanatory responses include the categories of justifications, excuses, accepting the blame.

One example of an evasive strategy employed by Russian incumbents is the case where officials in Prime Minister Viktor Chernomyrdin's office persuaded a Moscow bank to freeze the credit of the popular weekly magazine Ogonek after it had reported on Chernomyrdin's lavish bear-hunting expedition in Yaroslav (RFE/RL, February 13, 1997). Another example of an aggressive Russian evasive strategy is to attack the journalist making the accusation psychologically. On September 16, 1997, the newspaper Nezavisimaya gazeta published a report suggesting that First Deputy Prime Minister Chubais's team fabricated reports of an alleged assassination plot against Chubais (RFE/RL, September 15, 1997). Attempting to intimidate the investigative journalist Alexander

Khinshtein, the ministry attempted to force Khinshtein into in a psychiatric hospital.[20]

Type of Investigation

This variable records all investigations preceding and following the emergence of allegations. The variables are dichotomous and equal 1 if the respective forum investigates the allegation, and 0 if it does not. The types of investigations are as follows: parliamentary questions after the accusation; parliamentary questions prior to allegation; lower court reviews the emerged allegation, the accusation is part of a prior lawsuit, the alleged incumbent is threatened with a suit, the allegation is investigated by an international commission, the allegation is investigated by internal governmental department, the allegation is investigated by a parliamentary committee, the allegation is investigated in a party meeting.

Popularity

The popularity of the government, the opposition and the president in Russia's case is included to control for the reputational effects and public perception effects inherent in the contextual environment. Government, oppositional and presidential popularity is measured as the first available public approval rating after the allegation emerges. It is a continuous variable.

Position of the accused incumbent

The coding differentiates between the position of the prime minister versus the position of lower ranking ministers, government officials or the government as a whole. It is a dichotomous variable indicating 1 if the Prime minister is alleged, 0 if otherwise.

---

20 Ideally, the classification of government responses would consider the veracity of the allegation. However, the literature has, to our knowledge, not integrated this factor, probably because it is usually unknown whether the alleged deed is true or false.

Further Data and Analysis

Germany and Russia emerge as suitable candidates because they exhibit a variety on these two independent variables, which are the identity of the accuser and the nature of the allegation. Germany and Russia exhibit variation on the independent variables because Germany is a well-established democracy with relatively free press, while Russia is a managed democracy, where the media freedom is more restricted. The German democratic landscape is dominated by political competition over issues rather than personalities. The political parties are centred on existing cleavages in society rather than on personalities (Beyme 1996, Diamond and Plattner 2002). By contrast, in Russia, the dominant political parties have been created by powerful players around the Kremlin (Oates 2006, 72). The political opposition is weak (Oates 2003).

It can be expected that politicians in democratic countries are more attuned to estimate the extent of politicization inherent in the type of allegation than rulers in a managed democracy. Politicians have different awareness of the importance and availability of evidence in criticisms in both systems. In democracies, the political discourse is more issue oriented (Mair 2013). Attentiveness to issues means that the politicians place a higher premium on discussing actual policies rather than smearing personalities. That is why incumbents will likely take a fuller advantage of corruption and non-policy-oriented accusations to avoid blame.

The Russian and German media systems differ substantially. The German system is characterised as a democratic corporatist model with high media circulation, high political pluralism, high professionalization, and relatively high state intervention (Hallin and Mancini 2004). The Russian system best fits the polarised pluralism model with low professionalization, low development of mass press, high political pluralism and high state intervention (De Smaele 2007). The period examined in this article includes a stage (1996-2000) when the Russian media were partially free but other media outlets were brought by oligarchs who used their media assets to wage vicious kompromat[21] wars against each other and against Yeltsin's ailing government (Oates 2006, 112). It also includes a stage of media development (2000-2005), which started with Putin's rise to power, when the government assumed control over national media (Dunn 2011, 44). By contrast, the German media system is characterized by diversity of media sources. The ownership of media outlets is split roughly equally between private and public enterprises. There is a vibrant local press. Journalists enjoy editorial independence (Trappel et al 2007, 136).

Governments are more likely to attack journalists in the polarised corporatist model than the media in the democratic corporatist model for the following reasons: media outlets are more vulnerable because journalistic associations are weak; the state controls many outlets; alternative news sources are not financially independent enough (due to low circulation) to bolster the accusers claims against the government. Consequently, the government knows that if it attacks a media outlet, the chances that some other institution, such as the prosecutor, will take on the charge is small. In addition, the media sources are considered to convey the claims of the oligarchs owning them rather than the evidence contained in wrongdoing.

This chapter seeks to measure and explain government account-giving strategies in response to allegations made in and by the media based on an original database of 692 media allegations containing 1,890 articles that are critical of the governments in Russia and Germany. The content analysis encompasses the period from January 1995 to December 2005. While the data covers a limited and distant period of time, the data are valuable as being the first of its kind in terms of quantifying the intractable situation, where all the following conditions are upheld simultaneously: there is information related to a long list of contextual factors, there is information for government responses, and the data uses the same coding to cover two very different countries. The available data enables the first of its kind statistical analysis between a large

---

21   Kompromat is Russian word for compromising material.

number of contextual factors and government responses. It can be replicated for more recent periods.

The German accusations were sampled manually from the newspaper Die Welt, which happens to be the only newspaper with an online archive at the time the content analysis was performed. Although Die Welt occupies the conservative end of the political spectrum, it is a suitable source because it expresses the views of the opposition for the better part of the period studied in the article. Arguably, the most numerous accusations can be found in oppositional newspapers. The information was double-checked against the contents of the more popular TV news program Die Tagesschau. The major stories from Die Welt were also present on national TV evening news broadcasts. Therefore, Die Welt stories containing accusations were relatively representative of a broader political discourse.

The Russian allegations were extrapolated from reading the daily press digests of Radio Free Europe Liberty (RFEL). RFEL was a suitable source of information because it sampled all available media sources. Single media sources in Russia do not produce enough criticisms. Additional sources were the Open Media Research Institute Daily Digest and the Jamestown Foundation Daily Monitor. Taken together, these three sources reach an expansive and representative sample of news outlets in Russia, the most important of which are: NTV, ITAR TASS, the newspapers Moskovsky Komsomolets, Nezavisimaya Gazeta, Izvestya the magazine Ogonek and radio Ekho Moskvy.

The unit of analysis is a media allegation of incompetence or malfeasance. One media allegation can be based on many articles. The characteristics of the data are described in appendix 8.1.

The content analysis was conducted through manual coding by the authors and two PhD students. All coders used the same coding scheme. The authors read the full length of all articles of each daily issue for each outlet for the full duration of the examined period. After the coding was finished, a new coding was carried out to determine intercoder reliability. The two PhD students with knowledge of German and Russian read the news for 12 randomly picked months of the websites of Die Welt and on RFLE respectively. These 12 months selected for checking inter-coder reliability constitute 10% of all available data, as is common practice. The Krippendorff's alpha for each indicator is listed in appendix 8.3.

Logistic Regression Analysis

Logistic regression analysis is used to examine reported changes in government responses due to various factors. Logistic regression analysis is a suitable statistical procedure for our case as it predicts a categorical outcome variable, which in this case pertains to whether the incumbent gave an evasive or explanatory answer, from a set of categorical and continuous independent variables, which in our model are the type of accuser, type of accusation, government popularity and others. The logistic analysis identifies which predictors are statistically significant and the exponentiated coefficients of the variables provide an estimate of the changes in the odds that an outcome will occur. The data are fully compliant with the requirements of a logistic regression.

Appendix 8.3: *Overview of Key Variables*

Type of variables	Variable name	Operationalisation	Germany Cronbach's alpha	Mean	SD	Russia Cronbach's alpha	Mean	SD
Dependent variable	Government responses	Dichotomous variable. Equals 1, when responses are evasive. Equals 0, when responses are explanatory (Kα = .69)	.70	.45	.49	.58	.52	.50
	Type of accusation	Dichotomous variable. If the accusation pertains to misconduct =1; If the accusation pertains to incompetence= 0 (Kα = .78)	.70	.79	.40	.59	.59	.49
Independent variables	Opposition as accuser	Dichotomous variable. If accuser is a member of Opposition= 1; Every other accuser = 0 (Kα = .80)	.72	.40	.49	.57	.37	.78
	Media as accuser	Dichotomous variable. If accuser is a journalist= 1 Every other accuser = 0 (Kα = .73)	.72	.30	.19	.55	.24	.43
	Number of articles	Number of articles pertaining to specific accusation (Kα = .78)	.70	10.10	18.12	.56	7.3	9.6
	Investigation: Parliamentary questions prior to allegation	Dichotomous variable. 1 if there is an investigation; 0 otherwise. (Kα = .78)	.72	.02	.14	.55	.26	.44
	Investigation: Parliamentary questions following the allegation	Dichotomous variable. 1 if there are questions after the accusation investigation; 0 otherwise. (Kα = .81)	.71	.16	.36	NA		
Control variables	Investigation: Court Lower court- Russia Supreme Court- Germany	Dichotomous variable. 1 if there is a lower court reviews the emerged after the allegation; 0 otherwise. (Kα = .92)	.71	.02	.14	.59	.05	.23
	Investigation: The accusation is part of a prior lawsuit	Dichotomous variable. 1 if there is an investigation; 0 otherwise. (Kα = .97)	.72	.01	.10	NA		
	The alleged incumbent is threatened with a suit	Dichotomous variable. 1 if there is an investigation; 0 otherwise. (Kα = .84)	.72	.05	.21	NA		
	Investigation: International commission	Dichotomous variable. 1 if there is an investigation; 0 otherwise. (Kα = .87)	.71	.02	.16	.59	.08	.27
	Investigation: Internal department	Dichotomous variable. 1 if there is an investigation; 0 otherwise. (Kα = .95)	.71	.06	.24	.58	.14	.35

Variable	Description						
Investigation: Parliamentary Committee	Dichotomous variable. 1 if there is an investigation; 0 otherwise. (Kα = .97)	.69	.14	.35	.59	.17	.38
Investigation: Party Meeting	Dichotomous variable. 1 if there is an investigation; 0 otherwise. (Kα = .76)	.72	.04	.20	NA		
Investigation: Security Forces	Dichotomous variable. 1 if FSB involved 0 otherwise. (Kα = .76)	NA			.58	.04	.21
Government Popularity	A number measured as soon as possible after the allegation emerges	.72	-.33	.77	NA		
Oppositional Popularit	A number measured as soon as possible after the allegation emerges	.72	-.01	.33	NA		
Presidential Popularit	A number measured as soon as possible after the allegation emerges	NA			.54	.40	29.9
Position of the accused	Dichotomous variable. 1 if the prime minister is accused; 0 if any other incumbent or the government as a whole (Kα = .95)	.72	.91	5.23	.55	.86	3.4
President in Power (Russia)	Dichotomous variable. 1 if Yeltsin, 0 otherwise	NA			.54	.43	.49

9 Future Research on Political Uncertainty
A Plea for a More Integrated Approach

Research on political uncertainty is currently under-developed, but, as demonstrated in the book, its underdevelopment harbours many opportunities. One future opportunity for growth is to conduct more integrated research on uncertainty. This would mean that scholars should consider how different types of uncertainty — institutional, inter-institutional, procedural, ontological, perceptual, etc — combine or compete to shape overall uncertainty. Such an approach will reverse the usual methodological course. Instead of preselecting a type of uncertainty, which in most cases is institutional uncertainty, and then apply it to various empirical processes, research should first select a process, and then examine all types of uncertainty inherent in it. In short, instead of following the logic of "one type of uncertainty — many processes," research should focus on a method embodying "one process-many types of uncertainty" logic. An exclusive focus on a preselected type of uncertainty entails the danger that different types of uncertainty, which reduce or increase overall uncertainty, remain disregarded. The effect would be to overestimate the importance of one preselected type of uncertainty, and to underestimate other types of uncertainty. This is not a purely taxonomical exercise. It makes sense to integrate various types of uncertainty because it is safe to assume that there is more than just one milieu, for example, institutions, or just one source of uncertainty, for example technological advancement, that are at play. Therefore, a more integrated, multi-dimensional approach will no doubt be more realistic.

The book made the first step towards such an integrated study of uncertainty by presenting a sequential view of uncertainty, where different types of uncertainty reveal themselves in consecutive phases in the process for holding the government to account for medial allegations. To begin with, the actor-based uncertainty refers to whether the accusers will go public with the incriminating information they have or they have fabricated. There is a verbally-induced uncertainty, which poses different accounts of the alleged wrong-doing and opens up the issue to doubt and contestation. Subsequently, a lot of inter-institutional uncertainty prevails as it is ambiguous which institution will take hold of the investigating and sanctioning process. Institutional uncertainty is relevant insofar it is unclear to what extent institutional rules will not be subverted by informal influences, as in the case of prosecutorial office being informally controlled by the president in Russia. Finally, there is substantive uncertainty not only about the range of the outcomes, but also about how to interpret outcomes, which claim to be repressive but in fact conceal a favourable attitude to the transgressors. This was evident in the cases in which the president seemingly punishes alleged ministers by first dismissing them but then appointing them to other attractive positions. Uncertainty in this process-oriented approach comes in gradual steps, which reflect the sequence of events. For example, sanctions may not come before the allegations. However, more research is needed to analyse the causal link between the various types of uncertainty invoked in the various stages of the process. Regardless of the early stage of the integrated approach in the book, it yielded some important insights. The book demonstrated that the degrees of uncertainty travel across types of uncertainty in a particular regime. In Russia, there was relatively low degree of inter-institutional uncertainty and substantive uncertainty. Institutional uncertainty and verbally induced uncertainty were higher. In Germany, the reverse was true.

The task of integrating verbal, inter-institutional, procedural, and other forms of uncertainty is fraught with challenges. The most apparent one is that it is impossible to estimate ontological or fundamental uncertainty because fundamental uncertainty by definition is hard to assess. Therefore, relating ontological uncertainty to perceptual or other forms of uncertainty would be challenging. But the less apparent reason, which is revealed by the critical analysis of the existing literature performed in chapter two, is that various types of uncertainty are gauged with a different criterion in mind. For example, ontological uncertainty assumes the view of an objective outside observer of real-world phenomena, while perceptual or actor-based uncertainty assumes the idiosyncratic point of view of inside players. Thus, the question arises, how should researchers relate these two different points of view on uncertainty of external and internal players? The lack of taxonomical overlap is evident in the categorisation of "effect uncertainty" (Milliken 1987), which estimates the impact on uncertainty on the one hand, and covid-induced uncertainty (Baker et al 2020), history-induced uncertainty, and verbally induced uncertainty, which point to the source of uncertainty, on the other hand.

Other examples of how typologies of uncertainty differ, and are therefore difficult to square, abound. For example, institutional uncertainty relates to the internal motivation and external behaviour of various actors to abide by the rules of various procedures. By contrast, the uncertainty posited by Bauman (2000) in his version of liquid modernity relates to the loneliness and the sense of helplessness resulting from the loss of overarching support structures. Continuing with exposing the different standards in categorising uncertainty, we should note that Beck (1992) and Giddens (1999) are concerned with the uncertainty experienced as doubt over the subjectification of science. Invariably, again and again, the same question arises: how should a researcher integrate these three types of uncertainty, manifested as readiness to follow rules, loneliness and doubt respectively?

Ultimately, a more integrated approach poses the issue of aggregation of various types of uncertainty. There are several possible avenues ahead. The most promising path is to deduce the causal relationship between various types of uncertainty. Such a relational approach to uncertainty has been attempted only and to a limited degree in regard to procedural and substantive uncertainty: "The close association between procedural legitimacy and substantive uncertainty poses the paradoxical challenge of "institutionalizing uncertainty" (Przeworksi 1988, p. 63). The relationship is causal, not only co-relational, because substantive uncertainty presupposes procedural certainty. It is this tight relationship between substantive and procedural uncertainty that defines the central task of electoral governance: organizing electoral uncertainty by providing institutional certainty (Mozaffar and Schedler 2002, p. 11). Figure 1.4.

in chapter one and figure 4.1. in chapter four suggested some patterns of various types of uncertainty. The advantage of these approaches is that they encompass more than two types of uncertainty but the disadvantage is that this relationship is mostly co-relational, i.e. these uncertainties come one after another, rather than casual, which would imply that one type of uncertainty causes another. Thus, the road of studying the causal relations between various types of uncertainty is very long. It should include inquiries, such as: if a process is underscored by a greater fundamental uncertainty, is perceptual uncertainty greater? Similarly, if fundamental uncertainty is greater, does that mean that verbally-induced uncertainty is bigger? If historical certainty is greater, is perceptual uncertainty smaller? Finally, if we put together verbally-induced uncertainty, historical uncertainty, inter-institutional uncertainty, and other types of uncertainty, what effect will they have on overall uncertainty? When speaking about the causality between these types of uncertainty, it is also very important to point out that one type of uncertainty may appear as the dependent variable in one process, but it may play the role of the independent variable in a subsequent process.

Integrating various types of uncertainty would be harder if the different types of uncertainty are self-negating and mutually exclusive. The answer to that question could possibly depend on the level of abstraction. As chapter six argued, democracy poses inherent antagonisms that make it fundamentally uncertain. These dichotomies between the promise and reality of democracy, between abstract solutions and vivid problems, and between individual autonomy and group empowerment, to name just a few of those listed in the chapter, are mutually opposing and present democracy as a zero-sum game. Uncertainty arises because it is permanently and invariably unclear which of these two sides of the dualities will prevail.

As chapter six further argued, fundamental uncertainty of democracy and the processual uncertainty of the accountability process are compatible because processual uncertainty is fickle, and it can thus manifest various sides of the antagonisms underlying fundamental uncertainty. On average, some cumulative patterns of uncertainty emerge. However, each stage of that process and each particular type of uncertainty embedded in that stage is non-linear because: it depends on the opinions of fickle vocal minorities and silent majorities, as opposed to a vocal majority, it involves numerous ways for imposing legitimacy, such as procedural, input, throughput, output as opposed to democratic legitimacy only. Uncertainty is also inherent because the principle "many people-one representative" is replaced by the principle "one person-many representatives" (Keane 2009). All these features decentralize political conflict. The transformation of a homogenous and monolithic dispute into a multi-faceted conflict invariably breeds uncertainty.

A fruitful avenue for research will involve a methodological switch from examining the explanatory weights of the determinants of an outcome to analysing the nature of the determinants themselves. At present, political science treats all explanatory variables as equivalent in nature, while their causal significance is presumed to vary. But what if not all causes are equally easy to perceive, estimate, change, etc? As chapter four argued, there are some uncertainty- reducing factors and some uncertainty reducing factors, and these observations have nothing to do with the coefficients attached to the causes. Rather, uncertainty was linked to the nature of the causes themselves. Uncertainty reducing causes are easier to observe. Observed either directly or on TV (such as earthquakes, massacres, terrorist plots, as opposed to corruption and infidelity), uncertainty reducing causes are not subjected to moral judgement and interpretation; they do not involve a cost-benefit analysis infused with many unknowns and individualistic preferences; they do not involve a process of aggregating the opinions of many people. Because of this, some causes, irrespective of and in addition to their causal weight, confidence interval and margin of error, contain a higher degree of uncertainty.

This assessment of uncertainty reducing and uncertainty inducing factors should be conceived as relative rather than absolute. As I write this book, Kamala Harris has just been announced as a vice-presidential candidate, and her blackness has already been questioned (Bouie 2020). Similarly, the shades of black of Barack Obama's skin have often been a matter of contention (Messing and

Plaut 2016), even though skin colour, according to the categorisations in this book, should be an uncertainty reducing factor as it is easy to observe, it is not a matter of ideological judgment and it is not a product of the aggregation of public opinion. More research is needed to increase the certainty of classifying factors as uncertainty-reducing or uncertainty-inducing.

A productive path for future research will also involve a methodological switch from analysing the probability of the occurrence of an outcome to the uncertainty of the occurrence of the projected outcome. Such an analytical shift is quite consequential. Instead of inquiring why wars occur, we will ask why it is hard to know why wars occur. Instead of asking why some cities are infested with crime, we will inquire why we do not know well enough how and why levels of crime increase. With so much effort dedicated to exclusively refining the precision of scholarly explanations and predictions, coming clear about the lack of precision, and the determinants of this lack of precision, would be counter intuitive. It will not be counter-productive, however. An open and rigorous conversation about the reasons why scholars failed to predict the end of communism may lead to understanding the reasons why our knowledge is limited, and how to overcome these limitations: was the study of the Soviet Union too ideological during the Cold War, did it suffer from a lack of reliable data, or was the nature of communism miscalculated? What lessons from this failure of prediction could be drawn from understanding other regimes to which scholars do not have a direct and open access? Perhaps such a conversation would uncover in-built biases. Talking about uncertainty in a systematic fashion will inject a healthy degree of reflexivity into political science.

We need to embed uncertainty more explicitly in substantive debates in political science by (1) thinking through the links between types of uncertainty; (2) switching the approach from selecting a type of uncertainty and applying it to an empirical process to selecting a process and extrapolating various types of uncertainty from it; (3) changing the object of analysis from predicting an outcome to analysing why these outcomes are hard to predict. As I have briefly noted before, uncertainty has already been discussed explicitly in the context of legislative voting, Supreme Court decisions, democratic transitions, and others. In this book, I demonstrated how integrating uncertainty in substantive debates can produce new insights about the impact of the president in the accountability process (chapter three), the impact of the EU in the accountability process (chapter four) and the multiple accountability disorder (chapter five). Thus, starting from what we do not know rather from what knowledge has already been accumulated can increase our understanding of the subject matter.

In the end, political science should think about how to report and present uncertainty to the public, to politicians and to businesses. In recent decades, the discipline has made substantial progress in refining the art of political risk analysis as far as financial investments in foreign countries are concerned. But this research on uncertainty, funded by big corporate clients, has not been matched by a comparable progress in terms of discussing the nature of opinion polls and electoral predictions. Most importantly, a lot of progress needs to be done in terms of discussing how to report predictions and findings to the public. If the confidence intervals are too wide, the predictions and explanations may be useless. If they are too narrow, the predictions and explanations may be wrong. If no uncertainty is reported, the public is being misled. If a lot of uncertainty is reported, the public may begin to doubt the scientific and immutable aspects of political science. If uncertainty is reported in a convoluted way, media consumers get overwhelmed (Blastland and Dilnot 2009). The good news is that after completing the methodological research agenda outlined above, the answers to these questions should become more obvious.

I want to end on a positive note. Despite all concerns that uncertainty is highly unsettling and hard to predict, uncertainty can be a source of inspiration and ingenuity:

> Humans thrive in conditions of radical uncertainty when creative individuals can draw on collective intelligence, hone their ideas in communication with others, and operate in an environment which permits a stable reference narrative. Within the context of a secure reference narrative, uncertainty is to be welcomed rather than feared. In personal matters—friends, holidays, leisure—stationarity is boring. In politics and business, uncertainty is a

source of opportunity for the enterprising... In the arts, uncertainty and creativity are inseparable (Kay and King 2020).

Uncertainty over electoral outcomes in democracy is inherently encouraging. In the midst of a lack of clarity over outcomes, candidates can hope that they may win. It is this uncertainty and the resulting hope that propel people to follow the rules of the game and, consequently, to resolve conflicts in a peaceful manner (Alexander2016; Lake and Rothchild1996). This peaceful resolution of conflicts is one of the greatest achievements of our civilisation. In a paradoxical way, when there is uncertainty, there is hope. There is always hope.

Bibliography

Alexander, G. (2016) Institutionalized Uncertainty, The Rule of Law, and The Sources of Democratic Stability. *Comparative Political Studies 35* (10), pp. 1145–1170. Available at: https://journals.sagepub.com/doi/abs/10.1177/001041402237946?journalCode=cpsa.

Baker, S.R., Bloom, N., Davis, S.J., Terry, S.J. (2020) Covid-Induced Economic Uncertainty. *National Bureau of Economic Research, No. w26983*, pp. 1-17. Available at: https://www.nber.org/system/files/working_papers/w26983/w26983.pdf [Accessed: February 8, 2023].

Bauman, Z. (2000) *Liquid Modernity*. Cambridge: Polity Press.

Beck, U. (1992) *Risk Society: Towards a New Modernity*. Frankfurt: Sage Publications.

Blastland, M., Dilnot, A.W. (2009) *The Numbers Game: The Commonsense Guide to Understanding Numbers in the News, in Politics, and in Life*. London: Penguin Books.

Bouie, J. (2020) Black Like Kamala. *The New York Times*. Available at: https://www.nytimes.com/2020/08/14/opinion/kamala-harris-black-identity.html [Accessed: July 32, 2020].

Kay, J.A., King, M.A. (2020) *Radical Uncertainty: Decision-Making for an Unknowable Future*. London: Bridge Street Press.

Keane, J. (2009) Monitory Democracy and Media-Saturated Societies. *Griffith Review*, Edition 24: Participation Society. Available at: https://core.ac.uk/download/pdf/30685323.pdf [Accessed November 20, 2013].

Lake, D., Rothchild, D. (1996). Containing Fear: The Origins and Management of Ethnic Conflict. *International Security 21* (2), pp. 41-75. Available at: https://doi.org/10.2307/2539070.

Messing, S., Plaut, E. (2016) What Colour is Obama? These Researchers Examined Reactions When His Skin Looks Darker. *The Washington Post.* Available at: https://www.washingtonpost.com/news/monkey-cage/wp/2016/01/11/what-color-is-obama-these-researchers-examined-reactions-when-his-skin-looks-darker/ [Accessed: July 3, 2020].

Milliken, F.J. (1987) Three Types of Perceived Uncertainty about the Environment: State, Effect, and Response Uncertainty. *Academy of Management Review* 12 (1), pp. 133-143. Available at: https://doi.org/10.2307/257999.

Mozaffar, S., Schedler, A. (2002) The Comparative Study of Electoral Governance — Introduction. *International Political Science Review* 23 (1), pp. 5-27. Available at: https://doi.org/10.1177/0192512102023001001.

Przeworski, A. (1988) *Democracy as a Contingent Outcome of Conflicts. In Constitutionalism and Democracy.* Cambridge: Cambridge University Press. Available at: https://www.cambridge.org/core/books/abs/constitutionalism-and-democracy/democracy-as-a-contingent-outcome-of-conflicts/8CB5719713F4177C1EFB2FAA611C2112 [Accessed: February 8, 2023].

SOVIET AND POST-SOVIET POLITICS AND SOCIETY
Edited by Dr. Andreas Umland | ISSN 1614-3515

1 *Андреас Умланд (ред.)* | Воплощение Европейской конвенции по правам человека в России. Философские, юридические и эмпирические исследования | ISBN 3-89821-387-0

2 *Christian Wipperfürth* | Russland – ein vertrauenswürdiger Partner? Grundlagen, Hintergründe und Praxis gegenwärtiger russischer Außenpolitik | Mit einem Vorwort von Heinz Timmermann | ISBN 3-89821-401-X

3 *Manja Hussner* | Die Übernahme internationalen Rechts in die russische und deutsche Rechtsordnung. Eine vergleichende Analyse zur Völkerrechtsfreundlichkeit der Verfassungen der Russländischen Föderation und der Bundesrepublik Deutschland | Mit einem Vorwort von Rainer Arnold | ISBN 3-89821-438-9

4 *Matthew Tejada* | Bulgaria's Democratic Consolidation and the Kozloduy Nuclear Power Plant (KNPP). The Unattainability of Closure | With a foreword by Richard J. Crampton | ISBN 3-89821-439-7

5 *Марк Григорьевич Меерович* | Квадратные метры, определяющие сознание. Государственная жилищная политика в СССР. 1921 – 1941 гг | ISBN 3-89821-474-5

6 *Andrei P. Tsygankov, Pavel A. Tsygankov (Eds.)* | New Directions in Russian International Studies | ISBN 3-89821-422-2

7 *Марк Григорьевич Меерович* | Как власть народ к труду приучала. Жилище в СССР – средство управления людьми. 1917 – 1941 гг. | С предисловием Елены Осокиной | ISBN 3-89821-495-8

8 *David J. Galbreath* | Nation-Building and Minority Politics in Post-Socialist States. Interests, Influence and Identities in Estonia and Latvia | With a foreword by David J. Smith | ISBN 3-89821-467-2

9 *Алексей Юрьевич Безугольный* | Народы Кавказа в Вооруженных силах СССР в годы Великой Отечественной войны 1941-1945 гг. | С предисловием Николая Бугая | ISBN 3-89821-475-3

10 *Вячеслав Лихачев и Владимир Прибыловский (ред.)* | Русское Национальное Единство, 1990-2000. В 2-х томах | ISBN 3-89821-523-7

11 *Николай Бугай (ред.)* | Народы стран Балтии в условиях сталинизма (1940-е – 1950-е годы). Документированная история | ISBN 3-89821-525-3

12 *Ingmar Bredies (Hrsg.)* | Zur Anatomie der Orange Revolution in der Ukraine. Wechsel des Elitenregimes oder Triumph des Parlamentarismus? | ISBN 3-89821-524-5

13 *Anastasia V. Mitrofanova* | The Politicization of Russian Orthodoxy. Actors and Ideas | With a foreword by William C. Gay | ISBN 3-89821-481-8

14 *Nathan D. Larson* | Alexander Solzhenitsyn and the Russo-Jewish Question | ISBN 3-89821-483-4

15 *Guido Houben* | Kulturpolitik und Ethnizität. Staatliche Kunstförderung im Russland der neunziger Jahre | Mit einem Vorwort von Gert Weisskirchen | ISBN 3-89821-542-3

16 *Leonid Luks* | Der russische „Sonderweg"? Aufsätze zur neuesten Geschichte Russlands im europäischen Kontext | ISBN 3-89821-496-6

17 *Евгений Мороз* | История «Мёртвой воды» – от страшной сказки к большой политике. Политическое неоязычество в постсоветской России | ISBN 3-89821-551-2

18 *Александр Верховский и Галина Кожевникова (ред.)* | Этническая и религиозная интолерантность в российских СМИ. Результаты мониторинга 2001-2004 гг. | ISBN 3-89821-569-5

19 *Christian Ganzer* | Sowjetisches Erbe und ukrainische Nation. Das Museum der Geschichte des Zaporoger Kosakentums auf der Insel Chortycja | Mit einem Vorwort von Frank Golczewski | ISBN 3-89821-504-0

20 *Эльза-Баир Гучинова* | Помнить нельзя забыть. Антропология депортационной травмы калмыков | С предисловием Кэролайн Хамфри | ISBN 3-89821-506-7

21 *Юлия Лидерман* | Мотивы «проверки» и «испытания» в постсоветской культуре. Советское прошлое в российском кинематографе 1990-х годов | С предисловием Евгения Марголита | ISBN 3-89821-511-3

22 *Tanya Lokshina, Ray Thomas, Mary Mayer (Eds.)* | The Imposition of a Fake Political Settlement in the Northern Caucasus. The 2003 Chechen Presidential Election | ISBN 3-89821-436-2

23 *Timothy McCajor Hall, Rosie Read (Eds.)* | Changes in the Heart of Europe. Recent Ethnographies of Czechs, Slovaks, Roma, and Sorbs | With an afterword by Zdeněk Salzmann | ISBN 3-89821-606-3

24 *Christian Autengruber* | Die politischen Parteien in Bulgarien und Rumänien. Eine vergleichende Analyse seit Beginn der 90er Jahre | Mit einem Vorwort von Dorothée de Nève | ISBN 3-89821-476-1

25 *Annette Freyberg-Inan with Radu Cristescu* | The Ghosts in Our Classrooms, or: John Dewey Meets Ceauşescu. The Promise and the Failures of Civic Education in Romania | ISBN 3-89821-416-8

26 *John B. Dunlop* | The 2002 Dubrovka and 2004 Beslan Hostage Crises. A Critique of Russian Counter-Terrorism | With a foreword by Donald N. Jensen | ISBN 3-89821-608-X

27 *Peter Koller* | Das touristische Potenzial von Kam"janec'–Podil's'kyj. Eine fremdenverkehrsgeographische Untersuchung der Zukunftsperspektiven und Maßnahmenplanung zur Destinationsentwicklung des „ukrainischen Rothenburg" | Mit einem Vorwort von Kristiane Klemm | ISBN 3-89821-640-3

28 *Françoise Daucé, Elisabeth Sieca-Kozlowski (Eds.)* | Dedovshchina in the Post-Soviet Military. Hazing of Russian Army Conscripts in a Comparative Perspective | With a foreword by Dale Herspring | ISBN 3-89821-616-0

29 *Florian Strasser* | Zivilgesellschaftliche Einflüsse auf die Orange Revolution. Die gewaltlose Massenbewegung und die ukrainische Wahlkrise 2004 | Mit einem Vorwort von Egbert Jahn | ISBN 3-89821-648-9

30 *Rebecca S. Katz* | The Georgian Regime Crisis of 2003-2004. A Case Study in Post-Soviet Media Representation of Politics, Crime and Corruption | ISBN 3-89821-413-3

31 *Vladimir Kantor* | Willkür oder Freiheit. Beiträge zur russischen Geschichtsphilosophie | Ediert von Dagmar Herrmann sowie mit einem Vorwort versehen von Leonid Luks | ISBN 3-89821-589-X

32 *Laura A. Victoir* | The Russian Land Estate Today. A Case Study of Cultural Politics in Post-Soviet Russia | With a foreword by Priscilla Roosevelt | ISBN 3-89821-426-5

33 *Ivan Katchanovski* | Cleft Countries. Regional Political Divisions and Cultures in Post-Soviet Ukraine and Moldova | With a foreword by Francis Fukuyama | ISBN 3-89821-558-X

34 *Florian Mühlfried* | Postsowjetische Feiern. Das Georgische Bankett im Wandel | Mit einem Vorwort von Kevin Tuite | ISBN 3-89821-601-2

35 *Roger Griffin, Werner Loh, Andreas Umland (Eds.)* | Fascism Past and Present, West and East. An International Debate on Concepts and Cases in the Comparative Study of the Extreme Right | With an afterword by Walter Laqueur | ISBN 3-89821-674-8

36 *Sebastian Schlegel* | Der „Weiße Archipel". Sowjetische Atomstädte 1945-1991 | Mit einem Geleitwort von Thomas Bohn | ISBN 3-89821-679-9

37 *Vyacheslav Likhachev* | Political Anti-Semitism in Post-Soviet Russia. Actors and Ideas in 1991-2003 | Edited and translated from Russian by Eugene Veklerov | ISBN 3-89821-529-6

38 *Josette Baer (Ed.)* | Preparing Liberty in Central Europe. Political Texts from the Spring of Nations 1848 to the Spring of Prague 1968 | With a foreword by Zdeněk V. David | ISBN 3-89821-546-6

39 *Михаил Лукьянов* | Российский консерватизм и реформа, 1907-1914 | С предисловием Марка Д. Стейнберга | ISBN 3-89821-503-2

40 *Nicola Melloni* | Market Without Economy. The 1998 Russian Financial Crisis | With a foreword by Eiji Furukawa | ISBN 3-89821-407-9

41 *Dmitrij Chmelnizki* | Die Architektur Stalins | Bd. 1: Studien zu Ideologie und Stil | Bd. 2: Bilddokumentation | Mit einem Vorwort von Bruno Flierl | ISBN 3-89821-515-6

42 *Katja Yafimava* | Post-Soviet Russian-Belarussian Relationships. The Role of Gas Transit Pipelines | With a foreword by Jonathan P. Stern | ISBN 3-89821-655-1

43 *Boris Chavkin* | Verflechtungen der deutschen und russischen Zeitgeschichte. Aufsätze und Archivfunde zu den Beziehungen Deutschlands und der Sowjetunion von 1917 bis 1991 | Ediert von Markus Edlinger sowie mit einem Vorwort versehen von Leonid Luks | ISBN 3-89821-756-6

44 *Anastasija Grynenko in Zusammenarbeit mit Claudia Dathe* | Die Terminologie des Gerichtswesens der Ukraine und Deutschlands im Vergleich. Eine übersetzungswissenschaftliche Analyse juristischer Fachbegriffe im Deutschen, Ukrainischen und Russischen | Mit einem Vorwort von Ulrich Hartmann | ISBN 3-89821-691-8

45 *Anton Burkov* | The Impact of the European Convention on Human Rights on Russian Law. Legislation and Application in 1996-2006 | With a foreword by Françoise Hampson | ISBN 978-3-89821-639-5

46 *Stina Torjesen, Indra Overland (Eds.)* | International Election Observers in Post-Soviet Azerbaijan. Geopolitical Pawns or Agents of Change? | ISBN 978-3-89821-743-9

47 *Taras Kuzio* | Ukraine – Crimea – Russia. Triangle of Conflict | ISBN 978-3-89821-761-3

48 *Claudia Šabić* | „Ich erinnere mich nicht, aber L'viv!" Zur Funktion kultureller Faktoren für die Institutionalisierung und Entwicklung einer ukrainischen Region | Mit einem Vorwort von Melanie Tatur | ISBN 978-3-89821-752-1

49 *Marlies Bilz* | Tatarstan in der Transformation. Nationaler Diskurs und Politische Praxis 1988-1994 | Mit einem Vorwort von Frank Golczewski | ISBN 978-3-89821-722-4

50 *Марлен Ларюэль (ред.)* | Современные интерпретации русского национализма | ISBN 978-3-89821-795-8

51 *Sonja Schüler* | Die ethnische Dimension der Armut. Roma im postsozialistischen Rumänien | Mit einem Vorwort von Anton Sterbling | ISBN 978-3-89821-776-7

52 *Галина Кожевникова* | Радикальный национализм в России и противодействие ему. Сборник докладов Центра «Сова» за 2004-2007 гг. | С предисловием Александра Верховского | ISBN 978-3-89821-721-7

53 *Галина Кожевникова и Владимир Прибыловский* | Российская власть в биографиях I. Высшие должностные лица РФ в 2004 г. | ISBN 978-3-89821-796-5

54 *Галина Кожевникова и Владимир Прибыловский* | Российская власть в биографиях II. Члены Правительства РФ в 2004 г. | ISBN 978-3-89821-797-2

55 *Галина Кожевникова и Владимир Прибыловский* | Российская власть в биографиях III. Руководители федеральных служб и агентств РФ в 2004 г.| ISBN 978-3-89821-798-9

56 *Ileana Petroniu* | Privatisierung in Transformationsökonomien. Determinanten der Restrukturierungs-Bereitschaft am Beispiel Polens, Rumäniens und der Ukraine | Mit einem Vorwort von Rainer W. Schäfer | ISBN 978-3-89821-790-3

57 *Christian Wipperfürth* | Russland und seine GUS-Nachbarn. Hintergründe, aktuelle Entwicklungen und Konflikte in einer ressourcenreichen Region| ISBN 978-3-89821-801-6

58 *Togzhan Kassenova* | From Antagonism to Partnership. The Uneasy Path of the U.S.-Russian Cooperative Threat Reduction | With a foreword by Christoph Bluth | ISBN 978-3-89821-707-1

59 *Alexander Höllwerth* | Das sakrale eurasische Imperium des Aleksandr Dugin. Eine Diskursanalyse zum postsowjetischen russischen Rechtsextremismus | Mit einem Vorwort von Dirk Uffelmann | ISBN 978-3-89821-813-9

60 *Олег Рябов* | «Россия-Матушка». Национализм, гендер и война в России XX века | С предисловием Елены Гощило | ISBN 978-3-89821-487-2

61 *Ivan Maistrenko* | Borot'bism. A Chapter in the History of the Ukrainian Revolution | With a new Introduction by Chris Ford | Translated by George S. N. Luckyj with the assistance of Ivan L. Rudnytsky | Second, Revised and Expanded Edition ISBN 978-3-8382-1107-7

62 *Maryna Romanets* | Anamorphosic Texts and Reconfigured Visions. Improvised Traditions in Contemporary Ukrainian and Irish Literature | ISBN 978-3-89821-576-3

63 *Paul D'Anieri and Taras Kuzio (Eds.)* | Aspects of the Orange Revolution I. Democratization and Elections in Post-Communist Ukraine | ISBN 978-3-89821-698-2

64 *Bohdan Harasymiw in collaboration with Oleh S. Ilnytzkyj (Eds.)* | Aspects of the Orange Revolution II. Information and Manipulation Strategies in the 2004 Ukrainian Presidential Elections | ISBN 978-3-89821-699-9

65 *Ingmar Bredies, Andreas Umland and Valentin Yakushik (Eds.)* | Aspects of the Orange Revolution III. The Context and Dynamics of the 2004 Ukrainian Presidential Elections | ISBN 978-3-89821-803-0

66 *Ingmar Bredies, Andreas Umland and Valentin Yakushik (Eds.)* | Aspects of the Orange Revolution IV. Foreign Assistance and Civic Action in the 2004 Ukrainian Presidential Elections | ISBN 978-3-89821-808-5

67 *Ingmar Bredies, Andreas Umland and Valentin Yakushik (Eds.)* | Aspects of the Orange Revolution V. Institutional Observation Reports on the 2004 Ukrainian Presidential Elections | ISBN 978-3-89821-809-2

68 *Taras Kuzio (Ed.)* | Aspects of the Orange Revolution VI. Post-Communist Democratic Revolutions in Comparative Perspective | ISBN 978-3-89821-820-7

69 *Tim Bohse* | Autoritarismus statt Selbstverwaltung. Die Transformation der kommunalen Politik in der Stadt Kaliningrad 1990-2005 | Mit einem Geleitwort von Stefan Troebst | ISBN 978-3-89821-782-8

70 *David Rupp* | Die Rußländische Föderation und die russischsprachige Minderheit in Lettland. Eine Fallstudie zur Anwaltspolitik Moskaus gegenüber den russophonen Minderheiten im „Nahen Ausland" von 1991 bis 2002 | Mit einem Vorwort von Helmut Wagner | ISBN 978-3-89821-778-1

71 *Taras Kuzio* | Theoretical and Comparative Perspectives on Nationalism. New Directions in Cross-Cultural and Post-Communist Studies | With a foreword by Paul Robert Magocsi | ISBN 978-3-89821-815-3

72 *Christine Teichmann* | Die Hochschultransformation im heutigen Osteuropa. Kontinuität und Wandel bei der Entwicklung des postkommunistischen Universitätswesens | Mit einem Vorwort von Oskar Anweiler | ISBN 978-3-89821-842-9

73 *Julia Kusznir* | Der politische Einfluss von Wirtschaftseliten in russischen Regionen. Eine Analyse am Beispiel der Erdöl- und Erdgasindustrie, 1992-2005 | Mit einem Vorwort von Wolfgang Eichwede | ISBN 978-3-89821-821-4

74 *Alena Vysotskaya* | Russland, Belarus und die EU-Osterweiterung. Zur Minderheitenfrage und zum Problem der Freizügigkeit des Personenverkehrs | Mit einem Vorwort von Katlijn Malfliet | ISBN 978-3-89821-822-1

75 *Heiko Pleines (Hrsg.)* | Corporate Governance in post-sozialistischen Volkswirtschaften | ISBN 978-3-89821-766-8

76 *Stefan Ihrig* | Wer sind die Moldawier? Rumänismus versus Moldowanismus in Historiographie und Schulbüchern der Republik Moldova, 1991-2006 | Mit einem Vorwort von Holm Sundhaussen | ISBN 978-3-89821-466-7

77 *Galina Kozhevnikova in collaboration with Alexander Verkhovsky and Eugene Veklerov* | Ultra-Nationalism and Hate Crimes in Contemporary Russia. The 2004-2006 Annual Reports of Moscow's SOVA Center | With a foreword by Stephen D. Shenfield | ISBN 978-3-89821-868-9

78 *Florian Küchler* | The Role of the European Union in Moldova's Transnistria Conflict | With a foreword by Christopher Hill | ISBN 978-3-89821-850-4

79 *Bernd Rechel* | The Long Way Back to Europe. Minority Protection in Bulgaria | With a foreword by Richard Crampton | ISBN 978-3-89821-863-4

80 *Peter W. Rodgers* | Nation, Region and History in Post-Communist Transitions. Identity Politics in Ukraine, 1991-2006 | With a foreword by Vera Tolz | ISBN 978-3-89821-903-7

81 *Stephanie Solywoda* | The Life and Work of Semen L. Frank. A Study of Russian Religious Philosophy | With a foreword by Philip Walters | ISBN 978-3-89821-457-5

82 *Vera Sokolova* | Cultural Politics of Ethnicity. Discourses on Roma in Communist Czechoslovakia | ISBN 978-3-89821-864-1

83 *Natalya Shevchik Ketenci* | Kazakhstani Enterprises in Transition. The Role of Historical Regional Development in Kazakhstan's Post-Soviet Economic Transformation | ISBN 978-3-89821-831-3

84 *Martin Malek, Anna Schor-Tschudnowskaja (Hgg.)* | Europa im Tschetschenienkrieg. Zwischen politischer Ohnmacht und Gleichgültigkeit | Mit einem Vorwort von Lipchan Basajewa | ISBN 978-3-89821-676-0

85 *Stefan Meister* | Das postsowjetische Universitätswesen zwischen nationalem und internationalem Wandel. Die Entwicklung der regionalen Hochschule in Russland als Gradmesser der Systemtransformation | Mit einem Vorwort von Joan DeBardeleben | ISBN 978-3-89821-891-7

86 *Konstantin Sheiko in collaboration with Stephen Brown* | Nationalist Imaginings of the Russian Past. Anatolii Fomenko and the Rise of Alternative History in Post-Communist Russia | With a foreword by Donald Ostrowski | ISBN 978-3-89821-915-0

87 *Sabine Jenni* | Wie stark ist das „Einige Russland"? Zur Parteibindung der Eliten und zum Wahlerfolg der Machtpartei im Dezember 2007 | Mit einem Vorwort von Klaus Armingeon | ISBN 978-3-89821-961-7

88 *Thomas Borén* | Meeting-Places of Transformation. Urban Identity, Spatial Representations and Local Politics in Post-Soviet St Petersburg | ISBN 978-3-89821-739-2

89 *Aygul Ashirova* | Stalinismus und Stalin-Kult in Zentralasien. Turkmenistan 1924-1953 | Mit einem Vorwort von Leonid Luks | ISBN 978-3-89821-987-7

90 *Leonid Luks* | Freiheit oder imperiale Größe? Essays zu einem russischen Dilemma | ISBN 978-3-8382-0011-8

91 *Christopher Gilley* | The 'Change of Signposts' in the Ukrainian Emigration. A Contribution to the History of Sovietophilism in the 1920s | With a foreword by Frank Golczewski | ISBN 978-3-89821-965-5

92 *Philipp Casula, Jeronim Perovic (Eds.)* | Identities and Politics During the Putin Presidency. The Discursive Foundations of Russia's Stability | With a foreword by Heiko Haumann | ISBN 978-3-8382-0015-6

93 *Marcel Viëtor* | Europa und die Frage nach seinen Grenzen im Osten. Zur Konstruktion ‚europäischer Identität' in Geschichte und Gegenwart | Mit einem Vorwort von Albrecht Lehmann | ISBN 978-3-8382-0045-3

94 *Ben Hellman, Andrei Rogachevskii* | Filming the Unfilmable. Casper Wrede's 'One Day in the Life of Ivan Denisovich' | Second, Revised and Expanded Edition | ISBN 978-3-8382-0044-6

95 *Eva Fuchslocher* | Vaterland, Sprache, Glaube. Orthodoxie und Nationenbildung am Beispiel Georgiens | Mit einem Vorwort von Christina von Braun | ISBN 978-3-89821-884-9

96 *Vladimir Kantor* | Das Westlertum und der Weg Russlands. Zur Entwicklung der russischen Literatur und Philosophie | Ediert von Dagmar Herrmann | Mit einem Beitrag von Nikolaus Lobkowicz | ISBN 978-3-8382-0102-3

97 *Kamran Musayev* | Die postsowjetische Transformation im Baltikum und Südkaukasus. Eine vergleichende Untersuchung der politischen Entwicklung Lettlands und Aserbaidschans 1985-2009 | Mit einem Vorwort von Leonid Luks | Ediert von Sandro Henschel | ISBN 978-3-8382-0103-0

98 *Tatiana Zhurzhenko* | Borderlands into Bordered Lands. Geopolitics of Identity in Post-Soviet Ukraine | With a foreword by Dieter Segert | ISBN 978-3-8382-0042-2

99 *Кирилл Галушко, Лидия Смола (ред.)* | Пределы падения – варианты украинского будущего. Аналитико-прогностические исследования | ISBN 978-3-8382-0148-1

100 *Michael Minkenberg (Ed.)* | Historical Legacies and the Radical Right in Post-Cold War Central and Eastern Europe | With an afterword by Sabrina P. Ramet | ISBN 978-3-8382-0124-5

101 *David-Emil Wickström* | Rocking St. Petersburg. Transcultural Flows and Identity Politics in the St. Petersburg Popular Music Scene | With a foreword by Yngvar B. Steinholt | Second, Revised and Expanded Edition | ISBN 978-3-8382-0100-9

102 *Eva Zabka* | Eine neue „Zeit der Wirren"? Der spät- und postsowjetische Systemwandel 1985-2000 im Spiegel russischer gesellschaftspolitischer Diskurse | Mit einem Vorwort von Margareta Mommsen | ISBN 978-3-8382-0161-0

103 *Ulrike Ziemer* | Ethnic Belonging, Gender and Cultural Practices. Youth Identitites in Contemporary Russia | With a foreword by Anoop Nayak | ISBN 978-3-8382-0152-8

104 *Ksenia Chepikova* | ‚Einiges Russland' - eine zweite KPdSU? Aspekte der Identitätskonstruktion einer postsowjetischen „Partei der Macht" | Mit einem Vorwort von Torsten Oppelland | ISBN 978-3-8382-0311-9

105 *Леонид Люкс* | Западничество или евразийство? Демократия или идеократия? Сборник статей об исторических дилеммах России | С предисловием Владимира Кантора | ISBN 978-3-8382-0211-2

106 *Anna Dost* | Das russische Verfassungsrecht auf dem Weg zum Föderalismus und zurück. Zum Konflikt von Rechtsnormen und -wirklichkeit in der Russländischen Föderation von 1991 bis 2009 | Mit einem Vorwort von Alexander Blankenagel | ISBN 978-3-8382-0292-1

107 *Philipp Herzog* | Sozialistische Völkerfreundschaft, nationaler Widerstand oder harmloser Zeitvertreib? Zur politischen Funktion der Volkskunst im sowjetischen Estland | Mit einem Vorwort von Andreas Kappeler | ISBN 978-3-8382-0216-7

108 *Marlène Laruelle (Ed.)* | Russian Nationalism, Foreign Policy, and Identity Debates in Putin's Russia. New Ideological Patterns after the Orange Revolution | ISBN 978-3-8382-0325-6

109 *Michail Logvinov* | Russlands Kampf gegen den internationalen Terrorismus. Eine kritische Bestandsaufnahme des Bekämpfungsansatzes | Mit einem Geleitwort von Hans-Henning Schröder und einem Vorwort von Eckhard Jesse | ISBN 978-3-8382-0329-4

110 *John B. Dunlop* | The Moscow Bombings of September 1999. Examinations of Russian Terrorist Attacks at the Onset of Vladimir Putin's Rule | Second, Revised and Expanded Edition | ISBN 978-3-8382-0388-1

111 *Андрей А. Ковалёв* | Свидетельство из-за кулис российской политики I. Можно ли делать добро из зла? (Воспоминания и размышления о последних советских и первых послесоветских годах) | With a foreword by Peter Reddaway | ISBN 978-3-8382-0302-7

112 *Андрей А. Ковалёв* | Свидетельство из-за кулис российской политики II. Угроза для себя и окружающих (Наблюдения и предостережения относительно происходящего после 2000 г.) | ISBN 978-3-8382-0303-4

113 *Bernd Kappenberg* | Zeichen setzen für Europa. Der Gebrauch europäischer lateinischer Sonderzeichen in der deutschen Öffentlichkeit | Mit einem Vorwort von Peter Schlobinski | ISBN 978-3-89821-749-1

114 *Ivo Mijnssen* | The Quest for an Ideal Youth in Putin's Russia I. Back to Our Future! History, Modernity, and Patriotism according to Nashi, 2005-2013 | With a foreword by Jeronim Perović | Second, Revised and Expanded Edition | ISBN 978-3-8382-0368-3

115 *Jussi Lassila* | The Quest for an Ideal Youth in Putin's Russia II. The Search for Distinctive Conformism in the Political Communication of Nashi, 2005-2009 | With a foreword by Kirill Postoutenko | Second, Revised and Expanded Edition | ISBN 978-3-8382-0415-4

116 *Valerio Trabandt* | Neue Nachbarn, gute Nachbarschaft? Die EU als internationaler Akteur am Beispiel ihrer Demokratieförderung in Belarus und der Ukraine 2004-2009 | Mit einem Vorwort von Jutta Joachim | ISBN 978-3-8382-0437-6

117 *Fabian Pfeiffer* | Estlands Außen- und Sicherheitspolitik I. Der estnische Atlantizismus nach der wiedererlangten Unabhängigkeit 1991-2004 | Mit einem Vorwort von Helmut Hubel | ISBN 978-3-8382-0127-6

118 *Jana Podßuweit* | Estlands Außen- und Sicherheitspolitik II. Handlungsoptionen eines Kleinstaates im Rahmen seiner EU-Mitgliedschaft (2004-2008) | Mit einem Vorwort von Helmut Hubel | ISBN 978-3-8382-0440-6

119 *Karin Pointner* | Estlands Außen- und Sicherheitspolitik III. Eine gedächtnispolitische Analyse estnischer Entwicklungskooperation 2006-2010 | Mit einem Vorwort von Karin Liebhart | ISBN 978-3-8382-0435-2

120 *Ruslana Vovk* | Die Offenheit der ukrainischen Verfassung für das Völkerrecht und die europäische Integration | Mit einem Vorwort von Alexander Blankenagel | ISBN 978-3-8382-0481-9

121 *Mykhaylo Banakh* | Die Relevanz der Zivilgesellschaft bei den postkommunistischen Transformationsprozessen in mittel- und osteuropäischen Ländern. Das Beispiel der spät- und postsowjetischen Ukraine 1986-2009 | Mit einem Vorwort von Gerhard Simon | ISBN 978-3-8382-0499-4

122 *Michael Moser* | Language Policy and the Discourse on Languages in Ukraine under President Viktor Yanukovych (25 February 2010–28 October 2012) | ISBN 978-3-8382-0497-0 (Paperback edition) | ISBN 978-3-8382-0507-6 (Hardcover edition)

123 *Nicole Krome* | Russischer Netzwerkkapitalismus Restrukturierungsprozesse in der Russischen Föderation am Beispiel des Luftfahrtunternehmens „Aviastar" | Mit einem Vorwort von Petra Stykow | ISBN 978-3-8382-0534-2

124 *David R. Marples* | 'Our Glorious Past'. Lukashenka's Belarus and the Great Patriotic War | ISBN 978-3-8382-0574-8 (Paperback edition) | ISBN 978-3-8382-0675-2 (Hardcover edition)

125 *Ulf Walther* | Russlands „neuer Adel". Die Macht des Geheimdienstes von Gorbatschow bis Putin | Mit einem Vorwort von Hans-Georg Wieck | ISBN 978-3-8382-0584-7

126 *Simon Geissbühler (Hrsg.)* | Kiew – Revolution 3.0. Der Euromaidan 2013/14 und die Zukunftsperspektiven der Ukraine | ISBN 978-3-8382-0581-6 (Paperback edition) | ISBN 978-3-8382-0681-3 (Hardcover edition)

127 *Andrey Makarychev* | Russia and the EU in a Multipolar World. Discourses, Identities, Norms | With a foreword by Klaus Segbers | ISBN 978-3-8382-0629-5

128 *Roland Scharff* | Kasachstan als postsowjetischer Wohlfahrtsstaat. Die Transformation des sozialen Schutzsystems | Mit einem Vorwort von Joachim Ahrens | ISBN 978-3-8382-0622-6

129 *Katja Grupp* | Bild Lücke Deutschland. Kaliningrader Studierende sprechen über Deutschland | Mit einem Vorwort von Martin Schulz | ISBN 978-3-8382-0552-6

130 *Konstantin Sheiko, Stephen Brown* | History as Therapy. Alternative History and Nationalist Imaginings in Russia, 1991-2014 | ISBN 978-3-8382-0665-3

131 *Elisa Kriza* | Alexander Solzhenitsyn: Cold War Icon, Gulag Author, Russian Nationalist? A Study of the Western Reception of his Literary Writings, Historical Interpretations, and Political Ideas | With a foreword by Andrei Rogatchevski | ISBN 978-3-8382-0589-2 (Paperback edition) | ISBN 978-3-8382-0690-5 (Hardcover edition)

132 *Serghei Golunov* | The Elephant in the Room. Corruption and Cheating in Russian Universities | ISBN 978-3-8382-0570-0

133 *Manja Hussner, Rainer Arnold (Hgg.)* | Verfassungsgerichtsbarkeit in Zentralasien I. Sammlung von Verfassungstexten | ISBN 978-3-8382-0595-3

134 *Nikolay Mitrokhin* | Die „Russische Partei". Die Bewegung der russischen Nationalisten in der UdSSR 1953-1985 | Aus dem Russischen übertragen von einem Übersetzerteam unter der Leitung von Larisa Schippel | ISBN 978-3-8382-0024-8

135 *Manja Hussner, Rainer Arnold (Hgg.)* | Verfassungsgerichtsbarkeit in Zentralasien II. Sammlung von Verfassungstexten | ISBN 978-3-8382-0597-7

136 *Manfred Zeller* | Das sowjetische Fieber. Fußballfans im poststalinistischen Vielvölkerreich | Mit einem Vorwort von Nikolaus Katzer | ISBN 978-3-8382-0757-5

137 *Kristin Schreiter* | Stellung und Entwicklungspotential zivilgesellschaftlicher Gruppen in Russland. Menschenrechtsorganisationen im Vergleich | ISBN 978-3-8382-0673-8

138 *David R. Marples, Frederick V. Mills (Eds.)* | Ukraine's Euromaidan. Analyses of a Civil Revolution | ISBN 978-3-8382-0660-8

139 *Bernd Kappenberg* | Setting Signs for Europe. Why Diacritics Matter for European Integration | With a foreword by Peter Schlobinski | ISBN 978-3-8382-0663-9

140 *René Lenz* | Internationalisierung, Kooperation und Transfer. Externe bildungspolitische Akteure in der Russischen Föderation | Mit einem Vorwort von Frank Ettrich | ISBN 978-3-8382-0751-3

141 *Juri Plusnin, Yana Zausaeva, Natalia Zhidkevich, Artemy Pozanenko* | Wandering Workers. Mores, Behavior, Way of Life, and Political Status of Domestic Russian Labor Migrants | Translated by Julia Kazantseva | ISBN 978-3-8382-0653-0

142 *David J. Smith (Eds.)* | Latvia – A Work in Progress? 100 Years of State- and Nation-Building | ISBN 978-3-8382-0648-6

143 *Инна Чувычкина (ред.)* | Экспортные нефте- и газопроводы на постсоветском пространстве. Анализ трубопроводной политики в свете теории международных отношений | ISBN 978-3-8382-0822-0

144 *Johann Zajaczkowski* | Russland – eine pragmatische Großmacht? Eine rollentheoretische Untersuchung russischer Außenpolitik am Beispiel der Zusammenarbeit mit den USA nach 9/11 und des Georgienkrieges von 2008 | Mit einem Vorwort von Siegfried Schieder | ISBN 978-3-8382-0837-4

145 *Boris Popivanov* | Changing Images of the Left in Bulgaria. The Challenge of Post-Communism in the Early 21st Century | ISBN 978-3-8382-0667-7

146 *Lenka Krátká* | A History of the Czechoslovak Ocean Shipping Company 1948-1989. How a Small, Landlocked Country Ran Maritime Business During the Cold War | ISBN 978-3-8382-0666-0

147 *Alexander Sergunin* | Explaining Russian Foreign Policy Behavior. Theory and Practice | ISBN 978-3-8382-0752-0

148 *Darya Malyutina* | Migrant Friendships in a Super-Diverse City. Russian-Speakers and their Social Relationships in London in the 21st Century | With a foreword by Claire Dwyer | ISBN 978-3-8382-0652-3

149 *Alexander Sergunin, Valery Konyshev* | Russia in the Arctic. Hard or Soft Power? | ISBN 978-3-8382-0753-7

150 *John J. Maresca* | Helsinki Revisited. A Key U.S. Negotiator's Memoirs on the Development of the CSCE into the OSCE | With a foreword by Hafiz Pashayev | ISBN 978-3-8382-0852-7

151 *Jardar Østbø* | The New Third Rome. Readings of a Russian Nationalist Myth | With a foreword by Pål Kolstø | ISBN 978-3-8382-0870-1

152 *Simon Kordonsky* | Socio-Economic Foundations of the Russian Post-Soviet Regime. The Resource-Based Economy and Estate-Based Social Structure of Contemporary Russia | With a foreword by Svetlana Barsukova | ISBN 978-3-8382-0775-9

153 *Duncan Leitch* | Assisting Reform in Post-Communist Ukraine 2000–2012. The Illusions of Donors and the Disillusion of Beneficiaries | With a foreword by Kataryna Wolczuk | ISBN 978-3-8382-0844-2

154 *Abel Polese* | Limits of a Post-Soviet State. How Informality Replaces, Renegotiates, and Reshapes Governance in Contemporary Ukraine | With a foreword by Colin Williams | ISBN 978-3-8382-0845-9

155 *Mikhail Suslov (Ed.)* | Digital Orthodoxy in the Post-Soviet World. The Russian Orthodox Church and Web 2.0 | With a foreword by Father Cyril Hovorun | ISBN 978-3-8382-0871-8

156 *Leonid Luks* | Zwei „Sonderwege"? Russisch-deutsche Parallelen und Kontraste (1917-2014). Vergleichende Essays | ISBN 978-3-8382-0823-7

157 *Vladimir V. Karacharovskiy, Ovsey I. Shkaratan, Gordey A. Yastrebov* | Towards a New Russian Work Culture. Can Western Companies and Expatriates Change Russian Society? | With a foreword by Elena N. Danilova | Translated by Julia Kazantseva | ISBN 978-3-8382-0902-9

158 *Edmund Griffiths* | Aleksandr Prokhanov and Post-Soviet Esotericism | ISBN 978-3-8382-0963-0

159 *Timm Beichelt, Susann Worschech (Eds.)* | Transnational Ukraine? Networks and Ties that Influence(d) Contemporary Ukraine | ISBN 978-3-8382-0944-9

160 *Mieste Hotopp-Riecke* | Die Tataren der Krim zwischen Assimilation und Selbstbehauptung. Der Aufbau des krimtatarischen Bildungswesens nach Deportation und Heimkehr (1990-2005) | Mit einem Vorwort von Swetlana Czerwonnaja | ISBN 978-3-89821-940-2

161 *Olga Bertelsen (Ed.)* | Revolution and War in Contemporary Ukraine. The Challenge of Change | ISBN 978-3-8382-1016-2

162 *Natalya Ryabinska* | Ukraine's Post-Communist Mass Media. Between Capture and Commercialization | With a foreword by Marta Dyczok | ISBN 978-3-8382-1011-7

163 *Alexandra Cotofana, James M. Nyce (Eds.)* | Religion and Magic in Socialist and Post-Socialist Contexts. Historic and Ethnographic Case Studies of Orthodoxy, Heterodoxy, and Alternative Spirituality | With a foreword by Patrick L. Michelson | ISBN 978-3-8382-0989-0

164 *Nozima Akhrarkhodjaeva* | The Instrumentalisation of Mass Media in Electoral Authoritarian Regimes. Evidence from Russia's Presidential Election Campaigns of 2000 and 2008 | ISBN 978-3-8382-1013-1

165 *Yulia Krasheninnikova* | Informal Healthcare in Contemporary Russia. Sociographic Essays on the Post-Soviet Infrastructure for Alternative Healing Practices | ISBN 978-3-8382-0970-8

166 *Peter Kaiser* | Das Schachbrett der Macht. Die Handlungsspielräume eines sowjetischen Funktionärs unter Stalin am Beispiel des Generalsekretärs des Komsomol Aleksandr Kosarev (1929-1938) | Mit einem Vorwort von Dietmar Neutatz | ISBN 978-3-8382-1052-0

167 *Oksana Kim* | The Effects and Implications of Kazakhstan's Adoption of International Financial Reporting Standards. A Resource Dependence Perspective | With a foreword by Svetlana Vlady | ISBN 978-3-8382-0987-6

168 *Anna Sanina* | Patriotic Education in Contemporary Russia. Sociological Studies in the Making of the Post-Soviet Citizen | With a foreword by Anna Oldfield | ISBN 978-3-8382-0993-7

169 *Rudolf Wolters* | Spezialist in Sibirien Faksimile der 1933 erschienenen ersten Ausgabe | Mit einem Vorwort von Dmitrij Chmelnizki | ISBN 978-3-8382-0515-1

170 *Michal Vít, Magdalena M. Baran (Eds.)* | Transregional versus National Perspectives on Contemporary Central European History. Studies on the Building of Nation-States and Their Cooperation in the 20th and 21st Century | With a foreword by Petr Vágner | ISBN 978-3-8382-1015-5

171 *Philip Gamaghelyan* | Conflict Resolution Beyond the International Relations Paradigm. Evolving Designs as a Transformative Practice in Nagorno-Karabakh and Syria | With a foreword by Susan Allen | ISBN 978-3-8382-1057-5

172 *Maria Shagina* | Joining a Prestigious Club. Cooperation with Europarties and Its Impact on Party Development in Georgia, Moldova, and Ukraine 2004–2015 | With a foreword by Kataryna Wolczuk | ISBN 978-3-8382-1084-1

173 *Alexandra Cotofana, James M. Nyce (Eds.)* | Religion and Magic in Socialist and Post-Socialist Contexts II. Baltic, Eastern European, and Post-USSR Case Studies | With a foreword by Anita Stasulane | ISBN 978-3-8382-0990-6

174 *Barbara Kunz* | Kind Words, Cruise Missiles, and Everything in Between. The Use of Power Resources in U.S. Policies towards Poland, Ukraine, and Belarus 1989–2008 | With a foreword by William Hill | ISBN 978-3-8382-1065-0

175 *Eduard Klein* | Bildungskorruption in Russland und der Ukraine. Eine komparative Analyse der Performanz staatlicher Antikorruptionsmaßnahmen im Hochschulsektor am Beispiel universitärer Aufnahmeprüfungen | Mit einem Vorwort von Heiko Pleines | ISBN 978-3-8382-0995-1

176 *Markus Soldner* | Politischer Kapitalismus im postsowjetischen Russland. Die politische, wirtschaftliche und mediale Transformation in den 1990er Jahren | Mit einem Vorwort von Wolfgang Ismayr | ISBN 978-3-8382-1222-7

177 *Anton Oleinik* | Building Ukraine from Within. A Sociological, Institutional, and Economic Analysis of a Nation-State in the Making | ISBN 978-3-8382-1150-3

178 *Peter Rollberg, Marlene Laruelle (Eds.)* | Mass Media in the Post-Soviet World. Market Forces, State Actors, and Political Manipulation in the Informational Environment after Communism | ISBN 978-3-8382-1116-9

179 *Mikhail Minakov* | Development and Dystopia. Studies in Post-Soviet Ukraine and Eastern Europe | With a foreword by Alexander Etkind | ISBN 978-3-8382-1112-1

180 *Aijan Sharshenova* | The European Union's Democracy Promotion in Central Asia. A Study of Political Interests, Influence, and Development in Kazakhstan and Kyrgyzstan in 2007–2013 | With a foreword by Gordon Crawford | ISBN 978-3-8382-1151-0

181 *Andrey Makarychev, Alexandra Yatsyk (Eds.)* | Boris Nemtsov and Russian Politics. Power and Resistance | With a foreword by Zhanna Nemtsova | ISBN 978-3-8382-1122-0

182 *Sophie Falsini* | The Euromaidan's Effect on Civil Society. Why and How Ukrainian Social Capital Increased after the Revolution of Dignity | With a foreword by Susann Worschech | ISBN 978-3-8382-1131-2

183 *Valentyna Romanova, Andreas Umland (Eds.)* | Ukraine's Decentralization. Challenges and Implications of the Local Governance Reform after the Euromaidan Revolution | ISBN 978-3-8382-1162-6

184 *Leonid Luks* | A Fateful Triangle. Essays on Contemporary Russian, German and Polish History | ISBN 978-3-8382-1143-5

185 *John B. Dunlop* | The February 2015 Assassination of Boris Nemtsov and the Flawed Trial of his Alleged Killers. An Exploration of Russia's "Crime of the 21st Century" | ISBN 978-3-8382-1188-6

186 *Vasile Rotaru* | Russia, the EU, and the Eastern Partnership. Building Bridges or Digging Trenches? | ISBN 978-3-8382-1134-3

187 *Marina Lebedeva* | Russian Studies of International Relations. From the Soviet Past to the Post-Cold-War Present | With a foreword by Andrei P. Tsygankov | ISBN 978-3-8382-0851-0

188 *Tomasz Stępniewski, George Soroka (Eds.)* | Ukraine after Maidan. Revisiting Domestic and Regional Security | ISBN 978-3-8382-1075-9

189 *Petar Cholakov* | Ethnic Entrepreneurs Unmasked. Political Institutions and Ethnic Conflicts in Contemporary Bulgaria | ISBN 978-3-8382-1189-3

190 *A. Salem, G. Hazeldine, D. Morgan (Eds.)* | Higher Education in Post-Communist States. Comparative and Sociological Perspectives | ISBN 978-3-8382-1183-1

191 *Igor Torbakov* | After Empire. Nationalist Imagination and Symbolic Politics in Russia and Eurasia in the Twentieth and Twenty-First Century | With a foreword by Serhii Plokhy | ISBN 978-3-8382-1217-5

192 *Aleksandr Burakovskiy* | Jewish-Ukrainian Relations in Late and Post-Soviet Ukraine. Articles, Lectures and Essays from 1986 to 2016 | ISBN 978-3-8382-1210-4

193 *Natalia Shapovalova, Olga Burlyuk (Eds.)* | Civil Society in Post-Euromaidan Ukraine. From Revolution to Consolidation | With a foreword by Richard Youngs | ISBN 978-3-8382-1216-6

194 *Franz Preissler* | Positionsverteidigung, Imperialismus oder Irredentismus? Russland und die „Russischsprachigen", 1991–2015 | ISBN 978-3-8382-1262-3

195 *Marian Madeła* | Der Reformprozess in der Ukraine 2014-2017. Eine Fallstudie zur Reform der öffentlichen Verwaltung | Mit einem Vorwort von Martin Malek | ISBN 978-3-8382-1266-1

196 *Anke Giesen* | „Wie kann denn der Sieger ein Verbrecher sein?" Eine diskursanalytische Untersuchung der russlandweiten Debatte über Konzept und Verstaatlichungsprozess der Lagergedenkstätte „Perm'-36" im Ural | ISBN 978-3-8382-1284-5

197 *Victoria Leukavets* | The Integration Policies of Belarus and Ukraine vis-à-vis the EU and Russia. A Comparative Analysis Through the Prism of a Two-Level Game Approach | ISBN 978-3-8382-1247-0

198 *Oksana Kim* | The Development and Challenges of Russian Corporate Governance I. The Roles and Functions of Boards of Directors | With a foreword by Sheila M. Puffer | ISBN 978-3-8382-1287-6

199 *Thomas D. Grant* | International Law and the Post-Soviet Space I. Essays on Chechnya and the Baltic States | With a foreword by Stephen M. Schwebel | ISBN 978-3-8382-1279-1

200 *Thomas D. Grant* | International Law and the Post-Soviet Space II. Essays on Ukraine, Intervention, and Non-Proliferation | ISBN 978-3-8382-1280-7

201 *Slavomír Michálek, Michal Štefansky* | The Age of Fear. The Cold War and Its Influence on Czechoslovakia 1945–1968 | ISBN 978-3-8382-1285-2

202 *Iulia-Sabina Joja* | Romania's Strategic Culture 1990–2014. Continuity and Change in a Post-Communist Country's Evolution of National Interests and Security Policies | With a foreword by Heiko Biehl | ISBN 978-3-8382-1286-9

203 *Andrei Rogatchevski, Yngvar B. Steinholt, Arve Hansen, David-Emil Wickström* | War of Songs. Popular Music and Recent Russia-Ukraine Relations | With a foreword by Artemy Troitsky | ISBN 978-3-8382-1173-2

204 *Maria Lipman (Ed.)* | Russian Voices on Post-Crimea Russia. An Almanac of Counterpoint Essays from 2015–2018 | ISBN 978-3-8382-1251-7

205 *Ksenia Maksimovtsova* | Language Conflicts in Contemporary Estonia, Latvia, and Ukraine. A Comparative Exploration of Discourses in Post-Soviet Russian-Language Digital Media | With a foreword by Ammon Cheskin | ISBN 978-3-8382-1282-1

206 *Michal Vít* | The EU's Impact on Identity Formation in East-Central Europe between 2004 and 2013. Perceptions of the Nation and Europe in Political Parties of the Czech Republic, Poland, and Slovakia | With a foreword by Andrea Petö | ISBN 978-3-8382-1275-3

207 *Per A. Rudling* | Tarnished Heroes. The Organization of Ukrainian Nationalists in the Memory Politics of Post-Soviet Ukraine | ISBN 978-3-8382-0999-9

208 *Kaja Gadowska, Peter Solomon (Eds.)* | Legal Change in Post-Communist States. Progress, Reversions, Explanations | ISBN 978-3-8382-1312-5

209 *Pawel Kowal, Georges Mink, Iwona Reichardt (Eds.)* | Three Revolutions: Mobilization and Change in Contemporary Ukraine I. Theoretical Aspects and Analyses on Religion, Memory, and Identity | ISBN 978-3-8382-1321-7

210 *Pawel Kowal, Georges Mink, Adam Reichardt, Iwona Reichardt (Eds.)* | Three Revolutions: Mobilization and Change in Contemporary Ukraine II. An Oral History of the Revolution on Granite, Orange Revolution, and Revolution of Dignity | ISBN 978-3-8382-1323-1

211 *Li Bennich-Björkman, Sergiy Kurbatov (Eds.)* | When the Future Came. The Collapse of the USSR and the Emergence of National Memory in Post-Soviet History Textbooks | ISBN 978-3-8382-1335-4

212 *Olga R. Gulina* | Migration as a (Geo-)Political Challenge in the Post-Soviet Space. Border Regimes, Policy Choices, Visa Agendas | With a foreword by Nils Muižnieks | ISBN 978-3-8382-1338-5

213 *Sanna Turoma, Kaarina Aitamurto, Slobodanka Vladiv-Glover (Eds.)* | Religion, Expression, and Patriotism in Russia. Essays on Post-Soviet Society and the State. ISBN 978-3-8382-1346-0

214 *Vasif Huseynov* | Geopolitical Rivalries in the "Common Neighborhood". Russia's Conflict with the West, Soft Power, and Neoclassical Realism | With a foreword by Nicholas Ross Smith | ISBN 978-3-8382-1277-7

215 *Mikhail Suslov* | Geopolitical Imagination. Ideology and Utopia in Post-Soviet Russia | With a foreword by Mark Bassin | ISBN 978-3-8382-1361-3

216 *Alexander Etkind, Mikhail Minakov (Eds.)* | Ideology after Union. Political Doctrines, Discourses, and Debates in Post-Soviet Societies | ISBN 978-3-8382-1388-0

217 *Jakob Mischke, Oleksandr Zabirko (Hgg.)* | Protestbewegungen im langen Schatten des Kreml. Aufbruch und Resignation in Russland und der Ukraine | ISBN 978-3-8382-0926-5

218 *Oksana Huss* | How Corruption and Anti-Corruption Policies Sustain Hybrid Regimes. Strategies of Political Domination under Ukraine's Presidents in 1994-2014 | With a foreword by Tobias Debiel and Andrea Gawrich | ISBN 978-3-8382-1430-6

219 *Dmitry Travin, Vladimir Gel'man, Otar Marganiya* | The Russian Path. Ideas, Interests, Institutions, Illusions | With a foreword by Vladimir Ryzhkov | ISBN 978-3-8382-1421-4

220 *Gergana Dimova* | Political Uncertainty. A Comparative Exploration | With a foreword by Todor Yalamov and Rumena Filipova | ISBN 978-3-8382-1385-9

221 *Torben Waschke* | Russland in Transition. Geopolitik zwischen Raum, Identität und Machtinteressen | Mit einem Vorwort von Andreas Dittmann | ISBN 978-3-8382-1480-1

222 *Steven Jobbitt, Zsolt Bottlik, Marton Berki (Eds.)* | Power and Identity in the Post-Soviet Realm. Geographies of Ethnicity and Nationality after 1991 | ISBN 978-3-8382-1399-6

223 *Daria Buteiko* | Erinnerungsort. Ort des Gedenkens, der Erholung oder der Einkehr? Kommunismus-Erinnerung am Beispiel der Gedenkstätte Berliner Mauer sowie des Soloveckij-Klosters und -Museumsparks | ISBN 978-3-8382-1367-5

224 *Olga Bertelsen (Ed.)* | Russian Active Measures. Yesterday, Today, Tomorrow | With a foreword by Jan Goldman | ISBN 978-3-8382-1529-7

225 *David Mandel* | "Optimizing" Higher Education in Russia. University Teachers and their Union "Universitetskaya solidarnost'" | ISBN 978-3-8382-1519-8

226 *Mikhail Minakov, Gwendolyn Sasse, Daria Isachenko (Eds.)* | Post-Soviet Secessionism. Nation-Building and State-Failure after Communism | ISBN 978-3-8382-1538-9

227 *Jakob Hauter (Ed.)* | Civil War? Interstate War? Hybrid War? Dimensions and Interpretations of the Donbas Conflict in 2014–2020 | With a foreword by Andrew Wilson | ISBN 978-3-8382-1383-5

228 *Tima T. Moldogaziev, Gene A. Brewer, J. Edward Kellough (Eds.)* | Public Policy and Politics in Georgia. Lessons from Post-Soviet Transition | With a foreword by Dan Durning | ISBN 978-3-8382-1535-8

229 *Oxana Schmies (Ed.)* | NATO's Enlargement and Russia. A Strategic Challenge in the Past and Future | With a foreword by Vladimir Kara-Murza | ISBN 978-3-8382-1478-8

230 *Christopher Ford* | Ukapisme – Une Gauche perdue. Le marxisme anti-colonial dans la révolution ukrainienne 1917-1925 | Avec une préface de Vincent Présumey | ISBN 978-3-8382-0899-2

231 *Anna Kutkina* | Between Lenin and Bandera. Decommunization and Multivocality in Post-Euromaidan Ukraine | With a foreword by Juri Mykkänen | ISBN 978-3-8382-1506-8

232 *Lincoln E. Flake* | Defending the Faith. The Russian Orthodox Church and the Demise of Religious Pluralism | With a foreword by Peter Martland | ISBN 978-3-8382-1378-1

233 *Nikoloz Samkharadze* | Russia's Recognition of the Independence of Abkhazia and South Ossetia. Analysis of a Deviant Case in Moscow's Foreign Policy | With a foreword by Neil MacFarlane | ISBN 978-3-8382-1414-6

234 *Arve Hansen* | Urban Protest. A Spatial Perspective on Kyiv, Minsk, and Moscow | With a foreword by Julie Wilhelmsen | ISBN 978-3-8382-1495-5

235 *Eleonora Narvselius, Julie Fedor (Eds.)* | Diversity in the East-Central European Borderlands. Memories, Cityscapes, People | ISBN 978-3-8382-1523-5

236 *Regina Elsner* | The Russian Orthodox Church and Modernity. A Historical and Theological Investigation into Eastern Christianity between Unity and Plurality | With a foreword by Mikhail Suslov | ISBN 978-3-8382-1568-6

237 *Bo Petersson* | The Putin Predicament. Problems of Legitimacy and Succession in Russia | With a foreword by J. Paul Goode | ISBN 978-3-8382-1050-6

238 *Jonathan Otto Pohl* | The Years of Great Silence. The Deportation, Special Settlement, and Mobilization into the Labor Army of Ethnic Germans in the USSR, 1941–1955 | ISBN 978-3-8382-1630-0

239 *Mikhail Minakov (Ed.)* | Inventing Majorities. Ideological Creativity in Post-Soviet Societies | ISBN 978-3-8382-1641-6

240 *Robert M. Cutler* | Soviet and Post-Soviet Foreign Policies I. East-South Relations and the Political Economy of the Communist Bloc, 1971–1991 | With a foreword by Roger E. Kanet | ISBN 978-3-8382-1654-5

241 *Izabella Agardi* | On the Verge of History. Life Stories of Rural Women from Serbia, Romania, and Hungary, 1920–2020 | With a foreword by Andrea Pető | ISBN 978-3-8382-1602-7

242 *Sebastian Schäffer (Ed.)* | Ukraine in Central and Eastern Europe. Kyiv's Foreign Affairs and the International Relations of the Post-Communist Region | With a foreword by Pavlo Klimkin and Andreas Umland | ISBN 978-3-8382-1615-7

243 *Volodymyr Dubrovskyi, Kalman Mizsei, Mychailo Wynnyckyj (Eds.)* | Eight Years after the Revolution of Dignity. What Has Changed in Ukraine during 2013–2021? | With a foreword by Yaroslav Hrytsak | ISBN 978-3-8382-1560-0

244 *Rumena Filipova* | Constructing the Limits of Europe Identity and Foreign Policy in Poland, Bulgaria, and Russia since 1989 | With forewords by Harald Wydra and Gergana Yankova-Dimova | ISBN 978-3-8382-1649-2

245 *Oleksandra Keudel* | How Patronal Networks Shape Opportunities for Local Citizen Participation in a Hybrid Regime A Comparative Analysis of Five Cities in Ukraine | With a foreword by Sabine Kropp | ISBN 978-3-8382-1671-3

246 *Jan Claas Behrends, Thomas Lindenberger, Pavel Kolar (Eds.)* | Violence after Stalin Institutions, Practices, and Everyday Life in the Soviet Bloc 1953–1989 | ISBN 978-3-8382-1637-9

247 *Leonid Luks* | Macht und Ohnmacht der Utopien Essays zur Geschichte Russlands im 20. und 21. Jahrhundert | ISBN 978-3-8382-1677-5

248 *Iuliia Barshadska* | Brüssel zwischen Kyjiw und Moskau Das auswärtige Handeln der Europäischen Union im ukrainisch-russischen Konflikt 2014-2019 | Mit einem Vorwort von Olaf Leiße | ISBN 978-3-8382-1667-6

249 *Valentyna Romanova* | Decentralisation and Multilevel Elections in Ukraine Reform Dynamics and Party Politics in 2010–2021 | With a foreword by Kimitaka Matsuzato | ISBN 978-3-8382-1700-0

250 *Alexander Motyl* | National Questions. Theoretical Reflections on Nations and Nationalism in Eastern Europe | ISBN 978-3-8382-1675-1

251 *Marc Dietrich* | A Cosmopolitan Model for Peacebuilding. The Ukrainian Cases of Crimea and the Donbas | With a foreword by Rémi Baudouï | ISBN 978-3-8382-1687-4

252 *Eduard Baidaus* | An Unsettled Nation. Moldova in the Geopolitics of Russia, Romania, and Ukraine | With forewords by John-Paul Himka and David R. Marples | ISBN 978-3-8382-1582-2

253 *Igor Okunev, Petr Oskolkov (Eds.)* | Transforming the Administrative Matryoshka. The Reform of Autonomous Okrugs in the Russian Federation, 2003–2008 | With a foreword by Vladimir Zorin | ISBN 978-3-8382-1721-5

254 *Winfried Schneider-Deters* | Ukraine's Fateful Years 2013–2019. Vol. I: The Popular Uprising in Winter 2013/2014 | ISBN 978-3-8382-1725-3

255 *Winfried Schneider-Deters* | Ukraine's Fateful Years 2013–2019. Vol. II: The Annexation of Crimea and the War in Donbas | ISBN 978-3-8382-1726-0

256 *Robert M. Cutler* | Soviet and Post-Soviet Russian Foreign Policies II. East-West Relations in Europe and the Political Economy of the Communist Bloc, 1971–1991 | With a foreword by Roger E. Kanet | ISBN 978-3-8382-1727-7

257 *Robert M. Cutler* | Soviet and Post-Soviet Russian Foreign Policies III. East-West Relations in Europe and Eurasia in the Post-Cold War Transition, 1991–2001 | With a foreword by Roger E. Kanet | ISBN 978-3-8382-1728-4

258 *Paweł Kowal, Iwona Reichardt, Kateryna Pryshchepa (Eds.)* | Three Revolutions: Mobilization and Change in Contemporary Ukraine III. Archival Records and Historical Sources on the 1990 Revolution on Granite | ISBN 978-3-8382-1376-7

259 *Mikhail Minakov (Ed.)* | Philosophy Unchained. Developments in Post-Soviet Philosophical Thought. | With a foreword by Christopher Donohue | ISBN 978-3-8382-1768-0

260 *David Dalton* | The Ukrainian Oligarchy After the Euromaidan. How Ukraine's Political Economy Regime Survived the Crisis | With a foreword by Andrew Wilson | ISBN 978-3-8382-1740-6

261 *Andreas Heinemann-Grüder (Ed.)* | Who are the Fighters? Irregular Armed Groups in the Russian-Ukrainian War in 2014–2015 | ISBN 978-3-8382-1777-2

262 *Taras Kuzio (Ed.)* | Russian Disinformation and Western Scholarship. Bias and Prejudice in Journalistic, Expert, and Academic Analyses of East European and Eurasian Affairs | ISBN 978-3-8382-1685-0

263 *Darius Furmonavicius* | LithuaniaTransforms the West. Lithuania's Liberation from Soviet Occupation and the Enlargement of NATO (1988–2022) | With a foreword by Vytautas Landsbergis | ISBN 978-3-8382-1779-6

264 *Dirk Dalberg* | Politisches Denken im tschechoslowakischen Dissens. Egon Bondy, Miroslav Kusý, Milan Šimečka und Petr Uhl (1968-1989) | ISBN 978-3-8382-1318-7

265 *Леонид Люкс* | К столетию «философского парохода». Мыслители «первой» русской эмиграции о русской революции и о тоталитарных соблазнах XX века | ISBN 978-3-8382-1775-8

266 *Daviti Mtchedlishvili* | The EU and the South Caucasus. European Neighborhood Policies between Eclecticism and Pragmatism, 1991-2021 | With a foreword by Nicholas Ross Smith | ISBN 978-3-8382-1735-2

267 *Bohdan Harasymiw* | Post-Euromaidan Ukraine. Domestic Power Struggles and War of National Survival in 2014–2022 | ISBN 978-3-8382-1798-7

268 *Nadiia Koval, Denys Tereshchenko (Eds.)* | Russian Cultural Diplomacy under Putin. Rossotrudnichestvo, the "Russkiy Mir" Foundation, and the Gorchakov Fund in 2007–2022 | ISBN 978-3-8382-1801-4

269 *Izabela Kazejak* | Jews in Post-War Wrocław and L'viv. Official Policies and Local Responses in Comparative Perspective, 1945-1970s | ISBN 978-3-8382-1802-1

270 *Jakob Hauter* | Russia's Overlooked Invasion. The Causes of the 2014 Outbreak of War in Ukraine's Donbas | With a foreword by Hiroaki Kuromiya | ISBN 978-3-8382-1803-8

271 *Anton Shekhovtsov* | Russian Political Warfare. Essays on Kremlin Propaganda in Europe and the Neighbourhood, 2020-2023 | With a foreword by Nathalie Loiseau | ISBN 978-3-8382-1821-2

272 *Андреа Пето* | Насилие и Молчание. Красная армия в Венгрии во Второй Мировой войне | ISBN 978-3-8382-1636-2

ibidem.eu